Winter/Spring 1991
Volume 5, Numbers 1–2

American Art

published by Oxford University Press in association with the
National Museum of American Art, Smithsonian Institution

Redefining National Culture

Elizabeth Broun

Director
National Museum of American Art
Smithsonian Institution

This journal was begun four years ago with a declaration that American art had "come of age" in the decade since the 1976 Bicentennial. Soaring market values, hundreds of new collectors, millions of museum visitors, and a proliferation of research methods created a lot of excitement that seemed symptomatic of the expansive 1980s. Yet even in the midst of the boom, Charles C. Eldredge wrote in his preface to the first issue, "Never before have we been faced with so many perplexing questions and so few incontrovertible answers." Four years later, events in the arts and public life have moved so rapidly that even the idea of incontrovertible answers seems wishful.

When American art scholars stopped seeing their art as a mirror of European work, they began to link it specifically to the development and history of the nation. Suddenly a lot of "masters" appeared in a new light, which, like the record of all human experience, is shot through with shadows. Some of those shadows are now being explored, and in doing so, new questions have emerged about the purpose of our art, who it serves, what it means, and why it is made.

These are shadows cast over two centuries of national experience. America began as a utopia and continues today to represent an ideal, a place where we are taught to believe that one's personal experience will be validated in an open democracy. But for many who came to these shores—willingly or in bondage, seeking new opportunities, fleeing oppression, or simply surviving—the utopia was structured in favor of a dominant culture. A fierce competition among groups began that has played itself out in the arena of art as well as in economics and politics. Personal expression has often been crowded to the margins by those who believed their own experience should be writ large as national destiny.

We find evidence of this competition in almost every phase of American history. The Mexican War, for instance, was more than a political event: it was an occasion for easterners of Anglo-Saxon descent to claim victory over the older Hispanic traditions that began with Catholic missions in the West and Southwest. Just three years after the eastern "victory," Emerson propounded a special relationship between the United States and its English ancestors, one that went to the heart of the democratic experiment in America. He claimed that the

American is only the continuation of the English genius into new conditions, more or less propitious. . . . It is in the deep traits of race that the fortunes of nations are written, and however derived . . . here exists the best stock in the world. . . . Hence we say that only the English race can be trusted with freedom,—freedom which is double-edged and dangerous to any but the wise and robust.[1]

To hear Emerson, who we have imagined to be uncompromisingly committed to native experience, propose freedom as the endowment of a single race is to confront our current dilemma full-face. Who will define national culture? A glance backwards tells us that winners have always written the histories, reshaping the past as energetically as they have set the stage for the future. In art no less than in war or history, those in power have defined success and failure, establishing the boundaries of mainstream and margin.

Historical art that today is evaluated primarily as stylistic expression may in fact contain coded messages that we have forgotten how to read. For instance, a half-century after the Mexican War, Childe Hassam was in Cuba on the eve of a doomed insurrection that led to the withdrawal of Spanish governors from the Caribbean. The painting he made from this experience seems at first only a placid impressionist view, but by Hassam's own words, it commemorated the last day the Spanish flag flew in the Western Hemisphere. Contemporary critics probably caught the message, just as they clearly heard the Anglophiliac undercurrents of his nostalgic evocations of Old Lyme and British colonialism. Today we see his art merely as style—the high point of Impressionism in America.

At the Chicago World's Fair of 1893, American artists exhibited their very best work in an effort to rival the accomplishments of European masters. They knew that American industry could go only so far in gaining a position on the international stage; the ultimate test of a nation rested on its "higher" accomplishments in art and civilization. To prove themselves, they relentlessly imitated European styles and subjects, excluding what was specific to America or related to other non-European traditions. However much we may regret this ideology of cultural dominance, their ambition led to extraordinary accomplishments within the framework of their standards. The work shown in the American section of the Chicago World's Fair reached a new pinnacle of excellence, though it expressed only the segment of American society modeled on European civilization. To the extent that the very idea of excellence or quality in art depends on having clear standards reflecting a common view, the aesthetic theories of Europe gave Americans a straighter path to success, but one that we now see as exclusionary.

What room is left for a theory of cultural dominance? The black slave trade that predated the birth of the nation is no minor subtext to history but a central fact whose legacy continues to press against our sense of national identity. American Indians, once dismissed as a "vanishing race," show an almost incredible ability to survive as separate sovereign nations against the combined forces of the United States armed forces, punitive government treaties, and outrageous neglect. Hispanic citizens demand overdue recognition of their early investment in America and their burgeoning role in society. Asians, who have entered every area of society in a triumph of assimilation, have often had to trade off strong cultural traditions for upward mobility.

We are rewriting history again to conform to an urgent new understanding of our past, redefined according to present needs, inspired in part by the growing presence of minority cultures in American society and the awareness of past injustices to many groups. As we uncover and disperse the old ideologies operating in our art, there is the possibility that new ones will emerge to take their place. Diversity, however, spells the end of those standards of quality that depend on shared cultural values. What will take their place? Even asking that question now, when forces of fragmentation overwhelm those of consolidation, is premature—rather like asking for the resolutions of Synthetic Cubism when the analytic stage was barely under way. What does seem certain, however, is that mourning antiquated standards will only delay new ones.

The 1890 census, which demonstrated that immigration was threatening Anglo-Saxon hegemony in the United States, led to a generation of shrill texts about "race suicide" and culminated in the 1924 immigration laws that greatly restricted blacks, orientals, Eastern Europeans, and other "undesirables."[2] A century later, the 1990 census has shown that

minority populations may soon form a new majority, engendering some of the same fears and feelings of competition. But we can also find in these statistics a liberating realization that through diversity comes invigoration and strength. Assimilation is on the retreat from Miami to Armenia, replaced by an appreciation of the most intimate aspects of personal and community identity. Those who warn against a "new tribalism" fear the fragmentation of culture, but such fragmentation is equally a source of energy in a society that has been superficially homogenized through mass communications.

Centuries are sometimes viewed as biological organisms, with optimistic beginnings followed by a confident maturity that leads ultimately to reflections of old age. American art of this century fits the pattern—born in high ambitions for a modernism expressive of new industrial power, enjoying remarkable international influence at mid-century, and now beset by questions and the sifting of priorities. In post-Vietnam, post-Watergate, post-Drexel America, we find that national purpose is no longer defined only by military, political, or economic initiatives. "Incontrovertible answers" may recede rapidly over the horizon, but the infinitely nuanced visual arts, contemporary and historical, offer an avenue to self-knowledge for those willing to look.

This journal invites a fresh approach to the present and the past. We construe our mandate to encompass culture as well as art, for we believe that art is not understood outside of culture and history. The times are right for openness—much that is relevant lies beyond yesterday's definitions.

1   Ralph Waldo Emerson, *English Traits* (Boston and New York: Houghton, Mifflin and Co., 1903), pp. 36, 134, 304.

2   Madison Grant, *The Passing of the Great Race* (New York: Charles Scribner's Sons, 1916).

Childe Hassam, *Place Centrale and Fort Cabanas, Havana,* 1895. Oil on canvas, 21 1/4 x 26 1/4 in. Detroit Institute of Arts, City of Detroit purchase

"Righting" Today's Art History

Stephen Polcari

The turn in art history toward the examination of art in context was decisive in the 1980s. Few art historians, particularly young art historians, still focus on stylistic issues alone. Formalism, the extreme and selective mode of stylistic analysis, no longer entices them.

This change is to be welcomed. Scholars now seek the larger ramifications and meanings of art. A key factor, perhaps *the* key factor, of this new art history is the study of art as an agent in local politics. New scholarship examines art as political history, placing art within social, political, and ideological conflicts. Again, this change is to be welcomed (although politics, the study of governance and interest groups, is often confused with history, the study of everything). For too long art has been seen simply as personal and subjective expression in a vacuum and, at best, as private philosophical musing.

There are, however, major problems with this new scholarship. What is often being written is not about art and history but the political and ideological agendas of the current university generation. Much as Clement Greenberg rewrote art history to suit his formalist theory of development, scholars are now rewriting it in ways that support the political wishes of the 1960s generation who now rule the university. The problem, however, is not only the evaluation of art merely in terms of today's notorious ideological warfare or "political correctness," but something else.

Art historians generally know very little about politics and history. In this they are like most Americans. Recent studies (*New York Times*, 15 July 1990) indicate that it is not only today's high school students who "know less and care less about news and public affairs" than students of previous generations but also those educated Americans between twenty and fifty years of age—in other words, those writing the new art history. The result is that the average younger art historian today is more naively idealistic, politically inexperienced, and historically unaware than previous writers. Moreover, the academic personality is often an iconoclastic one; that is, it delights in and seeks to set itself in opposition to whatever is politically and intellectually established. This tendency seems instinctual, a virtual knee-jerk stance. While such automatic opposition may be necessary to break new ground, it also has a dark side. It can be thoughtless and superficial. When combined with political ignorance and naïveté, it is foolish and even dangerous.

In general, graduate training does not prepare art historians to write about the intersection of art and history. Graduate training in art history usually consists of a major and two minors in the same discipline. Nowhere is there any requirement that students know their era historically, politically, socially, and intellectually as well as they do artistically. Even in terms of events of today, most art historians' standard of knowledge is no more comprehensive than reading the *New York Times* and watching the nightly news once in a while. This is more equivalent to staying up on "current events" than to making a serious, responsible study of contemporary events and their meanings.

Sometimes I give my graduate students a test. I ask them about significant modern

Members of an international medical commission view remains of exhumed bodies at a mass grave at Katyn, Soviet Union, 28 April 1943.

events and their meanings. I ask them if they know of the Kronstadt Affairs, the Katyn Forest (even after today's news stories), Brest-Litovsk, Bukharin, Shanghai, Verdun, Kursk, Japan's defeat of a major Western power and emergence as an Asian power long before today, and more. Most do not know. Nor do they know or have they ever read—or, even more disturbing, ever heard of—the basic books of politics and history, such as Hans Morgenthau's *Politics among Nations*, or the basic magazines of international relations, such as *Foreign Affairs* and *Foreign Policy*. The CIA is likened to the gestapo on many university campuses today, but few students know much about the nature of intelligence gathering or are aware of professional journals about it, such as the *International Journal of Intelligence and Counterintelligence*. Most art historians, too, would not do well in these areas.

In my field, modern art at mid-century, I am appalled by the simple ignorance of most critics about the central event of modern and perhaps all of Western history—the Second World War. In the writing on Abstract Expressionism, my particular interest, the war—if mentioned at all—is covered in a sentence or two. When I discuss the war with colleagues, I hear only remarks about the A-bomb and the Holocaust. These are less war issues than postwar issues: the A-bomb is really about current fears of nuclear annihilation, and the Holocaust is about racism, another contemporary concern. For most young art historians, the Second World War is just some distant conflict with combat, as remote in implication, meaning, and experience as the Civil War. Its torments, humiliations, violations, and catastrophes for humanity and what humanity long thought of itself are never mentioned or even acknowledged, even though these elements changed the course of the world and Western civilization.

Three recent books highlight the problem. One is about American artists' opposition to fascism. Reflecting the current mania to position (and valorize) people according to the left-right spectrum, FDR is characterized as merely a liberal-interventionist who was most likely maneuvering the United States into war before Pearl Harbor. While there is some truth in this statement, the characterization is extremely reductive, interpreting Roosevelt's actions in the narrowest and most negative way. It fails to discern the nuances and foresight of Roosevelt's position, in which he recognized the dangers of nazism and tried to prepare for it despite the opposition of many Americans. (Before Pearl Harbor, Congress voted for the draft by only one vote.) Portraying Roosevelt as a virtual pro-Britain warmonger is a heedless idea emanating from university pacifism.

Another recent book is about a political American artist in the postwar period. It is a relentless assault on America as the center of evil in the world. So relentless is it that I breathed a sigh of relief when the author admitted that the North Koreans did indeed invade South Korea and start the Korean War. My relief from that one sentence was short-lived, however, for what followed was a harangue about America's consequent unnecessary buildup of its armed forces. Later the United States is portrayed as a big bully destroying Korea in fighting the war. Nowhere is there a discussion of the geopolitical implications of North Korea's connivance with Stalin to begin a war, the definitions of defense perimeters by the United States, or what the invasion meant for Europe. The author merely presents a Vietnam-generation attitude extended to the Korean War. Sophisticated historians of international relations would not bother with such writing.

While the older generation (those over fifty) is generally more sophisticated, having had more historical experience than Vietnam, a third new book, written by old lefties, exhibits the same flaws. It purports to be an anthology of criticism of Abstract Expressionism and its politics and ideology from the 1930s to the 1950s. The book simply skips the period from 1939 to 1945 in its discussion. Apparently, nothing important happened then: it is a historical black hole.

And interestingly, there has been a recent spate of writing equating the Cold War defense of the individual with Abstract Expressionism's humanism. The artists are thus portrayed as Cold Warriors. Such a view reduces history and art to simplistic views of left-right politics once again. The idea of the defense of the individual and his freedom was not merely an American Cold War idea. Rather, it was revived all over the West during the Second World War when intellectuals realized their interwar dismissal of such concerns seemed to accord with fascism and its indifference to human rights. European intellectuals like Jean Paul Sartre, Albert Camus, Thomas Mann, Harold Laski, and others wrote of freedom and the individual during the war. In the period of transition from war to semi-peace that characterized the late 1940s, these ideas did not die. If anything they were reinforced for reasons ranging from the most profound to the most prosaic. The carnage of the war, the death camps, and the revelations of the Nazis' treatment of people made many in the West rededicate themselves to individual freedom. So did the return of millions of men and women who had "lost" their rights while serving in the armed forces. As the military historian John Keegan writes, the war "exposed over 12 million [Americans] to a system of subordination and autocracy entirely alien to American values," or as one soldier put it, "I joined the army to fight the fascists but I found it was full of 'em." Americans could not wait to retrieve their individual sense of self. To reduce the postwar assertion of the individual to merely a Cold War stance is silly and pernicious.

That is the crux. University humanists today know very little about real history, real politics, or real experience. What we are getting in the new writing about art and politics is a naive pacifist socialism and anarchism that rewrites history in a simplistic manner.

This state of affairs seems unacceptable. If art historians want to write about art and politics, graduate training should be changed so they are required to know something beyond today's headlines. Dump the second minor inside the discipline and replace it with a minor in history, international relations (with its study of diplomacy, economics, and global security systems), and the like. Only then will we see art historians who have a more seasoned, if not more professional, understanding of politics and, perhaps, even the beginnings of a wise art history full of serious, broad, and deep insights into human beings, their art, and their time.

How Museums Define Other Cultures

Ivan Karp

Toward the end of President Reagan's tenure, the *Miami News* published a remarkable cartoon by Don Wright, which showed silhouettes of Ronald and Nancy Reagan in grass skirts dancing around what appears to be a sacrificial shrine (fig. 1). Ronald holds a goat over his head, Nancy a chicken in each hand. Ronald says, "What's the astrologer say to do next, Nancy?" Answer: "Sacrifice the goat, singe the chickens and pound the lizard to powder!"

The cartoon's images of the Reagans echo, quite deliberately, the popular imagery of the witch doctor. Herbert Ward's 1890 Victorian travel book *Five Years with Congo Cannibals* contains a strikingly similar illustration, though drawn without the same satirical intent (fig. 2). It portrays a so-called witch doctor, similarly clothed in sketchy costume, dancing around a fire and holding over his head a fetish figure.

I do not suggest the cartoonist was copying Ward, but both draw upon a stock of deeply held and patently enduring cultural imagery about the "other"—the generalized conception of people on the losing side of the colonial and imperial encounter. Both the figures of the Reagans and the Ward witch doctor, for example, are depicted in classic ballet positions, a similarity that helps exemplify the paradox of representing the other: Difference can only be communicated in terms that are familiar.

Two strategies are used when representing other cultures or their works of art. Exoticizing showcases the differences between the cultural group being displayed and the cultural group doing the viewing, while assimilating highlights the similarities. Whether we are describing a text or an exhibition, otherness is either made strange by exoticizing or made familiar by assimilating.[1]

In exoticizing, the differences of the other are portrayed as an absence of qualities the dominant, often colonizing, cultural groups possess. In the cartoon and engraving, three features of civilized man are missing in the witch doctor character: rationality, symbolic (as opposed to true) animal sacrifice, and an orderly bourgeois sense of propriety. Imagine what little effect the *Miami News* cartoon would have had if the Reagans were dressed in vestments and placed primly behind a lectern with a holy book, "sacrificing" only bread and wine.

Both the editorial cartoon and the engraving represent so-called savages as controlled by emotions and unable to calculate rationally. Myth making here is not isolated from real life; it is part of the process whereby our beliefs about other people are shaped. Radio and television news, for example, report that black South Africans belong to tribes when they are in conflict with each other and to political parties when they dispute with the white regime. Likewise, journalists refer to the leaders of Columbia's Medellin cartel of cocaine dealers as part of a clan of closely knit persons who act in concert. If the other is different from us, one feature of that difference is his identification with social groups that claim his loyalties in ways that impede rational calculation.

1 Don Wright, *What's the Astrologer Say to Do Next, Nancy?* Cartoon published in the *Miami News*, 1988

2 S. Northcote, *Antics of the Charm Dancer.* Engraving published in Herbert Ward, *Five Years with Congo Cannibals* (London: Chatto and Windsor, 1890)

Conversely, otherness can also be positively valued. Recent writings about American Indians or definitions of Afrocentricity often romanticize minority and Third World cultures as possessing a less aggressive attitude toward nature and a more group-oriented attitude toward social life. Yet these assertions still embody a depressingly familiar set of beliefs: The other lacks the rationality of modern man, or the other's thought process is circular rather than linear. These images of the other are turned not so much on their head as on their side. Assigning positive values to the other may be novel, but the racial and ethnic stereotypes used to arrive at these conclusions are shockingly familiar.

The image of the other is derived not only from assertions about cultural differences. The use of a ballet pose to portray the Reagans and the African witch doctor was probably not consciously intended; neither was it accidental. Negative images need positive associations to make them work. If familiar devices were not used, the consumers of the image would have nothing onto which to graft cultural, racial, or ethnic differences. The politics of producing the image of the other requires a poetics of difference *and* similarity. The familiar becomes the bridge through which we understand the exotic.

While all museum exhibits draw on the resources of public culture and popular imagery to produce their effects, none draw on them more than exhibitions of the art and life of the other. And exhibits of exotic art and cultures are as much an arena of discourse about the other as editorial cartoons or travel books. However, because they draw on the authority of museums and the public's goodwill toward museums, exhibitions have a greater legitimacy than forms of popular culture defined as less highbrow. But all forms of communicating about the other use the organizing principles of difference and similarity to produce their imagery.[2] Which of these opposing principles dominates an exhibition's account or image of a cultural other often determines how the other is perceived. Although recent scholarship describes the other as being represented primarily through difference, similarity can be—and often is—used to assert that the people of other cultures are no different in principle than the producers and consumers of their images. Striking differences can then be interpreted as mere surface manifestations of underlying similarities.[3]

Exoticizing often works by inverting the familiar—showing how a well-known practice takes an inverted form among other peoples. The common belief that Africans practice

3   Richard Long, *Untitled*, 1989.
River Avon mud on black paper, 14 x
22 in. Collection of the artist

4   Earth and ochre sand painting by
six artists of the aboriginal
community of Yuendumu,
Australia

animism is an example. The anthropomorphic tendency of most Western
religious belief is inverted, thus creating
the notion that there is a class of people
who worship beings created not in their
own image, but in the image of nature.
That such beliefs have never been docu-
mented in a non-Western religion has not
stopped legions of writers from describing
Africans as animists.

Assimilating strategies are less easy to
read. They appeal to the audience's sense
of the familiar and natural. They don't
stop exhibit goers in their tracks with such
thoughts as "What in the world is that?"
Assimilating is inherently a more subtle
exhibiting strategy than exoticizing. In the
so-called primitive or tribal exhibits in
fine art museums, art objects are usually
isolated from any sort of context. Encased
in a vitrine, they are provided with a label
that reveals more about the collectors who
donated them than about their maker,
their iconography, or their history.[4] The
governing assumptions behind these
displays are that primitive objects mysteri-
ously embody the same aesthetics as
modern art forms and that curators and
museum audiences are able to appreciate
such objects because they are the heirs to
a familiar aesthetic tradition whose history
encompasses the primitives who make
primitive art. What they truly inherit is a
capitalist world system that has acquired
things from other peoples and transformed them into objects of modern art.

The controversial 1984 MOMA
exhibition " 'Primitivism' in 20th Century
Art" provides us with a classic example of the assimilating strategy. Objects were brought
together either because they were known to provide models for modern artists or because
they were known to exhibit perceived affinities. For William Rubin, the curator of the
exhibition, affinities exist because artists working independently on similar formal problems arrive at similar solutions. This is a pure structuralist interpretation. Considerations
of content, such as iconography, or questions about intention and purpose, such as the
religious role of an object, or even the examination of the contexts of production and
use are omitted as possible factors that influence the final form of the object. History
is omitted from consideration. Objects are defined as the products of individuals who
accidentally derive their work from a limited stock of available forms. The result is
assimilating because cultural and historical differences are obliterated from the exhibiting

record. Rubin's exhibit turns the African, American Indian, and Pacific makers of the objects displayed in his exhibition into modern artists who lack only the individual identity and history of modern art.[5] Given the curator's insistence that context is absolutely irrelevant to the exhibition of affinities between the primitive and the modern, the only place in history allowed for the artists of other cultures and their works is as a footnote to the development of art in the West.

Even Rubin's decision to retain the word *primitivism* stirs controversy. The sense that so-called primitives are what we once were, our "contemporary ancestors" whose only history is our past, can hardly be avoided. The author Anthony Burgess defines primitivism as the "sense of a stumbling amateur striving towards a hard-won perfection and not quite achieving it." No matter how Rubin chooses to define his terms, his methods of classification reveal the sense conveyed by Burgess's definition.[6]

Yet Rubin's intention is not to exclude primitive artists from the history of art. He simply desires to place primitive aesthetics on a par with modernist aesthetics. In the end, however, he merely assimilates the aesthetics of other cultural traditions into a particular moment within his own tradition.

Other aesthetic traditions take shape in cultural settings outside of such art museums as MOMA. There are, for example, aesthetics that use political or religious criteria in judgments about what is good and bad. In some aesthetic traditions, the experience of viewing an object may be more than just a sensory reaction to the visual, just as aesthetic idioms may be applied to objects and actions normally excluded from the realm of museums.

If Rubin had chosen to examine how "tribal" artists and Picasso used similar forms in combination with other forms, or if he had inquired about how these objects were judged by their users and makers in the context of their creation, he would have produced a more textured and culturally diverse exhibition, while still remaining faithful to his project.[7]

The Pompidou Center's answer to MOMA's "Primitivism" exhibition, the 1989 "Magiciens de la Terre" consisted of two entire halls of artworks derived from vastly different cultural traditions, yet the master narrative for the whole exhibition asserted a fundamental underlying similarity in spirit and intent among the producers of such disparate works of art.[8] In this sense, the curators of "Magiciens de la Terre" did no better than the curator of "Primitivism." By juxtaposing a work by Richard Long with a sand drawing by Australian aboriginal artists (figs. 3, 4), the curators conflated Long's attempt to return to the elemental with the Australian re-creation of an alternative universe—the "dream time" in which the cultural world was wrested from nature. Given the audience's lack of familiarity with Australian cosmology and art, the act of conflation becomes an act of assimilation: the Australian artists become echoes of Long. As Yogi Berra once said, "It's *déjà vu* all over again." There is, in effect, no substantial difference between the "Magiciens" exhibition's juxtaposition of Long's work with the Australian aborigines' sand drawing and the "Primitivism" show's juxtaposition of Kenneth Noland's *Circle* painting with a New Guinea shield exhibiting concentric motifs (fig. 5).[9]

Nevertheless, the curators of "Magiciens" could be seen as more egalitarian than the curator of "Primitivism." They deny that Third World artists and contemporary artists differ in self-consciousness. All, in their view, are equally conscious about the sources and meanings of the art they create; perhaps it would be fairer to say that all are equally naive about the magical and elemental sources of their art. The cost of this egalitarian strategy of assimilation, however, is the elimination of cultural context, motives, and resources from the record.

All exhibitions, in fact all representations of the other, simultaneously exoticize and assimilate, but some museums often emphasize both exhibiting devices within the same

5 Installation view of the exhibition " 'Primitivism' in 20th Century Art: Affinity of the Tribal with the Modern," 19 September 1984– 15 January 1985, The Museum of Modern Art, New York

setting. The history of the Smithsonian Institution illustrates this in a grand manner. The National Museum of American History was originally developed out of the National Museum, which was a museum of natural history. Unintentionally but nevertheless palpably, the Smithsonian maintains a nineteenth-century evolutionist distinction between modern cultures and those cultures that are best known and exhibited as part of nature. The latter, primarily American Indians and peoples of the Third World, are then subject to the interpretations and procedures of natural history scholars. In contrast, white middle-class Americans are defined as possessing science and technology and as having cultural and social history exempting them from a similar examination in terms of natural history.[10]

No genre of museum has been able to escape the problems of exoticizing and assimilating inherent in exhibiting other cultures. That includes museums that restrict themselves to examining diversity within their own societies. The same museums that make the products of others into a minor digression in the history of modern art also treat the art and artists of their own traditions the same way. What happens to an artist who moves outside of the Paris–New York orbit? How do so-called "regional" traditions get created in the stories curators tell in exhibitions? Cultural centers and peripheries are determined by museums, not by nature. The only hope is to develop more reflective exhibitions that question their own assumptions. This would have its parallel in the new research in anthropology and history, in what is coming to be called the "History of the Other" or the "Anthropology of the Imaginary," which is less about the examination of people's everyday lives than an examination of how images and ideas about imaginary and unknown worlds come to appear real and even effect what is real. This new field demonstrates how the image of the other is formed partly from images of class, ethnicity, and gender in Western cultures, partly from negation and inversion of Western self-images, and partly from images transmitted by explorers, colonials, and other occupants of cultural and imperial frontiers.[11]

The solution will not be to invent new tropes of representation or new exhibiting devices for museum displays. Every venture into the unknown is based on an analogy with the known. Exoticizing and assimilating are all we have to reach out to the unknown. At best, they enable us to approximate other experiences and to appreciate new forms of art; at worst, they prevent us from truly learning about other cultures and their works of art. The error is not in using these strategies, but in failing to reflect on our own work when making analogies with the other and in treating our works as if they were naturally occurring—as if they did not also carry the unacknowledged baggage of other associations.

Notes

This column is developed from material originally published by the author in *Exhibiting Cultures: The Poetics and Politics of Museum Displays*, ed. Ivan Karp and Steven D. Levine (Washington, D.C.: Smithsonian Institution Press, 1991). I want to thank Joanne Berelowitz, Corinne Kratz, Robert Leopold, Steven Lavine, Mary Jo Arnoldi, and Sue Warga for their comments.

1   See, for example, the essays in *Writing Culture*, ed. James Clifford and George Marcus (Berkeley: University of California Press, 1986). For an excellent account of how European travel writing about the other uses imagery that defines cultures as primitive by reducing them to nature, see Mary Louise Pratt's essay "Scratches on the face of the Land; Or what Mr. Barrow saw among the Bushmen."

2   I differ from the account of how the other is constructed in Edward Said's path-breaking book *Orientalism* (New York: Pantheon, 1978). Said stresses the *negation* of the imputed qualities of the West, while I emphasize the mutual dependence of the tropes of similarity and difference in the construction of any image of the other. I use similarity to refer to what other authors term identity, though both identity and similarity are asserted in the strategy of assimilation, discussed in note 5.

3   See Sally Price, *Primitive Art in Civilized Places* (Chicago: University of Chicago Press, 1989), or Marianna Torgovnick, *Gone Primitive* (Chicago: University of Chicago Press, 1990).

4   For an insightful account of how the identity of the collector tends to dominate the presentation of primitive arts in fine art museums, see Price.

5   My account of Rubin's interpretation of primitive artists shows why I prefer to use the term *similarity* rather than *identity*. Even assimilating strategies conclude that similarity, not identity, is modified by critical differences. Rubin's primitive artists, however, are "identical" to modern artists except for those features of modern art they do not have. Thus, his initial assertion of identity concludes with a declaration of difference.

6   Anthony Burgess, "Native Ground," *Atlantic Monthly* 261 (January 1988): 89.

7   See Rubin's introductory essay "Modernist Primitivism," in *"Primitivism" in 20th Century Art: Affinity of the Tribal with the Modern*, ed. William Rubin (New York: Museum of Modern Art, 1984), pp. 1–84, especially pp. 50–55.

8   See the sumptuous catalogue for this exhibition, *Magiciens de la Terre* (Paris: Editions du Centre Pompidou, 1989).

9   For a description of the *Circle* and New Guinea shield juxtaposition, see Karen Wilkin, "Making Sport of Modern Art," *New Criterion* 8 (November 1990): 75.

10 The National Museum of American History now includes exhibits on ethnic and racial groups, but it still exhibits them in terms of the master narrative of American history. For example, exhibitions on such topics as black migration and the internment of the Japanese define these people in terms of their relationship to the dominant groups in American society. Moreover, by locating their cultural origins in the National Museum of Natural History, the Smithsonian presents the message that these groups have escaped from inferior cultural status through migration to the United States.

    The establishment of the Museum of the American Indian does not solve the problem posed by the hierarchy of representations of cultures at the Smithsonian Institution. The master narrative of the museums still asserts the dominion of nature over *some* cultures. The emphasis on fine art in the National Museum of African Art and on the collection in what will be the National Museum of the American Indian only serves to underscore how the aesthetics and history of the dominant culture define the missions of these museums.

11 See the meticulous research in Peter Mason, *Deconstructing America: Representations of the Other* (London: Routledge and Kegan Paul, 1990).

Weegee's Unstaged Coney Island Dramas

David Corey

Pictures have taken the words right out of our mouths. Photographs are quicker than words, sexier. We'd rather see something than read or hear about it. Memory, imagination, the past, the present, and our ideas about the future have been transformed by photography. In the past fifty years, an endless stream of images has entered our consciousness, creating an image world with its own language.

The following narrative was taken from our work-in-progress, Talking Pictures: Oral Histories in a Visual World, *a collection of edited interviews by individuals who we asked to select and describe the single image that means the most to them. David Corey, who grew up in Brooklyn, New York, where he now teaches comparative literature and film, chose a photograph by Arthur Fellig (1899–1968), better known as Weegee. About this picture and his own life, Corey says, "Growing up in Coney Island in the 1940s was a Lewis Carroll experience, an oddity where traditional lines between the real and imaginary worlds were blurred—the perfect amalgam that Weegee's picture captures."*[1]

— Carole Kismaric
—Marvin Heiferman

Weegee, *Untitled,* n.d.
Gelatin silver print, 14 x 11 in.

My mother was pregnant with me when she watched Luna Park burn. The fire was at night, and she remembers worrying that it might not be safe when she began to feel the heat from the fire. She backed up but continued to watch it burn. That must have been in early 1944, and I was born in November.

We lived in Coney Island, and, in a funny way, Weegee was the court photographer. You would see his photographs with Coney Island settings in the newspapers, next to pictures of Harry Truman and public ceremonies. But there was always something different about a Weegee picture: the stockings had runs, the shirts had sweat under the arms, and everybody looked unshaven. A Weegee photograph was like a production still. If the mainstream world was MGM, Weegee was Warner Brothers—real grit.

My world did not tally with the mainstream news photographs of people in suburban families, living the kinds of lives that rematerialized on TV. A lot of what I saw by way of media culture, I later realized, was an idealized view of the world. Well, we were nothing like that. We lived in a house surrounded by rooming houses, largely occupied by carnival workers and sideshow freaks. A typical neighborhood scene was a 400-pound woman painting her toenails on the porch. The real world was the beach and what went on there. I lived there until I was eight.

Around the Fourth of July, the New York newspapers always ran an "anniversary" kind of Weegee picture of Coney Island above a caption like "One million people fill the beach at Coney Island." I remember looking at that picture very, very carefully—going cross-eyed staring at the grain in the newspaper because I was sure my face was in there. I looked for Weegee on the beach, but I never saw him. I guess I looked at his photographs and realized that that was how you engaged him. He was present to all of these faces staring back at him.

The beach was a giant theatrical construct. You see it in this photograph, where the most unstaged is the most operatic. This photograph is presumably about someone dragged out of the water. And it would not be strange for lifeguards to sing a duet. A figure is slumped over, people grabbing at it—typical Weegee people grabbing. There's the ever-present audience, the boardwalk as family circle. Like most Weegee photographs, people bulge, sweat, and look uncomfortable. The ugly parts of life are on display. The flesh really does speak. You wouldn't be surprised if somebody had two heads or an extra leg. Everything in the photograph affirms that it's part of a large human construct.

The guy with the tattoos was probably sitting there drinking beer for most of the day. The tattoos say he was presumably in the Navy and probably knew something about artificial respiration. He's got this sense that he's involved in something being recorded, a kind of friendly collaboration, like all of Weegee's photographs. No matter what craziness they're involved in, his subjects smile back. In a Weegee, there's a bonhomie that comes from shared class associations. You can imagine Weegee on the other side of the camera, sloppy, fat, and unshaven, having just rolled out of bed after the police radio called him, looking a lot like the people in front of the camera.

I could tell you just where this picture was taken—West 10th Street and the Board-walk. Behind Weegee is the Steeplechase Pier. These were the most crowded beaches, the terminus of four or five subway lines. All of New York poured in at Stillwell Avenue. There was not an afternoon on the beach when you did not have the spectacle of someone being dragged from the water and being given artificial respiration. Somebody would bounce on the victim's chest; there'd be jets of water—if he was lucky—pouring out of his mouth. He was either alive or dead. If he was dead, he was covered up and rushed off on a stretcher to a police ambulance waiting under the boardwalk. It was all entrances and exits. Sex and death. Everything was heightened.

New York had a lot of picture newspapers when I was growing up—the *News*, the *Mirror*, the *World Telegram*, and the *Herald Tribune*. The *News* and the *Mirror* were the natural settings for Weegee's photographs because his pictures were surrounded by ones that showed you what was going on in the world at the pedestrian level—jackknifed tractor trailers, secretaries with crossed legs on their way to Bermuda. It was a world of moderate aspirations. There was an optimism, a sense that one could act; people were hopeful. There were always parades. My grandmother bought a confetti machine. You fed the newspaper in and got bags of confetti. There was just a different sense of those newspapers and the world.

Weegee was romantic against his will. He didn't go off and set up a boho world for himself. He lived in a furnished room. It wasn't furnished as a bohemian atelier. It was a furnished room *as* a furnished room. It's the same in the world he records. In the midst of the most extraordinary crisis, human foibles make themselves known. He was witty about it, ironic. Very often, he did the same thing as Daumier when depicting human vanity—he managed to capture sin radiating through sanctimony. There's one photograph of Wally Simpson and the Duke of Windsor at the circus, and it's perfect because within the Weegee viewfinder they become part of the other nameless swells who slummed in the

slob-show world Weegee knew best, like the people from the opera who came down to Sammy's Bowery Follies. I think he liked the clash. He probably sensed that ultimately the glossier world was going to prevail. He was photographing Pompeii before the eruption.

Weegee was the mediator between us and his subjects—he allowed us to enjoy a kind of voyeurism with perfect safety. Rather than making us feel compelled or moved, Weegee fascinated us with his world's emotional and physical complexity. The situation he chose to depict is very serious to those involved; they're doing the best they can. You can see the single-mindedness in the faces of the two lifeguards wearing their green Department of Parks uniforms with orange trim. These people, running around in leotards, eroticizing the Coney Island landscape, were the official protectors of the beach. The figure in the middle is somewhat self-conscious; the tattoos tell you that. The cop knows perfectly well that the lifeguards are doing their job, and he's waiting to see if there's any need for an ambulance. He's satisfied simply to monitor the thing. There's a wonderful division of labor here. We're seeing the configuration of an elaborate drama, a kind of schema for intense physical and emotional energy in graphic terms. Weegee was simply, as his name implies, the Ouija board: he was the medium.

When people try to take these kinds of pictures today, they're more arch and arty. What's missing is spontaneity. The ante has been upped. If there's something truly heroic in scale or dramatic, it probably means that a vast number of lives are at stake or some enormous disaster is about to occur. These days, you want to flee from the picture; you don't stop to see the spectacle unfold. You just hope that the building isn't going to fall on you or that the machine gun isn't aimed at your corner of the sidewalk. We're more cynical, much less willing to believe. We look at a documentary photograph, and what it documents is the complete inscrutability of the physical world. But in this picture, you're a Weegee distance away. The scale of the heroism is very domestic, very human.

Now we have a roster of tragic situations in the world—horrendous situations—and photographs seem to replicate one another. Poverty looks like poverty everywhere; the figures look the same, the abjectness looks the same. Official visits look the same—snap off the Pope's head and put on Ronald Reagan's head. Pictures deliver the information that people want—the illustrations of what they're about to read—the standard view of an explosion, the courtroom, the auto crash. We read them all as glyphs. When you look at the space shuttle exploding, it takes a real, real push to energize yourself enough to imagine the emotions experienced by the astronauts' families.

Today, a Weegee stops you in your tracks. Instead of turning the page and going on, a Weegee photograph slows the clock and raises too many issues. These are not earth-shattering issues but simply issues that have to do with the way we process information. The Weegee doesn't tell you immediately what the specific crisis is. For all you know, the guy could be having an appendicitis attack. But that kind of ambiguity is not efficient today.

Today, imagination has been taken away. One of the things we've lost in a literate population is the notion of uncertainty. If we learn more and more about something, it's less easy to make the *easy* decision about it. The idea of knowledge coming in a hermetic package is really what we prefer; we want to learn things efficiently. It would be hilarious to think about this photograph in relation to a ten-page series of Ralph Lauren beachhouse pictures, because it's entirely possible that Ralph himself was on the beach the day that Weegee was taking this photograph. Ralph probably took the train down from the Bronx.

The photographs in Ralph's ads are all about memory and loss. There are all of these neo-Hapsburgs weeping over their chintz couches, looking empty-eyed and sad as if their whole world has vanished and they're the last preservers of a way of life. You realize what an extraordinary lie it is, what a creation, what a piece of carefully crafted information is being presented. Weegee's beach is the world Ralph lost, not the imaginary one Lauren invented.

It's not that you have a choice when you look at the Polo ads. You only have one choice, the choice of the marketer. You see bereavement and loss in all of those people with their bent heads. It's an anachronistic world—it's Fitzgerald's world, but even he had a detached irony about how it had faded.

Suddenly this world has been fully reinstated. The only thing you can do, if you want to be part of it at all, is to say, "Yes, it is terrible that those people moved into the next estate down the bay, but hopefully our daughter won't go sailing with their parvenu son." What the ads say is "We all know that it's slipping away from us day by day, but these products will make you feel better." It's a sense of bogus continuity. You know, there are the little Nazi babies on their chintz chairs, and there's the old grandfather, who looks like he was in the Boer War, wearing some fabulous outfit. I mean, come on, for him to be dressed the way he's dressed he'd have to be ninety-seven. Within their big house, they've managed to reinvent the myth.

It's crazy, a celebration of passivity. Now that Ralph can furnish the house with every piece of furniture, every fabric, every drape, you can be thoroughly passive. A wing chair is made to look like a wing-tip shoe, with all the associations of leather and patina and Englishness or American patricianness piled on. At this point, the myth reaches the psychotic phase, babbling associations in any order. Mattress ticking has become stylish upholstery, like anything else Ralph wants to haphazardly put together. You say "Yes, I'll take it." Bring an empty space that's just the right size emotionally, and such accoutrements fit right in. All you have to do is sign the charge slip for the stuff to be delivered to Zombieland the next day. It's the ultimate extrapolation. Mortality ceases to be an issue; timelessness prevails. What Ralph is giving you is the same as what the Pharaohs, who took all of their crap into the Pyramids with them, sought—a world that's going to protect you from death.

But in Weegee's world, all the physical laws of the universe—gravity, mortality, whatever—*are* at work. Regardless of what happens on Weegee's beach under siege, you know that once the fleeting activity is over, in perhaps five minutes the beach will heal itself. The people in this picture will finish their day and go on with the rest of their lives.

Notes

1   David Corey, interview with Carole Kismaric and Marvin Heiferman, New York, N.Y., 27 April 1987.

Turning the Mirrors Around—The Pre-Face

Lucy R. Lippard

So where we are now is that a whole country of people believe I'm a "nigger," and I don't, *and the battle's on! . . . Because if I am not what I've been told I am, then it means that* you're *not what you thought you were either! And that is the crisis.*

—James Baldwin[1]

These lines, written by James Baldwin in 1963, get more profound every time I read them. We have known about the battle for many years, but the reciprocity of racism and self-identification on both sides of the barricades has not yet been internalized by most white people. I've spent much of the last decade trying to understand how people of color are seen and how they see themselves and the world in their art, looking for a more "relational" theory of multiplicity. But it was Baldwin's statement that brought home to me the complexity of the task ahead of us. If we are not who we thought we were, who are we?

I was lucky, because the feminist movement had provided me with the impetus to explore my own class and cultural background within the framework of gender. As I wrote a book on the cross-cultural process in art (*Mixed Blessings*, 1990), I could answer affirmatively when I was asked if I'd thought to study my own culture before I started screwing around with other people's. My own culture is WASP New England, although it was not I but my parents who were raised there. Only now that the book is completed have I begun to understand what the last chapter should have been. The time seems to have come to scrutinize white consciousness of difference in *relation* to that of people of color. We all live in this culture, and it would behoove us to explore our own cultural assumptions as well as those of others.

This article is only a toe in the water, an exercise in turning the mirrors around. I was originally asked to write autobiographically about the development of my art ideas. In the interest of brevity and sanity I decided to concentrate on the cross-cultural aspects. Having done so, I see that the autobiographical ingredient is compulsory, if somewhat embarrassing, if the subject is to be treated honestly. As I start to peel away the top layer here, perhaps it will tap others' memories. The process is contagious. I find in my occasional work with students that the subjects of "race," class, and gender are best raised within the context of personal background.[2] When we go around the room and all the students tell something about their "cultural background," much is revealed about class in particular, though that word may never be used, since few students have been exposed to the notion of a class structure in the United States. Class is a key to understanding discrimination and alienation across the board. Stories about the ways the personal is political *and* the political is personal—how larger events affect families' and therefore individuals' lives—pave the way for an understanding of what different cultures or so-called races are experiencing within a time and place we all share. The master narratives are told from the bottom up instead of from the top down. The macrocosm is clarified by

Edna Davis Jackson, *Kaaswoot*, 1982. Handmade cast cedar paper, prismacolor pencil on a black silk, beaded box, 14 1/2 x 8 1/2 x 2 in. Collection of the artist

Jackson is a Tlingit living in a small town in Alaska. Kaaswoot is her Indian name, and this work is a self-portrait, reflecting her Indian and white heritages. She was inspired by the traditional Northwest carved masks and the local forests' cedar bark, which has long been a cultural staple for native peoples there.

Manuel Macarrulla, *Goat Song #1: Struggle*, 1986. Oil on canvas, 88 x 105 in. Collection of the artist

Macarrulla was raised in the Dominican Republic and now lives in New York. The *Goat Song* series refers to the United States' colonial presence in Latin America, especially in El Salvador, through the ominous presence of the white van that is a trademark of the death squads.

the microcosm. In visual art, lived experience offers the threads of communication through images, forms, colors, and sometimes words.

Over My Shoulder

I am often asked about my motivations, how I happened to plunge into the cross-cultural process. It's a long story. Sometimes I start with my grandparents, one side working-class Canadian and British, the other side a Congregational minister from Colorado who, assisted by his lively wife, was the last white president of Tougaloo College in Mississippi. (This was in the forties, when the faculty and student body was entirely African American.) Or I start with my mother, who worked in what was then called "race relations" in New Orleans in the late forties and early fifties, or with my father, who as dean integrated a southern university's medical school in the fifties. Sometimes I start with the fact that I'm an only child, always attracted to communities while relishing my own solitude. Or with the summer of 1958, which I spent in a poor Mexican village working with the American Friend Service Committee—my first experience of the Third World. Despite the obvious poverty, I loved it. Mexico and poverty both represented freedom, independence, rebellion, and a chance to break out of the white middle-class WASP culture in which I was raised.

When I got to New York in the fall of 1958 and took a job as a page in the Museum of Modern Art Library (where my immediate superior was Sylvia Williams, now director of the Smithsonian's National Museum of African Art), I fell wholeheartedly into the

Ming Fay, *Extinct Ancestors*, 1987.
Mixed media, 24 x 14 x 12 in.
Collection of the artist

Born in Shanghai and raised in
Hong Kong, Fay arrived in the
United States at age eighteen. His
naturalistic but not realistic
objects often recall ritual forms.
This sculpture refers to cultural
continuity and to the universal
inevitability of death.

margins of the art world for the same reasons. I was so enthralled with the romanticized
"freedom" of the artist's life that Freedom Summer, the freedom rides, the whole Civil
Rights movement, went right by me. While my liberal background should have prepared
me to participate in all these ground-shaking events, I was merely an absent-minded
onlooker and supporter, keeping my eyes glued to the white walls of studios, galleries, and
museums until the late sixties, when I was finally catapulted into the antiwar movement
and with it, the antiracist movement and, soon, the feminist movement. I was already
over thirty and a divorced mother when I discovered the sixties, but I was happy to defer
maturity.

The catalyst was another trip to the Third World. On a jurying job in Buenos Aires in
1968, I was exposed to large corporations that tried to tell us what to choose and to artists
working with striking laborers in the town of Tucaman and declaring that they would not
make art until the world changed. Politically naive as I was, this was an entirely new and
stunning idea. On the same trip I was deeply, emotionally impressed by Machu Picchu
and the Inca ruins around Cusco, where I hiked alone in a landscape that seemed more
ancient than any other I had known. I went back to New York with the idea of a "suitcase
exchange exhibition" that would be exported to and from Peru, Argentina, and the
United States by a single artist from each place with a donated plane ticket. This never
happened as such, but it was the kind of idea that was sparked internationally by the
Conceptual art conspiracy, which was where my heart and energies lay at the time.

In the Artworkers Coalition, which began in January 1969, I worked for the first time
with politically conscious artists of color, especially in the AWC Decentralization Committee, which planned art-based community centers in several New York boroughs.
Among our demands to the city's museums was increased representation of black and
Puerto Rican artists. But when a group of women within the AWC began to organize, I
resisted. Even though my parents had raised me to care about and genteelly protest
injustice, I never felt I belonged in their world. I had always overidentified (in their eyes)
with the underdog, but I was unprepared to *become* the underdog.

Nevertheless, I couldn't fend off the deluge of truths for long. The feminist movement,
with all its hugely disturbing and exhilarating insights about the oppression of women,
changed my life and my view of art, although I have told that story elsewhere (in *From the
Center*, 1976, and *Get the Message?* 1984) and need not repeat it here. In short, I had to
rethink my "critical criteria" from the ground up. In the process of rejecting standards
imposed from the outside and examining my own taste, I came to the conclusion that
quality (a word I had been battling for years) was art that moved me or others, that good
art used form with aesthetic integrity to communicate content, and that context was
always a crucial ingredient.

But it wasn't until a group of us founded the Heresies Collective in 1976 and I became
a member of a non-art feminist socialist group about the same time that my consciousness
was raised enough to take a new, less encumbered look at class and racism. I came to
understand that for all my liberal background, I, like virtually all my art-world colleagues,
was still a racist, because no white person in the United States, no matter how fine,
decent, and well intentioned, could escape the social construction of superiority—or at
least social supremacy. It was years, for instance, before I noticed the way we in the
women's movement talked about "women" and "women of color," as though white
women were generic women and everybody else was something else.

From 1972 to 1981, I lived with an artist who made mythical clay landscapes for an
imaginary "little people" in the streets of the Lower East Side, where he became involved
with black and Puerto Rican community activists. (I hung around on the margins.) He
also introduced me to the Southwest. Native American culture—petroglyphs, ancient

ruins, and contemporary dances, but not, tellingly, contemporary art—became an important part of an ongoing series of connections between myth and history. Today, having been introduced to contemporary Indian art in the early eighties, I find it an increasingly compelling part of my work—another long story, another product of the cross-cultural process that guarantees its own relational dilemmas.

During the seventies a number of my friends died "untimely" deaths, which forced me to think more about less "timely" events. In 1977–78 I lived on a farm in England, where virtually all of my ancestors came from. There I wrote a second novel (the first, written in 1970, was published in 1979). Although the novel was unrelated to the place where it was written—it was about three generations of American women and how politics affected their lives—I was being sucked into the history and energies of the surrounding land. The ubiquitous prehistoric stone markers became the medium for a new sense of what art could mean spiritually and communally. A later book called *Overlay: Contemporary Art and the Art of Prehistory* (1983) was the result. The speculative possibilities of prehistory offered a new arena within which to write about public art, which had been a major interest of mine since the sixties. While writing *Overlay*, I began to read widely outside the art arena about myth and world culture and began to form a new (for me) concept of culture that incorporated what I had learned from conceptual, political, and feminist art. Connections with the past, and therefore the future, began to make sense outside of the usually insular art historical domain.

When I got back to New York in the fall of 1978, I found a new and lively art scene brewing, a punk aesthetic that on the one hand was sensationalizing and offensive and on the other hand offered an accessible and even cathartic vehicle for anger at the world and the art world. During the next couple of years I did a performance called "Propaganda Fictions" in which I screamed at "You lousy artists" for decorating the world rather than changing it. I drew comic strips starring a black feminist superheroine called "Polly Tickle." Inspired by the analytical rigor of left-wing British art, I founded an archive of international political art that evolved into an activist art organization: Political Art Documentation/Distribution (PADD). It lasted from 1979 to 1987 and was the backbone of my art and political life until 1986, when I began to spend five months a year in Boulder, Colorado. Aside from the PADD archive of socially concerned art (now at the Museum of Modern Art in the care of an early PADD member, librarian Clive Philpot), we published a journal, *Upfront*, resisted Reaganism and interventionism with innovative street and demonstration art projects, and organized monthly evening forums that were determinedly "multicultural" (a word that had not yet been sullied by overuse and patronization).

Through PADD, I began a working partnership with Jerry Kearns, a white artist who had worked with Amiri Baraka's Anti-Imperialist Cultural Union, the Black United Front in Brooklyn, and CAFA (Committee Against *Fort Apache*, a racist movie about the Bronx). He introduced me to grassroots antiracist and media-oriented cultural organizing, and we collaborated on exhibitions (including several at District 1199, the primarily black and Latino hospital workers' union), articles, events, and occasionally art.

The years 1979 through 1984 were a time of incredible energy and resistance where we hung out on the fringes of the art world. The leaders were the young artists of Group Material, Fashion Moda, Colab, ABC No Rio, and PADD, who were unsettling the Lower East Side, working in the South Bronx, and making a new kind of public and collaborative art that often jumped class barriers. In 1979 the "Nigger Drawings" exhibition at Artists Space was a turning point that forced many of us to confront racism in the art world. An ambitious and insensitive (to put it mildly) young white artist named his

Ismael Frigerio, *In Nomine D. H. Jesu Christi*, 1987. Installation of burlap, Dacron, feathers, gold leaf, 108 x 504 x 96 in. INTAR, New York

Frigerio is a Chilean living in New York, and this installation is one of a series, to culminate in 1992, about Columbus's invasion of the Americas. A giant serpent confronts a green-on-white cross that is partially swallowed by a curtain of feathers, symbolizing the cultural clash of the conquest and the destruction of the indigenous worlds.

show with an eye to sensationalism and brought down on his head a storm of publicity (which he welcomed) and wrath from artists of color and white progressives, led by Howardena Pindell, who hasn't since stopped her elegant vendetta against art-world racists. The debate that followed ensured another leap in consciousness, since many white artists did not understand the depth of the insult and insisted on the artist's right to do anything at all. (This leads, of course, into the current censorship debates and the problems inherent in the art world's lack of communication with a general public.) The fact that the "Nigger Drawings" show consisted of innocuous abstract charcoal drawings and that the insult came not from the art but from the gratuitous title disarmed this argument, but that did not stop a polarization in the art world that made me, for one, take yet another step away from the "mainstream" value system.

The next year I was working on the journal *Heresies*'s "Racism is the Issue" volume (published in 1982) within a delightful, contentious, culturally mixed editorial collective of women artists who were struggling to create an un-American realm in which we could work together without our histories setting us at one another's throats. In 1982 I joined the multicultural Alliance for Cultural Democracy (ACD), where I learned that activist and community theater was far ahead of visual art and that the United States had no visible cultural policy. For almost five years I wrote a monthly piece on art and politics in the *Village Voice* that performed a networking function among activist and marginalized artists across the country. (I was fired in 1985 for reasons the editors were unable to articulate, although they assured me that it had nothing to do with my politics or the fact that I was writing "too much about the Third World.")

The early to mid eighties were a time of much hope and intense coalition building on the cultural Left. In 1981, through an exiled Salvadoran artist, I joined the Central America Solidarity movement, which exposed me to other baffling facets of cross-cultural organizing and eventually produced the national campaign Artists Call Against U.S. Intervention in Central America. Early in the decade I traveled to China, Cuba, Nicaragua, El Salvador, and Australia—all of which were eye-openers in different ways. At the

GUARDED CONDITIONS

SEX ATTACKS | SKIN ATTACKS | SEX ATTACKS | SKIN ATTACKS | SEX ATTACKS | SKIN ATTACKS | SEX ATTACKS | SKIN ATTACKS | SEX ATTACKS | SKIN ATTACKS
SEX ATTACKS | SKIN ATTACKS | SEX ATTACKS | SKIN ATTACKS | SEX ATTACKS | SKIN ATTACKS | SEX ATTACKS
SKIN ATTACKS | SEX ATTACKS | SKIN ATTACKS | SEX ATTACKS

Lorna Simpson, *Guarded Conditions*, 1989. Eighteen color Polaroid photographs with twenty-one plastic plaques, 91 x 131 in. La Jolla Museum of Contemporary Art, La Jolla, California

Lorna Simpson is an African-American photographer living in New York. This piece employs body language and cryptic phrases to draw attention to the imposed anonymity of the individual in many racist situations.

same time a very different kind of motivation, one that went deeper into my personal life, was emerging: the fact that I was/am looking for art that combines in some meaningful way both political and spiritual energies. Artists of color and artists in the Third World were the ones who were making that art. In New York I was acquainted with Latino, African, Native and Asian American artists; the time spent each year in Colorado made rural and Chicano culture real to a New Yorker. "Mixing It Up," an annual symposium of women artists of color that I organize ad hoc at the University of Colorado in Boulder, provides the kind of intellectual intensity and intimacy that I came to expect from feminist groups and encounters.

What then can be made of all this? Looking back over this sprint through a lifetime of cross-cultural relationships, I realize the powerful influences of the artists themselves, of the content rather than the form or formations of their art, and of the contexts in which it has been made. Increasingly since the sixties, I have become less and less interested in the machinations of the art world—in commerce and trends and the evil effects both have on the hearts of artists—and more and more interested in the kind of culture that reveals the world from different angles and moves people to change their own and others' lives or undermines the assumptions that keep people "in their places." Increasingly since the eighties, my concerns have grown broader and broader until sometimes I think I'll burst with fragmented emergencies. While I was working on *Mixed Blessings*, I had a dream in which I was told that I'd never finish the book. It scared me for a while, until I decided that it didn't mean I was going to die before the book came out (I didn't), but that the seeds sown in it would continue to sprout from now on.

The Return of the Critic

If those who have been made invisible by social forces are to represent themselves, white people at the same time must let go of the privilege of representing everybody. As Baldwin wrote, this is a reciprocal process. Every time people with whom we live—in both the personal and public sense—redefine themselves, we have to respond with our own reevaluations. It seems impossible for a white person working in this field to be totally free of cultural racism. Having spent the last five years or so trying to represent everybody, I now find myself in a peculiarly "liminal" area in regard to that process, realizing just how little I know about everything I thought I was an "expert" on and balancing on another threshhold when I'd expected to be in or out of the door by now.

One reason for this is that in the last two years the national discourse about racism, ethnocentrism, and intercultural/cross-cultural/multicultural art has intensified to a point few of us would have predicted five years ago. And we are finally hearing the "real stories" from an increasingly diverse group of intellectuals who are challenging the whole left-to-right spectrum of white cross-cultural conceptions.

Looking for the link that I missed, I see that we the critics and scholars concerned with cross-cultural discourse have not paid much attention to the development of *white* consciousness in relation to the development of the various ethnic consciousnesses. It has seemed immodest, self-indulgent, and even politically incorrect to focus on our own experience since its oceanic presence surrounds everyone. But what, for instance, was our contemporary response to art made in the context of the Civil Rights movement, Black Pride, or the Chicano Movimiento? I haven't read the last three decades' literature with this in mind, so I don't really know the specifics of our ignorance, but I do know that there were precious few exceptions to the general rule of indifference, dismissal, paternalism, and neglect.

I've been embarrassed to hear white folks (myself included) running on about the pain of racism, although it's true that I, and the dominant culture, suffer from it far more profoundly than is realized. Yet guilt cannot determine our approaches to the subject of racism. Responsibility is a better way of looking at it. There are obvious reasons why white people find themselves, or rather put ourselves, in the colonial position of being in control of the overview in a dominantly white society. If we weren't representing everybody there might be no overview. Would that be a disaster or a blessing or a mixed blessing? We say that we are making our texts porous and interrupted in order to give voice to others. But is it ours to give? Here we go again.

Another colonial gambit that can heighten the walls of the ghetto is the white enforcement of cultural apartheid by encouraging artists of color to stick to their cultural backgrounds, as though we do not share a dominant culture that affects all of us while representing few of us. For example, if white writers are going to subject everyone else to a naming process, identifying them as African American, Native American, from this or that place, with this or that life behind them, then it has to be reciprocal. It feels awkward at first to say "Jenny Holzer, a white artist, James Clifford, white ethnographer," because it is taken for granted that all artists and scholars are white, right? And only the exceptions need to be named?

Paralleling such Eurocentrism is another assumption that has not been sufficiently scrutinized: the feeling of many white people in this society that we've lost our roots, that we have no culture, or that our culture is just a lot less interesting than other people's. A kind of ethnocentric reversal has placed African-American, Latino, Native American, and Asian cultures in such a spotlight that there are white people envying—if with some condescension—those whose lives are often socially and economically unenviable. Rayna Green, a Cherokee writer who directs the American Indian program at the Smithsonian, looked out at the white people in a panel audience last June and said ironically, "You don't think you have a culture? Did you belong to a country club? Go to Boy Scouts? To church?" and so forth.

This is actually the kind of question white students like to answer, once they get used to the fact they are being asked. Variants might be: Look at the colloquial expressions you use, the way you dress, your habits of gift giving, ritual, family interaction, how you decorate your home, your yard, your car. How do these things reflect your culture? And if you think that none of this comes from your background, that it all comes from the foreground, then the dominant culture has become your culture.

All of this presents a dilemma both for white critics and for artists of color who still do not have the luxury of choosing to do whatever they want in art. If they are formalists, they may be accused of abandoning their roots and communities, although many African-American abstract artists in particular insist upon the African origins of their forms. If these artists are imagists, they can be accused of fulfilling the expectations of a white audience that prefers to ghettoize other cultures. Artists of color asked to participate in exhibitions, panels, etc., are expected to "speak for their people" and to concentrate on issues of culture, so-called race, and discrimination in the art world, or on "how I became a success against the odds." The most common response to the latter is "by going into my studio and forgetting the world," despite the fact that when the artist emerges, the world is not likely to have changed. A young black abstract painter will be seen as a young *black* painter, no matter how mainstream his work may be, just as a woman artist remains a woman artist and must also be better than good to attain even basic acceptance.

In addition, artists of color working however innocently from their cultural heritages or everyday lives (lived experience) are often perceived by the white mainstream as "political," as though anything with another flavor is by definition in opposition to the mainstream. And "political" isn't good news in art schools, galleries, and museums, unless it's the kind of (also valuable) generalized issue-oriented art that is not too angry and never names names or specifically locates corporate, governmental, or institutional guilt.

Why must one lose one's background to attain a foreground? The art world being what it is, there can only be ambivalence about a background—or a foreground—no matter how culturally rich and supportive, that is ignored or disdained by the dominant culture. I understand a lot better now the annoyance of some artists of color with those of us who have made too much of *their* cultural backgrounds and too little of *our* common foregrounds. And at the same time, overemphasis on the common foreground and underemphasis on the differences also cloud the issues as we enter what Exit Art founders Papo Colo and Jeanette Ingberman call the "hybrid state," with its "parallel cultures."

The goal, of course, must be a "multiculture" in which the artist is the one who chooses whether or not to deal with her or his cultural material and in which all good artists are recognized as such, no matter what subject matter they choose, according to multifaceted criteria. In a multiculture, people would know how to look at an artwork or an issue, not just from their own vantage point; they would know how to see in the round. However, in these touchy times, as we teeter on the brink between growing racism and growing understanding, a prime concern remains the relationship between the two.

There is an increased, and justified, mistrust of white audiences who are seeking, like tourists, only the "authentic," the "typical," the "exotic." But the other extreme is that sector of the mainstream that considers all culturally based art *de-based* art, non-art, folk art, crafts, etc., and only approves of art by people of color who have totally "escaped the

Clarissa Sligh, *Seeking Comfort, I Sucked My Thumb*, 1989. Cyanotype, 30 x 23 in. Collection of the artist

Sligh is an African-American photographer and book artist who often deals with the subject of childhood traumas, including incest and school segregation. This image is part of a "birth reenactment" series in which she tries to resurrect experiences buried in her subconscious.

ghetto" and have merged with the mainstream. Of course, once they get there, artists of color are often called "derivative" because white artists have already skimmed the surface of their cultural heritages.

This also poses a real problem for many white artists. The legend goes that artists can (as in the "Nigger Drawings") do anything without blame, that art is a realm in which anything goes. Yet, to paraphrase Amiri Baraka, some people have corporate support and millions of dollars to advertise in the *Times*, and we've got a pocket full of nickels for the Xerox machine. There may be a certain freedom of expression in the United States, but there is no equality of access for those who are financially unable to make their voices heard. Similarly, white artists are more likely to have access to education and travel and to feel comfortable in museums and libraries. In their/our journeys through other cultures, they/we innocently pick a flower here, a pattern there, an idea here, a prayer there.

Such Western borrowings range from the Cubists' appropriation of forms, to the Surrealists' appropriation of images, to the "primitivists'" and Conceptualists' appropriation of mythologies, ideas, and even belief systems, to the feminists' appropriation of ritual, to the leftists' appropriation of revolutionary imagery, and so forth. The territory may be thoroughly scavenged by the time an artist of color decides to nourish her or his art with fragments of tradition handed down through family or culture. Furthermore, if artists of color use the elements of their culture "differently," outside of the white consciousness of symbols or images, they may be accused not only of derivation, but of ineffectiveness.

Europeans and Euro-Americans do not have a god-given right to strip-mine world culture to their heart's content with rarely a credit or thank-you. (And credits and thank-yous don't heal the wounds either.) So what is the responsible position? What should all those white artists working with borrowed ritual, pattern, and imagery do about this? Must they disavow their work and stick to European sources or work only in the area of *inter*-action? As I've written before, there is a difference between homage and robbery, between mutual exchange and rape.[3] I don't think every white artist influenced by the power of other cultures should be overwhelmed with guilt at every touch, but a certain *humility* couldn't hurt. Such humility is uncommon among Western artists educated to express *themselves* rather than to be responsible for themselves in relation to society. It's all related to that old anthropological (and high art) habit of admiring the objects but disregarding the people who created them—a syndrome particularly common in relation to Native American art.

A major component of an enlightened attitude would be the acknowledgment of and familiarity with contemporary art being made by those whose pasts now appear to be common property. Lived experience is always a better source than second-hand experience, which does not mean that white artists should not look at, admire, and be influenced by Native American art. It simply means that white artists should look at Native American art *as white people* examining the interface rather than trying to pour themselves through the cracks.

We Shall See . . .

In 1992 the quincentennial of Columbus's accidental invasion of the Americas will be a battle royal of representations, with a focus on Native American culture. Alas, it could also mark the end of shortsighted American institutions' commitment to multiculturalism. White culture will be watched carefully for its responses. Turning the mirror around, native Canadian curators Lee-Ann Martin and Gerald McMaster have asked ironically about 1992, "Has history provided the perfect opportunity to assess Western rituals of celebration from a Native perspective?"[4]

Museums—bearers, for better or worse, of public assumptions about art—could play a key role in the development of white consciousness. What's in the museums, how it got there, and how it's displayed are all quincentennial issues. Four examples: in Santa Fe, which touts its touristic "triculturalism," Native American and Chicano artists are protesting the exclusion of artists of color from the Museum of Fine Arts's "Alcove Shows" of recent work; beginning in Florida, Indian anti-quincentennial activists have spearheaded imaginative protests around the NEH-funded traveling exhibition "First Encounters," with its rosy view of genocide; nationally, other institutions will be showing the "Submuloc Wohs" (Columbus Show) of progressive Native American art, curated by Flathead painter Jaune Quick-To-See Smith. In his 1986 *Artifact Piece*, an ironic

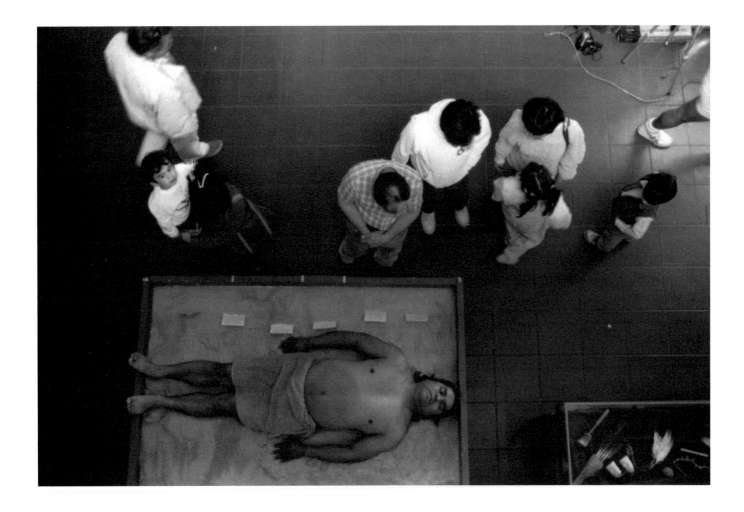

James Luna, *The Artifact Piece*, 1986.

Luna is a Luiseño/Diegueño from San Diego who lives on the La Jolla Reservation and calls himself a "contemporary traditionalist." This piece was first installed at the Museum of Man in San Diego, which has a large collection of Edward Curtis's photographs of "vanishing Americans" who, Luna counters, have not disappeared. Neighboring cases contained traditional artifacts and the Pop artifacts of a 1960s adolescence.

affirmation and reversal of the "vanishing Indian" (as photographer Edward Curtis once put it), Luiseño/Diegueño James Luna first raised these issues by exhibiting himself lying in a glass case at the Museum of Man in San Diego. Even when he vanished (left the case), he was very much there; his imprint remained in the bed of sand for the rest of the show.

Art museums are not only the receptacles but also the representation of our histories. They could also be the sites of historical reclamation. I keep asking myself what this continent would look like now if the government had honored all or any of the Native American treaties. Similarly, what would museums look like if the native, African, pre-Columbian, and Asian collections were administered, installed, and above all represented by those who made the art? Citing signage, docents' tours, exhibition design, etc., Chicana artist and educator Amalia Mesa Bains has insisted that "the issues of interpretation are as important as being able to be exhibited."[5] We need to take a radical tack on installation and display, an area in which all kinds of subliminally racist assumptions operate. One example is the remodeling of the American Indian collections at the Denver Art Museum. There are enlarged but unlabeled photographs of people and places (some apparently out of place, as when the Ohio Serpent Mound is placed in the "Southeast" section). They suggest a "generic Indian" approach to tribeless, nameless, placeless peoples. Then there are the gray, featureless "dummies" that wear the beautiful garments. These not only deny individuality but also demonstrate another colonial symptom: the pervasive notion that the objects are wonderful but the people who made them are either gone (those gray ghosts) or not very important (the ghosts are faceless).

Curators of American Indian exhibitions in particular need a new angle. White artist (and former anthropologist) Susan Hiller wrote of the 1977 touring exhibition "Sacred Circles: 2,000 Years of North American Indian Art": "It would have been educational, as well as providing badly needed 'context,' if the exhibition had attempted to make us aware of the interactions between the objects displayed and our own history; but instead, there has been an effort to empathize with the Native American world view."[6]

Museum people will also have to reconsider the whole question of what is art and what is not, expanding their notions to meet those of the cultures they exhibit. Anthropology's stranglehold on native art will have to be broken. Museum administrators will have to take responsibility for the return of Native American remains for respectful burial, the return of sacred objects for more appropriate use, and, though it's outside their purview, they should also consider the fate of indigenous sacred sites.

Lee-Ann Martin, who is surveying the treatment of native art in Canadian museums, has a radical suggestion that reflects a traditional lack of boundaries between art and life:

I think we should abolish the whole museum system. I don't think there should be an anthropology museum and an art museum. I think there should be institutes or cultural centers of human achievement. I don't think art should be separated from other aspects of human activity.[7]

This is not as off the wall (literally) as it sounds. Martin's viewpoint parallels the development of the most interesting strains of modern art, which have also been concerned with blurring boundaries and transcending borders between art and life. She also questions the presence of Indian art in her home institution, the Canadian Museum of Civilization:

If they want to go into Native art, why don't they show all historical art? Why don't they show the Group of Seven and put it in some sort of Canadian context? It's perfectly justified within their mandate. But they never do it. Because that's art. That's real art.[8]

Much of the responsibility lies with those of us for whom it is somewhat easier to be heard. I've been told to get out there and use my "white-skin privilege" to raise these issues, just as I've been told over the years by feminists of color to start proselytizing within my own community. There are a number of relatively easy ways for white people to ensure, selfishly, that we will have the privilege of working in a much more varied art context. White critic Moira Roth, who works intensively with and writes about women artists of color, has led the move for concerned whites to refuse to be on all-white panels, to write about all-white exhibitions, and so forth. The time is long overdue for artists of color to be included in exhibitions, magazines, and panels on all current aesthetic trends and issues that concern all artists—public art, appropriation, censorship, and Neo-everything. This need not exclude acknowledgment of racism in the art world nor the vastly different ways in which artists approach their own cultural backgrounds and foregrounds.

White consciousness cannot be developed in the white community alone. Perhaps a reciprocal, relational theory can be developed only in collaboration. And perhaps the collaboration is a social rather than a personal one. Now that so many more diverse voices are being heard, the possibilities are many. The danger is, as always, that these voices will only be heard briefly, as a trend rather than a necessity.

Tseng Kwong Chi, *Disneyland, California*, 1979. Gelatin silver print, 36 x 36 in.

Tseng was raised in Hong Kong, and his series of himself in prototypically "American" places examines exile and difference in a simultaneously deadpan and poignant framework.

Notes

1 James Baldwin, quoted in "A Talk to Teachers," in Scott Walker and Rick Simonson, eds., *Multicultural Literacy: The Graywolf Annual Five* (St. Paul: Graywolf Press, 1988), p. 8.

2 I follow the lead of Henry Louis Gates, Jr., and others in putting the term "race" in quotation marks since it is a historical rather than a scientific construct. See Gates, ed., *"Race," Writing and Difference* (Chicago: University of Chicago Press, 1986).

3 Lucy Lippard, "Give and Takeout," in Marcia Manhart and Tom Manhart, eds., *The Eloquent Object* (Tulsa: Philbrook Art Center, 1987).

4 Lee-Ann Martin and Gerald R. McMaster, "De-Celebration," *Artscraft* 2 (Spring 1990): 20.

5 Amalia Mesa-Bains, speech at the Western Museums Conference, San Jose, California, October 1990.

6 Susan Hiller, "Sacred Circles: 2,000 Years of North American Indian Art," *Studio International* 1 (1977): 56.

7 Lee-Ann Martin, quoted in Mike Anderson, "Where to Go From Here . . ." *Artscraft* 2 (Summer 1990): 15.

8 Ibid.

Frederic Remington

Within and Without the Past

Alex Nemerov

From behind the breastworks of his big desk the editor is banging at me to write about myself. I find the thought very chilly out here in the garish light, but his last shot says, "If you don't, I will send a person to interview you, and he will probably misquote you." Quite so—one doesn't need that character of help when about to play the fool; so if you find the going heavy, gentle reader, camp here.

I had brought more than ordinary schoolboy enthusiasm to Catlin, Irving, Gregg, Lewis and Clark, and others on their shelf, and youth found me sweating along their tracks. I was in the grand silent country following my own inclinations, but there was a heavy feel in the atmosphere. I did not immediately see what it portended, but it gradually obtruded itself. The times had changed.

Evening overtook me one night in Montana, and I by good luck made the camp-fire of an old wagon freighter. . . . I was nineteen years of age and he was a very old man. Over the pipes he developed that he was born in Western New York and had gone West at an early age. His West was Iowa. Thence during his long life he had followed the receding frontiers, always further and further West. "And now," said he, "there is no more West. In a few years the railroad will come along the Yellowstone and a poor man can not make a living at all." . . .

The old man had closed my very entrancing book almost at the first chapter. I knew the railroad was coming—I saw men already swarming into the land. I knew the derby hat, the smoking chimneys, the cord-binder, and the thirty-day note were upon us in a resistless surge. I knew the wild riders and the vacant land were about to vanish forever, and the more I considered the subject the bigger the Forever loomed.

Without knowing exactly how to do it, I began to try to record some facts around me, and the more I looked the more the panorama unfolded. . . . If the recording of a day which is past infringes on the increasing interest of the present, be assured there are those who will set this down in turn and everything will be right in the end. Besides, artists must follow their own inclinations unreservedly. It's more a matter of heart than head, with nothing perfunctory about it. I saw the living, breathing end of three American centuries of smoke and dust and sweat, and I now see quite another thing where it all took place, but it does not appeal to me.

—Frederic Remington[1]

In *Collier's Weekly* magazine for 18 March 1905, an issue devoted to the work of Frederic Remington (1861–1909), there appeared a statement by the artist entitled "A Few Words from Mr. Remington." These few words, however, say a great deal about the artist's role in documenting the Old West. In its openly figurative language, Remington's statement reveals an interest in a kind of representation that dealt less with faithfully documenting the past than with dramatizing the difficulty of its documentation at the turn of the century.

As a literary analogue to Remington's response to the difficulties he also confronted in painting scenes of the Old West, "A Few Words from Mr. Remington" is worth examining. Particularly noticeable is the seemingly sharp division between Remington's scene of writing and the historical scene he describes. The story opens with Remington meeting with his editor and then shifts to the young Remington's meeting with the old wagon freighter. (The editor's "banging" might well refer to typing, which would suggest that Remington is not actually meeting with his editor but reading a typewritten letter the editor has sent to him.) The sentence at the end of the second paragraph, "The times had changed," signals this apparently clean break between present and past. Immediately afterwards, we are transported back in time to the campfire scene.

Yet the second paragraph also suggests that the two realms are not in fact as easily separated as the simple declaration "The times had changed" would indicate. Despite the second paragraph's shift into the past tense and its reference to Remington with such words as *schoolboy* and *youth*, the second paragraph nonetheless evokes a library- or study-like setting where "Catlin, Irving, Gregg, Lewis and Clark, and others" reside in the form of volumes "on their shelf." This setting is similarly evoked in a subsequent paragraph, which refers to the old man in the historical scene as having "closed my very entrancing book almost at the first chapter."

More compellingly, the second paragraph also contains the sentence that begins "I was in the grand silent country following my own inclinations," an echo of which appears in the story's final paragraph: "Artists must *follow their own inclinations* unreservedly" (italics added). This second quotation reminds us that Remington regarded his career in terms of a dramatic separation between his earlier

work as an illustrator and his subsequent status as a fine artist who could choose his own subjects, or follow his "own inclinations." Accordingly, Remington's recollection about "following my own inclinations" in Montana may not represent his youthful wanderings so much as the artistic freedom—the imagination—with which Remington the established fine artist could render them. In this case it would amount to another intrusion of Remington's scene of writing, his present-day situation, upon his historical subject, for here he recalls his past using the very terms that express its imaginative representation, as if the image of the youthful Remington walking unfettered through the West were in fact a metaphor for the creative process, equally unfettered, by which this youthful Remington could be represented.[2] That Remington gained his artistic freedom thanks largely to *Collier's*, whose annual contract beginning in 1903 called for one original painting a month from his hand, only reinforces the idea that here, in the very pages of the magazine, he would unconsciously comment on his newfound artistic freedom.[3]

The story's relationship between the present and past becomes particularly clear when the opening scene is read against the historical scene set in Montana. In each scene Remington encounters another man (first the editor, then the old wagon freighter) who imparts disquieting information concerning the unwelcome intrusion of another party (first an interviewer, then the railroad). Further, there is the odd sentence in the first paragraph that begins "I find the thought very chilly out here in the garish light," which, as a description of Remington's scene of writing, resonates strangely with the scene in which the youthful Remington is illumined by a campfire ("garish light") out in the presumably cold ("chilly") night. As if to emphasize this connection, Remington ends his first paragraph by advising his reader—

oriented at that point to the author's study or library—to "camp here." In the story's final paragraph, moreover, he assures the reader that a representation of the past will not preclude a representation of the present—that "there are those who will set this [the present] down in turn and everything will be right in the end." Such a sentence epitomizes the confusion of past and present scenes that occurs throughout "A Few Words from Mr. Remington."

Of course, no one can be certain to what degree Remington unconsciously incorporated the imagery within his library or study into his historical narrative as he wrote it. But it seems fair to say that Remington's historical subject here is to some extent a representation of the scene in which it was written.[4] Remington as much as literalizes this assimilation when he describes the method of his historical documentation: "I began to try to record some facts around me." What this tells us is that on a subliminal level "A Few Words from Mr. Remington" is about the scene of representation—the writer's own situation—intruding upon and even determining the appearances of his historical subject matter.

What compelled Remington to design the past from the material of his own present-day situation? A certain self-reflexivity is always inherent in pictorial representation, for on some level within their work all artists must disclose information related to the circumstances in which their art took shape, even if this information concerns only the kinds of paint and canvas they used. In this way an artwork will always, if sometimes only nominally, allow us to conjure a vision of the artist in the act of its creation. So is this true, though in perhaps less direct ways, of a piece of writing. In "A Few Words from Mr. Remington," however, our sense of the writer's presence is quite explicit, and it is this explicitness that

prompts an explanation not in the problems inherent to the act of representation, but in a specific set of historical circumstances: namely, a widespread turn-of-the-century antimodernism that equated an idealized "Old America" with loss and distance and consequently contributed to an awareness of the *inherent* falsity of "realistic" historical representation.[5] The "Old America" required the preservationist representations of Remington and other history painters because it had largely disappeared; but, paradoxically, its representation could never ignore this disappearance and the problems it posed for realism or historical accuracy.

This nostalgic sense of disappearance was the central drama of Remington's life. "I sometimes feel," he wrote in his diary for 15 January 1908, "that I am trying to do the impossible in my pictures in not having a chance to work direct but as there are no people such as I paint it's 'studio' or nothing."[6] For Remington, as for others at the turn of the century, metaphors of loss and distance were inextricably bound with what it meant to imagine a historical scene.

A number of Remington paintings, particularly those executed in the last three years of his career, dramatize this sense of distance. Yet Remington's most prevalent metaphor for distance may surprise those who perceive him as possessing a maudlin, uncritical sentiment for days gone by, for distance in Remington's late paintings is most often conveyed as the distance between paint and what it represents. Despite all the forms it may take, paint for Remington is always and intractably just paint, and as such a powerful evocation of the absence of the very things it represents.

Two kinds of images of mere paintedness appear in Remington's work. The first is a figure coming to acknowledge itself—with varying degrees of concern, fear, or anger—as nothing more than

1 *The Old Stagecoach of the Plains,*
1901. Oil on canvas, 40 x 27 in.
Amon Carter Museum, Fort
Worth, Texas

paint. The second is a figure of Remington himself painting the very scenes in which he is metaphorically included.

This is not to argue that Remington *consciously* included images of mere paintedness in his work. In fact, Remington himself would undoubtedly tell us that his paintings are triumphant precisely because they contain no mere paint; that is, that all his paint successfully disguises itself as cowboys, Indians, horses, and other things of the world. Late in his life he wrote, "I stand for the proposition of 'subjects'—painting something worthwhile against painting *nothing* well—merely paint."[7] Yet perhaps Remington protests too much.

The Eternal West

Before the emergence of Remington's expressions of mere paint, his earlier works sought to preserve or document the Old West in a way that rigorously denied the distance between paint and what it represents. To do this, Remington depended upon a professedly transcriptive style in which accurate detail, graphic violence, and the dramatic incorporation of the space of the viewer all express his pictures' realism. Yet his later paintings downplay this literal realism in favor of a kind of *essential* realism—a realism less reliant on appearances than on essences. Detail and graphic violence are often absent in these later works, often described as expressing the "mystery," if not the literal truth, of Remington's western subjects.[8]

Such descriptions are correct insofar as they go, for Remington clearly intended something different—something less literal and more self-consciously imaginative—in his later works. Yet "mystery" is an imprecise word to describe these later paintings, for Remington specifically relied on themes from Christian and classical mythology as a means of suggest-

ing the essential or spiritual truth of the Old West.

In Remington's *The Old Stagecoach of the Plains*, for example, the stagecoach seems to move downhill in a generally straightforward way toward the space of the artist/viewer (fig. 1). Yet, as we realize that this downward movement is not the only action within the painting—that, in short, the stagecoach can be said to move *up* as well—the image becomes far from straightforward or literal, and its Christian meanings begin to unfold.

In several important respects the stagecoach is identified with the sky, or with the upper half of a picture that neatly divides into two realms: earth and heaven. Its lanterns mirroring the light of the stars, the stagecoach itself is dramatically silhouetted against the sky. Similarly, many of the delicate, wispy forms on or around the stagecoach—the hats, gun, and railing, for example—are literally "airier" than the blocky, solid forms below.

Nevertheless, the stage still moves downhill. The horses pull it precipitously downward, a movement accentuated by the figurative "weight"—the sheer two-dimensional bulk—of the horses and their shadows. The lower realm of the picture, as it were, "weighs" more than the airy, upper realm, and this formal device, as much as the picture's manifest action, enhances our sense of the stage's descent. Moreover, the heaviness of the forms is reflected in the manner of their depiction: Remington richly painted the lower registers of *Old Stagecoach*, making the horses' shadows, the roadside brush, and the road itself a turgid chop of paint whose lugubrious quality analogizes the weight of the forms it renders.

The stagecoach, rising as it sinks, black and lantern-lit, belongs to both heaven and earth. This interaction between realms suggests that Remington conceived of the spirituality of the Old West as born of its physical disappearance—a variation on the old idea that immortality comes

only in death. As the shadows of the horses adumbrate the shadow of the stagecoach, creating an ominous rhythm of departure, the stagecoach appears to ascend into the sky.[9]

This ascension represents the apotheosis of the Old West. Silhouetted against the sky, looking down on the earth with an omniscience afforded by his position atop the stagecoach, the gun-bearing figure calls to mind a deity rising into or already ensconced in the heavens. Given the relationship between the lanterns and stars, the apotheosized stagecoach also takes the form of a constellation. The prominent star to the right of the stagecoach falls into line with the parallel lights of the lanterns, making a row of three "stars" that suggests an already-constellated stage, its lanterns merely two points in its heavenly delineation.

Yet, however fixed that delineation appears, the stagecoach is still ascending. The star to its right leads our eye to another prominent star above, and, taken together, these two white points not only perfectly continue the upward trajectory of the stagecoach, adding to our sense of its movement from one realm to another, but also anticipate the stagecoach's final placement in the sky: they are its constellation, its sky-bound representation. They are the form *it will take*. If the topmost star now represents one of the stage's lanterns, it has then replaced a moving, flickering, extinguishable light—indeed, the very light of the West's memento mori—with a light that will not change. So too has the constellation as a whole arrested the stage's precipitous downward movement, its threat to disappear forever, and represented it in terms of a permanence that befits its identity as an icon of the West. The stagecoach, transfixed in the sky and on the canvas, is stopped in time.

By connecting a western icon to a certain conception of the eternal, Remington somewhat shrilly resolved the Old West's actual disappearance. The emblems of this connection include the reins that tie the horses to the stage, foreground to background, and earth to sky. But it is the gun-bearing figure atop the stagecoach that is perhaps the picture's most spectacular expression of connectedness. Indeed, the inextricability of his twin identities—seated cowboy and enthroned god—achieves a union of the physical and the spiritual that forgoes the need for links or any other manifestation of connectedness. Instead, the two, cowboy and god, connect in a way that effaces evidence of the connection. Following in the great romantic tradition of unity between the physical and spiritual worlds, they *are* one another.

This ultimate connection was crucial to Remington's attempt to eradicate historical distance and provide his viewers with an immediate view of the past, for, by extrapolation, such an emblem of connection helped him to deny the difference between the painting and its subject. On the painting's own terms, no medium links the painting and the past. Instead, the two entities *are* one another. As such, the alarming sense of separation occasioned by the actual making of the picture—the distance between paint and what it depicts, between present and past—is repressed. The movement of the stagecoach also confirms this: rolling into our space, the stage effectively joins the two worlds—that of the painting and the artist's space in front of the painting—in a way that seeks to deny the fundamental difference between the two.

Merely Paint

The strategies Remington employed in *The Old Stagecoach of the Plains*, painted in 1901, also appeared in paintings produced later in his career, specifically the years 1907–9. In *Night Halt of the Cavalry*, painted in 1908, the figure with

2 *Night Halt of the Cavalry*, 1908.
Oil on canvas, 27 x 40 in. Private
collection

head bowed, hat off, and hands clasped in
a prayerful gesture alerts us—even though
he himself, in his slumber, is not alert—to
the presence of Christian themes (fig. 2).
The importance of his gesture is under-
scored by its repetition throughout the
canvas: the leftmost figure clearly mirrors
the position of the hatless figure, as does
the solitary middleground figure directly
to the right of the most prominent horse's
rump. Equally significant are the two
curiously symbiotic figures whose whitish
gloves, together with the similarly colored
horse's head between them, create a
triangular shape that repeats the prayerful posture of the figure in the right
middleground.

Also striking is the resemblance
between the horses' heads, particularly
the two seen in profile, and the sculptural
ornamentation of medieval cathedrals,

which so intrigued Remington's culture.
This association is reinforced in the
stillness and rigidity of the horses' heads
and, perhaps most dramatically, in the
archlike spring of the nearest horse, from
its front hooves to its mouth.[10] Under this
"arch," appropriately, the image's most
conspicuous prayer takes place.

But it is in respect to another of the
picture's Christian references that we can
begin to measure its difference from the
earlier *Old Stagecoach*. The action of
Night Halt suggests another, holier halt—
namely, the Rest on the Flight into
Egypt—and in this suggestion the
painting betrays an overall theme of
stillness, or immobility, that markedly
contrasts with the flowing, dynamic
movement of *The Old Stagecoach*.

In *Night Halt* all of the soldiers except
one are motionless. The horses stand in

3 *Fired On*, 1907. Oil on canvas, 27 1/8 x 40 in. National Museum of American Art, Smithsonian Institution, Gift of William T. Evans

their sculptural rigidity. Even the picture's emphatic horizontal orientation denies another kind of movement—the spiritual movement from earth to sky. The horses and the dark band on the horizon effectively block any relationship between the figures and the heavens. In this way Remington can be said to have simultaneously posited and denied the transcendence of his subject matter, for his figures are cut off from the heavens by the very roofs under which they pray.

The picture's extreme stasis also extends into another realm. Whereas *The Old Stagecoach* annexes the space before itself, so that the stagecoach seems to be rolling into our space, in *Night Halt* this space is represented as threatening and foreign to the realm of the picture. The figure third from the left has noticed something in the space directly in front of the picture. He clutches his gun and prepares to investigate, placing his weight on his left leg as if he were about to stand. This action, it is true, might be seen as fundamentally no different from *The Old Stagecoach*'s evocation of the viewer's space as part of the depicted action. Yet,

on another level, *Night Halt* implies a presence considerably more disturbing than that of the western interloper suggested by the manifest narrative: the presence of the painter himself in the act of painting the very scene we see.

Several factors lead to this conclusion. The trooper's stare directly out of the picture is a traditional way of evoking the divide across which the stare takes place. Such a stare has the power to objectify a viewer (or painter) in front of a canvas as part of a world that is fundamentally different from the world "inside" that canvas.[11] As if to emphasize this difference, the trooper is uncertain about and perhaps even fearful of the foreign world he has seen. Moreover, his uncertainty about what is out there evokes the night—the literal impediment to his vision—as a *representation* of the fundamental divide across which he struggles to see. As such, the night may be read as corresponding to the picture plane, as if Remington had painted not only on this picture plane but also *the picture plane itself*, acknowledging it as a kind of barrier between his world and the world he depicts. The night may thus be interpreted here (and in certain other Remington nocturnes) as a kind of "surface" that, exactly like the picture plane itself, blocks movement in and out of the picture.

Other late Remington paintings raise the same issues more explicitly. In *Fired On*, gunshots have halted six horsemen at the edge of a body of water (fig. 3). The gunshots come from outside the picture, the realm that concerned the trooper in *Night Halt*, but here this threatening presence outside the picture is more forcefully linked to the painter himself—or, more specifically, to his act of painting.

The conspicuous fear of the white horse is the key to this link. The horse may not literally see itself in the water, but in a figurative sense it does: it is terrified by the splashes of water that formally correspond to its tail and mane. These splashes, appearing on the flat surface of the water, suggest by way of analogy paint applied to the surface of the canvas itself, much like the paint that composes the horse itself. Remington painted the horse's torso in a richly slathered impasto and other areas—primarily the neck—in a light, scumbly style that reveals the rough weave of the canvas, and it is this manifestly painted status that allows us to understand the horse's fear. In those paintlike sprays or strokes on the water it sees itself vaporized, abstracted, bodiless—as the "mere paint" that it is. Like the trooper in *Night Halt*, except more dramatically, it recognizes that it belongs to a world in which there are no rocks, water, or stars, but only paint. It is an awful recognition for the horse as well as for the artist whose emotions the horse embodies.

In Remington's art, a figure's recognition of its mere paintedness could also be hostile. In *Apache Scouts Listening*, which Remington worked on and completed simultaneously with *Night Halt*

in 1908, a group of frontiersmen and Apaches has stopped before an unidentified presence beyond the picture (fig. 4). Although this presence exists to the right of the picture plane and thus does not seem to correspond to the space of the painter, its ominous character is indicated by something that emerges from the painter's space: namely, the shadow that extends across the bottom of the picture.

This shadow tells us that the painter's realm is, appropriately, the realm from which images emerge, but what kind of image, in this case, is it? Or, better, *whose* image? As much as it might convincingly suggest the presence of a tree just outside the painting, the shadow is the only evidence of the tree's existence, a copy of something that we cannot see. Yet the shadow also evokes an actual presence before the picture: Remington himself in the act of painting his scene. Incorporating Remington's signature, the smaller pattern of shadow at right falls perfectly into the diagonal line defined by the shadows of the kneeling Apaches above. Formally, this shadow is like the shadows cast by all the figures in the painting, as if it too were cast by a human presence, specifically that implied by Remington's signature. This signature crucially provides a presence—an actual being casting the shadow—that is missing in the case of the tree.[12] Moreover, the "Remington" shadow appears in the general direction in which the scouts strain to see (and even hear) an alien presence.

This relationship between the painter and his painting is not merely one of curiosity but one of outright hostility. Like the horses in *Night Halt*, the Apaches seem to evoke the sculptural ornamentation on cathedral facades, but this time the ornamentation is monstrous: the three kneeling Apaches resemble crook-armed gargoyles squatting on their haunches. Oriented toward the picture plane, the gargoyle-like Apaches can thus be seen as further literalizations of the "facade" of

4 *Apache Scouts Listening,* 1908. Oil on canvas, 27 x 40 in. Private collection

this picture plane, analogizing the function of the night as an expression of surface. As gargoyle-like beings, the Apaches suggest a frightening, monstrous presence confronting the artist as he made his picture.

This same theme is crystallized in another late Remington painting, *Wolf in the Moonlight (Moonlight, Wolf)* (fig. 5). About 1909, when Remington made this picture, wolves had long functioned in his art as symbols of inveterate hostility within the natural world: the intractable otherness of nature.[13] In *Wolf in the Moonlight*, however, the hostile difference of the wolf is that of the painting itself.

Aligned with and centered within the picture plane and related both formally and tonally to the surrounding scene, the wolf condenses the painting's imagery within its body. Its eyes match the two prominent stars in the sky, its body is reflected in the water, the line of its back and head parallels the line of the distant sloping hill, and its white-tipped tail assumes the colors and elongated forms of the hill and sand. In short, the hostile presence of the wolf, with its threatening

squint at the painter-viewer, is synonymous with the painting as a whole.

The painting "is" a wolf. Remington expressed his painting's foreboding otherness—its fundamental difference from the world it represents—through what had been since early in his career the most powerful symbol of otherness within his art. Yet the wolf is now no longer a monster in the world but a monster of the artist's own creation, and like the gargoyle Apache scouts, it glowers at its maker.

Why in these two paintings would Remington paint monstrous or quasi-monstrous figures staring back at him? Perhaps it is because monstrousness or otherworldliness became one of Remington's ways of acknowledging that nothing could be literally more unlike the world it represents than paint itself.

That most important Romantic allegory of artistic creation, the Frankenstein myth, helps clarify this point. For having brought a monstrous otherness into the world—for having created a thing that only *represents* a living being—Dr. Frankenstein's punishment is to be forever haunted by his awful creation.

5   *Wolf in the Moonlight (Moonlight, Wolf)*, ca. 1909. Oil on canvas, 20 1/16 x 26 in. Addison Gallery of American Art, Phillips Academy, Andover, Massachusetts

In this tradition Remington represents himself as continually confronted by the monstrosity of his creation. The stroke that makes a figure "live"—the stroke of realism itself—also leaves the figure looking back from the oblivion of a merely painted world, a world monstrous because it only *seems* to be alive. Hence the wolf's stare. "I am alone and miserable; man will not associate with me" is the Frankenstein monster's hateful reproach to its creator.[14]

Thus, too, the "stare" of the entire painting. The stars, formally corresponding to the eyes of the wolf, become so many vigilant "eyes" subjecting the artist to a witheringly penetrative gaze. But it

is the wolf itself that most powerfully projects this scrutiny. Whereas the white horse dissolves into mere paint in *Fired On*, the figure of the wolf reverses this process: paint is gathered or coalesced, seemingly from the peripheries of the image, into the corporeal form at the center. Yet it is a form whose sinister stare expresses the continuing threat of its mere paintedness. Indeed, the wolf's stare is metaphorically the stare of paint itself at Remington, confronting him with its own brute materiality, with its status not as fur, eyes, water—those representations that allow us to suspend our disbelief—but as an opaque gunk that bears no relation to any of these things.

6   *His First Lesson*, 1903. Oil on
canvas, 27 1/4 x 40 in. Amon Carter
Museum, Fort Worth, Texas

Painter into Painting

The second metaphor of mere paintedness in Remington's work is the painter
himself represented within his very
paintings. In *His First Lesson*, a work
that on close inspection has more to
do with picture making than any other
Remington painting, the shadow of a
fence and its gate extends from outside
into the picture itself (fig. 6). The shadow
is more than just an illusionistic continuation of the scene, however; it also creates a
rectangle that corresponds to the rectangle
of the picture plane itself. Extending from
the realm of the painter, this shadow
amounts to a metaphorical representation
of the canvas itself on an easel in front of
the pictured scene, as if this canvas and
easel cast the shadow into the scene they

depict. This metaphorical canvas is like
an open window, however, since it is only
the *frame* and easel that cast a shadow.
Yet, from another perspective, this
metaphorical canvas is far from transparent, for there is a sense that canvas and
easel exist less as a mere shadow of
themselves than *as* themselves, as if
Remington painted into his picture the
very canvas on which his scene is depicted. Seen in this way, the painting
would amount to a finished painting of
itself within the landscape it depicts, as if
Remington showed us a view from behind
himself as he painted. In this sense, even
as it posits its own transparency, the
canvas would be represented as blocking
or covering the scene it depicts.

This ambivalence about painting
and paint itself—transparent yet really

opaque—is reinforced by the other "paintings" in *His First Lesson.* Along the walls behind the main figures are six windows and one doorway that suggest pictures on a wall. Like the gate, these shapes are both open and closed, transparent and opaque: although the windows are open, they allow us only an unsatisfying view of the building's darkened interior and appear as closed as the one that is shuttered.

The doorway is the most interesting of these simultaneously open and closed spaces. It shows the resolution of the picture's main action: a horse complacently under a man's domination. The man holds the horse's bridle, but his control is also registered by the tidy enclosure of man and horse within the "frame" of the doorway. In this sense the doorway scene is related to the work's main scene. Each depicts a horse "tamed" not only by ropes but also by the grid or box in which it is confined. While the main action depicts the taming as being still in process, the doorway scene depicts the taming as being complete. Between these two poles, serving as an intermediary between the wild and tame, is the man astride the white horse. Although he has his horse under control, it has not yet been literally domesticated like the horse framed within the doorway.

This drama of domestication is about picture making. In the step-by-step taming of the horse, the painting takes us through the analogous stages in which Remington subdued or tamed the wildness of his intransigent medium, until it made a "subdued" picture such as the one framed in the doorway.

Such concerns about picture making may have been especially important to Remington at the time. Peter Hassrick has pointed out that *His First Lesson* "was the first Remington painting which *Collier's* published in color. Shortly thereafter, Remington signed a contract with the magazine in which he agreed to furnish

them a dozen comparable paintings each year in return for $12,000 salary."[15] Given the pivotal moment of his career when Remington made the painting, it is possible that the impending challenge of becoming a fine artist, of "taming" a new field, helped determine the subject matter of the very picture that officially inaugurated this change in artistic status.

If the title of Remington's painting really refers to a kind of *art* lesson, what exactly has been learned about art? Has it been a lesson in making a painting, pure and simple; or has it been a lesson—a less than happy lesson—in recognizing that a finished painting, neat and tidy within its frame, is in fact the wildest thing imaginable because the paint of which it is made only *seems* tame? This is the question raised by *His First Lesson*. Does language—in this case, paint—reveal or obscure the world?

Possible answers can be found in the foreground and doorway figure groups, each of which is organized on a threshold, a boundary between exterior and interior space, that can be likened to the picture plane itself. As openings that transport the viewer from one realm to another, both the gate and doorway function like the threshold of the picture plane according to the classical definition of painting. Yet in each case this role is questioned. Just as the closed gate shuts us off from the action, as an image of the canvas itself it also represents the opacity of this canvas by its projection into the scene in a way that paradoxically conceals the very reality it wishes to display. The canvas is only a sham or shadow gateway. So too is the doorless doorway, an otherwise inviting image of entry, closed to the viewer by both its pitch blackness and the man and horse. Standing exactly on its threshold, the man seems to guard this doorway: his body becomes another boundary beyond which the viewer cannot pass. In the doorway scene Remington's first lesson ends with an image of a finished painting

7 Diego Velázquez, *Las Meninas (The Maids of Honor)*, 1656. Oil on canvas, 125 x 108 in. The Prado, Madrid

not as a pure and simple creation but as a hostile otherness.

Several other points are worth noting about *His First Lesson*. The doorway portrait, like the darkened windows, could more specifically be called a nocturne, a status that links its themes still further to those in Remington's nighttime scenes. The man and horse stare from their nocturne like the wolf in *Wolf in the Moonlight*. Also noteworthy is how these doorway figures appear as a mirror image of the standing Apache and horse to the right in *Apache Scouts Listening*, a correspondence that precisely links the doorway group to the confrontation at work in *Apache Scouts*. This hostile confrontation—only implied in *Wolf, Apache Scouts*, and the doorway scene—actually takes place in the foreground of *His First Lesson*, where the horse's defiance has repelled a man who strikingly resembles a painter painting the very thing that repels him. The man's right hand is connected to the horse via a taut rope that suggests a paintbrush umbilically linking the two. His defensive stance away from the horse is exactly like the posture of an artist standing back from his work to survey it, as though this traditional gesture of connoisseurial appraisal also announced the artist's repulsion at the monstrous otherness he had created. Indeed, in the lines of the harness traversing the horse's head, we even see where the artist's metaphorical paintbrush has just traveled, as though the drag of the brush upon the horse's head—the process of being manufactured—were provoking its hostility.

Lastly, as might befit an image so thoroughly concerned with picture making, *His First Lesson* contains several unexpected and startling affinities with Diego Velázquez's *Las Meninas (The Maids of Honor)*, perhaps the most famous painting about picture making (fig. 7). For example, the fenced enclosure in Remington's painting, suggested in the background fence that is presumably connected to the fence implied by the gate shadow, evokes the pictorial space as a "room" like the room in *Las Meninas*. Along the back walls of this room, as in Velázquez's painting, dark "pictures" are arranged. One of these pictures—the shuttered window—is different from the others, much as the mirror reflecting the king and queen differs from the surrounding paintings in *Las Meninas*. In both paintings, too, a man looks into the scene as he stands in a doorway along the right side of the back wall, and a painter or painterlike figure stands on the left. Finally, the taming of the horse could be likened to the social training of the infanta. Whether or not Remington knew of *Las Meninas*, his use of Velázquez's motifs would have aligned him with Thomas Eakins, John Singer Sargent, and other contemporaries who quoted from *Las Meninas* in their paintings.[16]

A little landscape painting Remington made late in his career offers a comparable image of his art-making presence. *Chippewa Bay* represents the sheltered inlet off the St. Lawrence where Remington had his summer island home (fig. 8). (The island would be just off the left edge of the canvas.) At first glance the picture seems to offer a deep and virtually unlimited view into one of Remington's beloved scenes of the "Old America." Painted from a commanding vantage point atop a local hill, the picture shows the Canadian shore clearly in the distance, a view that seems to celebrate the possibility of almost limitless seeing, of gazing into the historical distance in a way that Remington's other late pictures generally deny.

The pictorial structure of *Chippewa Bay* underscores this sense of union with the distance—and more particularly with the historical distance—that the scene evokes. Ostensibly disparate objects assume one another's properties, thereby evincing relationships or connections that

cross boundaries and consequently reflect the work's larger sense of historical connectedness. The chimney of the distant farmhouse, for example, is mirrored in the similar "chimney" on the island directly behind it. The barn, long and low against the water, likewise resembles one of the similarly shaped islands. The irregular rectangles of the islands resonate with the shapes of the clouds, as do the splotches of sunlight on the foreground rocks. Finally, the big, rectangular rock in the left foreground matches the shape of the barn in the distance, creating a wonderful rush of space in which foreground and background, the space of the painter and the distant old-time farm, are magically united.

The foreground ledge in *Chippewa Bay* is also an expression—far more literal than any we have seen so far—

of Remington's vantage point, for it is certainly on this ledge that he painted this picture. Because the ledge's big rectangular rock relates not only to the shape of the distant barn but also to the shape of the canvas itself, it can also be seen as another metaphorical representation of Remington's canvas strangely depicted into the very scene it depicts. Indeed, in several ways the rock is distinctly canvas-like. With Remington's signature and the swaths and splotches across its surface, the rock has the appearance of having been not only "painted upon," but also painted upon in a suggestively abstract way—"merely" painted upon. But it is the rock's dark left side that best identifies it as a "canvas," for this side is visible from the front, suggesting that the rock, like a canvas, is flat. Remington's signature and the words "Chippewa Bay" extend in perfect flatness from the rock's

9　*Shotgun Hospitality*, 1908. Oil on canvas, 27 x 40 in. Hood Museum of Art, Dartmouth College, Hanover, New Hampshire, Gift of Judge Horace Russell, Class of 1865

side to front, heightening our sense of its two-dimensionality. In its curious representation, then, the rock summarizes the picture as a whole—its illusion of three dimensions, even of heaviness and solidity, on what is really only a two-dimensional surface.

In this respect, the foreground ledge is represented as fundamentally different from the virtually limitless scene extending beyond it. The painter's access to the distance is posited only so that it may be denied. His position atop a cliff mitigates the connection between his act of painting and what he sees. Within *Chippewa Bay*, he literally cannot get from the cliff to the house in the distance,

a dislocation reinforced by the worm fence that intrudes, like the fence in *His First Lesson*, between realms. Similarly, Remington's exaggeration of his actual vantage point (from a gentle hill on the William Cuthbert farm into the foreboding cliff in the picture) emphasizes the difference between the painting and the world it represents.[17] (So too are the darkened windows of the little white house, a return to the visual device used in *His First Lesson*, a statement of pictorial difference.) Actually, it would have been easy for Remington to reach the distance represented in his picture. To read this or any other Remington painting literally, however, is to miss its meaning. *Chippewa*

10 *The Biggest Thing in Shafter's Army Was My Pack.* Published in *Harper's Monthly* 97 (November 1898): 962. Helen L. Card Collection, Thomas J. Watson Library, Metropolitan Museum of Art

Bay is about a *figurative* inability to bridge distance—the distance between paint and the world it shows but cannot touch.

One other painting from 1908 provides us with perhaps the most dramatic example of this theme in Remington's art. In *Shotgun Hospitality*, it is now not a canvas but a shadowy human presence that intrudes onto the scene (fig. 9). Like the gate and the open windows in *His First Lesson* and the rock in *Chippewa Bay*, this figure that establishes our point of entry into the scene also paradoxically blocks our access to what is depicted. Yet, despite the figure's concealing blanket and turned back, his intrusive presence is in fact Remington's most complete dramatization of his own presence within one of his paintings. The picture shows us the artist himself, figuratively standing before the very picture in which he is included. His shadowy figure does in fact stand directly in front of a "canvas," manifest in the collapsed (perhaps significantly) canvas atop the wagon. Moreover, he stands before a flat rectangle—the right

side of the wagon—that approximates the shape of the painting itself.

Although such an interpretation may presuppose a curious viewpoint—the artist depicting himself fully from behind —precedents exist within Remington's art for just such a self-portrait. In *The Biggest Thing in Shafter's Army Was My Pack* (fig. 10), an illustration Remington made for one of his *Harper's Monthly* stories on the Spanish-American War, the artist represented himself in a manner similar to that of the foreground figure in *Shotgun Hospitality*. Likewise, in an informal drawing accompanying a letter to his friend Joel Burdick, he explicitly showed himself from behind in the act of representation (fig. 11).

The kneeling man staring at the intruder in *Shotgun Hospitality*, then, plays the role we have seen so often: the figure perceiving the artist and thus coming to perceive himself as nothing more than the artist's creation, as having no reality beyond the image in which he is confined. Here the moment of perception is

11 Untitled cartoon, 1889. Ink on paper, 7 x 9 in. Joel Wakeman Burdick Papers, Essex County Historical Society, Elizabethtown, New York

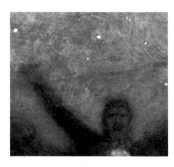

12 *Fired On*, (detail), 1907. Oil on canvas, 27 1/8 x 40 in. National Museum of American Art, Smithsonian Institution, Gift of William T. Evans

13 Jacques-Louis David, *Bonaparte Crossing the Great St. Bernard*, 1801. Oil on canvas. Musée National Du Château, Malmaison

particularly intense. It is as if the kneeling figure strokes his chin not in mere wonderment but in self-exploration, as though the sight of the painter were causing him to feel the paint of which he is made.[18]

Crossing Boundaries: Ambition and Failure

The greatest expression of this anxiety in Remington's art is the boundary. We can no sooner cross into the world of the wolf or pass through the doorway enclosing the man and horse than these figures may cross into ours. Paintings such as *Fired On* and *Wolf in the Moonlight* even literalize the idea of uncrossable boundaries by representing their figures conspicuously stopped on the very border separating their own from other worlds. These paintings contrast forcefully with the flowing connectedness—the denial of boundaries—that characterized an earlier work like *The Old Stagecoach of the Plains*. If in the *The Old Stagecoach* the stagecoach illusionistically moves into the viewer's space as a continuation of the picture, in Remington's late paintings his figures stop and stare before this same, yet very alien, space.

Yet, examples of boundary crossing do emerge in certain later paintings. In the background of Fired On, for example, is a strange figure whose head and arm conspicuously transgress the boundary between hill and sky (fig. 12). The implied quickness of the figure's move-ment, together with his primal yell, suggest that this transgression is exhilarat-ing. Indeed, he appears metaphorically freed from the flat, dark oblivion by which his own body and much of the lower portion of the picture is repre-sented, as though he were freed from the paint itself.

Yet there is also a sense of futility about the figure's transgression. He literally reaches for the stars, a reach that is paradigmatic of Remington's conception of the hopelessness of reaching for that which is faraway—the past—with paint. This sense of futility is perhaps best expressed in Remington's ironic use of the figure's heroic gesture—beloved by earlier Romantic artists as an expression of untrammeled power and bravado (fig. 13)—in a context that manifestly con-cerns doubt, fear, and confusion.

The gesture recurs in other Remington paintings, where it similarly connotes the desire, continually questioned or denied, to refer beyond a painting's boundaries. *Moonlight Scouting Party*, in many ways like *Fired On*, depicts a similar boundary-crossing figure, whose outstretched right arm and reaching hand, cast once more in a play with the distant stars, appear to feel the picture's limits, as though he were straining to touch the frame within which he is enclosed (fig. 14). In *With Eye of the Mind*, an Indian explicitly attempts to interpret and copy the shape of a distant cloud with his raised hand, inviting a comparison to Remington's own task of interpreting and copying a past he thought of as murky and unclear (fig. 15).[19] In *Trail of the Shod Horse*, the standing Indian scout similarly attempts to recount a prior event with a sign that copies what he has seen (fig. 16). Taken from the *Hellenistic Dancing Faun* (fig. 17), a plaster cast of which Remington saw at the Yale School of Fine Arts, the pose represents not only Remington's conception of the sensuous faunlike wildness of the Indian scout, but also his own similar conception of historical interpretation itself.[20] The picture equates its own copying of the past—epitomized in the scout's interpretive gesture—with the stereotypical sensuousness or illogic of the Indian cultures Remington professed to distrust.

It may seem arbitrary that this gesture, above all others, most concisely expresses Remington's doubts about representing

14 *Moonlight Scouting Party*, ca.
1907. Oil on canvas, 27 x 40 in. The
Thomas Gilcrease Institute of
American History and Art, Tulsa,
Oklahoma

15 *With the Eye of the Mind*, 1908.
Oil on canvas, 27 x 40 in. The
Thomas Gilcrease Institute of
American History and Art, Tulsa,
Oklahoma

55 *American Art*

16 *Trail of the Shod Horse*, 1907. Oil
on canvas, 27 x 40 in. The Philip
Ashton Rollins Collection of Western
Americana, Princeton University
Library

17 Drawing class at the School of
Fine Arts, Yale College, ca. 1879,
with a plaster cast of the *Dancing
Faun* in the foreground.

the past. In another sense, however, it could not be more appropriate, for it resembles Remington's act of painting itself—the right-handed gesture with which he applied paint to canvas (fig. 18).

Fired On's figure with raised arm is especially revealing here, for the way it both crosses and does not cross boundaries bears more than a formal resemblance to Remington's act of painting. Like the figure's reach across boundaries, the very act of placing paintbrush on canvas creates a kind of flow between the world of the painting and that of the painter, a dynamic connection in which the brush itself is the conduit. By his brush, as by a magic wand, the nostalgic artist could know that which is both faraway and heavenly: the past.

Yet this same gesture in *Fired On* identifies the act of painting more cynically as a "reach" that reveals nothing except the boundaries it is supposed to break down. For Remington, as he subliminally represented his act of painting, the placement of paintbrush on canvas revealed an absolute boundary, a block in the magical flow between the painter and the past. This inviolable boundary was the painting itself. The gesture that makes a figure live is also the gesture that acknowledges the palpable otherness of the materials of representation: paint and canvas.

"There is no more West"

Remington's expressions of the inadequacy of his "realistic" representations of the past arose from his sense of utter dislocation from an idealized American past. He attempted to describe the feeling in the ending of "A Few Words from Mr. Remington": "I saw the living, breathing end of three American centuries of smoke and dust and sweat, and I now see quite another thing where it all took place, but it does not appeal to me." Likewise, in his diary he lamented the modernity of an Indian model:

"Kinrade" my indian came to pose. Says he is a Sac and Fox—he had a good figure but dont know how to put on a G string and is innocent of indian business. He acts tongue bred and dresses "western" actor fashion.[21]

Remington was not alone in his perception of an old and new America, but rather part of an entire culture that considered itself hopelessly dislocated from an idealized, sentimentalized pre-industrial time.[22]

"There is no more West," said the old wagon freighter to the young Remington, who then began to paint his western scenes. Yet what came to interest Remington was not "the West" but the "no more"—that great Romantic theme that determined, more than any cowboy or Indian, his way of thinking. And Remington's most eloquent statement of this "no more," this Romantic distance, was his sustained unconscious expression of his paintings as, in his own words, "merely paint." For at no time was something further away for Remington than at just that moment when he wanted to bring it close.

Notes

1   Frederic Remington, "A Few Words from Mr. Remington," *Collier's Weekly* 34 (18 March 1905): 16, reprinted in Peggy and Harold Samuels, eds., *The Collected Writings of Frederic Remington* (Garden City, N.Y.: Doubleday, 1979), pp. 550–51.

2   The very description of his historical meeting similarly summons the process of its imaginative creation: "I by good luck *made* the campfire of an old wagon freighter" (italics added).

3   On the *Collier's* contract, see, for example, Peggy and Harold Samuels, *Frederic Remington: A Biography* (Garden City, N.Y.: Doubleday, 1982), 344–45.

4   For this interpretation of "A Few Words from Mr. Remington," I am deeply indebted to Michael Fried's *Realism, Writing, Disfiguration: On Thomas Eakins and Stephen Crane* (Chicago: University of Chicago Press, 1987), particularly the chapter on Crane, and *Courbet's Realism* (Chicago: University of Chicago

Press, 1989). Here I would also like to acknowledge Fried's influence on my entire interpretation of Remington's art. Edward Snow's wonderful book *A Study of Vermeer* (Berkeley: University of California Press, 1979) was also influential.

5   Remington used the phrase "Old America" in a letter to another western painter, Carl Rungius: "We fellows who are doing the 'Old America' which is so fast passing will have an audiance [sic] in posterity whether we do at present or not"; quoted in Brian W. Dippie, *Remington and Russell* (Austin: University of Texas Press, 1982), p. 11.

6   Frederic Remington diary, 15 January 1908, Frederic Remington Art Museum, Ogdensburg, N.Y.

7   Remington to Al Brolley, 8 December [1909], quoted in Allen P. and Marilyn D. Splete, eds., *Frederic Remington: Selected Letters* (New York: Abbeville, 1988), p. 435.

8   See, for example, Peter Hassrick, "Remington: The Painter," in Hassrick et al., *Frederic Remington: The Masterworks* (New York: Harry N. Abrams and the St. Louis Art Museum in conjunction with the Buffalo Bill Historical Center, 1987), p. 126.

9   The exaggerated verticality of *The Old Stagecoach of the Plains* is emphasized not only in the stagecoach's simultaneous upward and downward movement but also in the canvas itself, reoriented from Remington's customary horizontal pictorial format. The dimensions of *The Old Stagecoach*—forty by twenty-seven inches—tell us that Remington took one of the regularly sized canvases on which he often made his horizontal compositions, measuring twenty-seven by forty inches, and turned it on its end. Thus before Remington had even made a mark on his canvas, its very orientation on his easel might well have struck him as something turned on its end, so that the picture's painted up-and-down action—the movement of the stagecoach—might be said to be merely a recapitulation, or

expression, of the primary "action" of the blank canvas.

10 As a sculptor himself, Remington was familiar with a large body of precedents for his work. He collected photographs of some of these sculptures in a scrapbook, now at the Frederic Remington Art Museum in Ogdensburg, N.Y. It is therefore likely that Remington knew of the sculptural ornamentation on European cathedrals and that he employed, consciously or unconsciously, forms evoking this ornamentation in paintings such as *Night Halt of the Cavalry*. It is also worth noting that, like many others at the time, Remington was interested in medieval culture. In 1908 he read a six-volume set of Jean Froissart's Chronicles. For a detailed account of the turn-of-the-century interest in medievalism, see "The Morning of Belief: Medieval Mentalities in a Modern World," in T. J. Jackson Lears, *No Place of Grace: Antimodernism and the Transformation of American Culture 1880–1920* (New York: Pantheon Books, 1981).

11 The two front horses in *The Old Stagecoach of the Plains*, particularly the one on the right, look out of the picture in a way that is similar to the trooper's gaze in *Night Halt of the Cavalry*. Yet in *The Old Stagecoach* the self-consciousness engendered by such a stare is mitigated by the fact that the two horses are depicted as having crossed partly into the realm they look at—a device that imaginatively activates this realm as part of the picture and not part of the painter's separate world.

12 The representation of human shadows extending into the picture from outside the picture plane is a relatively common motif in Remington's art. See, for

example, *Well in the Desert* (ca. 1897, Stark Museum of Art, Orange, Texas) and *The Hungry Moon* (1906, Thomas Gilcrease Institute of American History and Art, Tulsa, Oklahoma). The motif may have been suggested to Remington by the way photographers' shadows sometimes extend into their photographs as "signatures." Because Remington took photographs as preparatory studies for many of his paintings, it is possible that his photographs may have prompted his unconscious expression of self-incorporation in the form of a shadow, as in *Apache Scouts Listening*.

13 See, for example, *Broncos and Timber Wolves*, reproduced in *Century Magazine* 37 (January 1889): 336, and *The Last March* (1906, Frederic Remington Art Museum, Ogdensburg, New York). See also Frederic Remington, "The Curse of the Wolves," *Collier's Weekly* 21 (27 January 1898).

14 Mary Shelley, *Frankenstein* (Harmondsworth, England: Penguin, 1985), p. 185. On Remington's ability to make a figure "live," Theodore Roosevelt wrote, "The soldier, the cow-boy and rancher, the Indian, the horse and the cattle of the plains will live in [Remington's] pictures and bronzes, I verily believe, for all time"; quoted in "Frederic Remington: An Appreciation," *Pearson's Magazine* 18 (October 1907): 394.

15 Peter Hassrick, *Frederic Remington: Paintings, Drawings, and Sculpture in the Amon Carter Museum and the Sid W. Richardson Foundation Collections* (New York: Abrams by arrangement with Harrison House and in association with the Amon Carter Museum of Western Art, 1973), p. 146.

16 I am grateful to Harry Rand for calling

my attention to the affinities between *His First Lesson* and *Las Meniñas*.

17 A visit to the area leaves little doubt that Remington made his painting from the Cuthbert farm. It also reveals how Remington exaggerated his viewpoint on the gentle hill to the left of the Cuthbert house and barn (these buildings were to Remington's right as he painted).

18 Omitted from this essay for reasons of length is what I consider to be another spectacular example of Remington's presence within his art, the beautiful *Radisson and Groseilliers* (1905, Buffalo Bill Historical Center, Cody, Wyoming). For a detailed account of Remington's inclusion of himself within *Radisson and Groseilliers*, see my essay in William Truettner, ed., *The West as America: Reinterpreting Images of the Frontier, 1820–1920* (Washington, D.C.: Smithsonian Institution Press, 1991).

19 Ben Merchant Vorpahl makes the same point in his book *Frederic Remington and the West: With the Eye of the Mind* (Austin: University of Texas, 1972), p. 282.

20 Michael Shapiro points out Remington's reliance on the *Dancing Faun* in such sculptures as *Coming through the Rye* (1902, Art Museum, Princeton University). See Shapiro, "Remington: the Sculptor," in Peter Hassrick et al., *The Masterworks*, p. 176.

21 Remington diary, 6 January 1908.

22 Many evocations similar to Remington's of a lost American past might be adduced here. Henry James's *The American Scene*, published in 1907, is a good example.

Captain Gallant

David Levinthal

From a post–Desert Storm vantage point, what comes to mind most immediately in regard to David Levinthal's *Captain Gallant* project is that exemplary postmodern inversion: art imitates life/life imitates art, the exegesis of which can be as entertaining as a Miller Lite commercial—"less filling/tastes great."

While *Captain Gallant* is not unrelated to the events in the Middle East preceding and following 17 January 1991, Levinthal's formative interest begins earlier—in adolescence, throughout his career, certainly as far back as the British partitioning of the Ottoman Empire, if not the Crusades of the eleventh century.

One of Levinthal's first projects as an art student at Yale in the early seventies was *Hitler Moves East*, a collaboration with Garry "Doonesbury" Trudeau. His photographs of toy Nazi soldiers in various states of attack and Trudeau's fictional commentary ostensibly chronicled the German invasion of Russia during World War II. An extremely shallow depth of field in the photographs, which has since become almost a trademark of Levinthal's images, helped blur the lines between fake soldiers in an ersatz landscape and a documentary believability—not unlike the illegibility of many photographs transmitted by satellite and printed on cheap newsprint in the likes of the *New York Times*.

After Hitler, however, Levinthal moved from tabletop photography of the mise-en-scène in service of a narrative to working with the twenty-by-twenty-four-inch Polaroid camera and focusing—or not—on what might be called stills from a movie of American popular culture's collective unconscious: *American Beauties* that might be Betty Grable pinups or Madonna magazine covers or Walter Mitty fantasies; *Cowboys and Western Landscapes* that could be Butch and Sundance or just a home movie of when you were eleven and tied your sister to a tree and whooped around her; *Modern Romance*, *UFOs*; or his most recent series, *Desire*—women in bondage.

Captain Gallant, specially produced for *American Art*, is part of a larger project-in-process in which Levinthal returns to the tabletop and photographs various staged events using a variety of play sets created in the fifties and sixties. Like the Captain Gallant play set (1956), many of these—War of the Worlds (1953), Davy Crockett at the Alamo (1955), Skyscraper (1957), Cape Canaveral (1961), The Untouchables (1961), and Tales of Wells Fargo (1959)—were based on television shows, comics, film characters, or myth-shrouded historical events. Levinthal writes about his play-set project:

Today as we look back at play sets we can see how they were mirrors of society's image of itself, much like a Norman Rockwell painting for the Saturday Evening Post. *Play sets reinforced the popular culture and the beliefs and stereotypes of America. Battleground play sets allowed children of the 50s and 60s to once again "win" World War II on the beaches of Normandy or the sands of North Africa or conquer the wild west from Ft. Apache*

or, we might add, vanquish the evil Saracens.—*Ed.*

CAPTAIN GALLANT
of the FOREIGN LEGION

THIS IS **CAPTAIN GALLANT**, SOLDIER OF FORTUNE, LEADER OF THE FOREIGN LEGION AT FORT YUSAN-BAH. HE SPEAKS SELDOM AND ONLY WHEN HE HAS SOMETHING TO SAY. HE SHOOTS FAST AND DEADLY, BUT ONLY TO PROTECT AND DEFEND. THE DESERT KNOWS HIM AS A TRUE FRIEND AND A FIERCE ENEMY.

AT EASE, BOYS AND GIRLS! MEET OUR MASCOT, CUFFY!

HI THERE, I'M RIDING "BABA", THE BEST PONY IN THE DESERT — MAYBE, IN THE WHOLE WORLD!

FUZZY, OVER THERE, RIDES A CAMEL WHOSE NAME IS "JOSEPHINE"! HE'S VERY FUNNY.

I ADORE YOU "JOSEPHINE"! YOU HAVE THE MOST BEAUTIFUL EYES AND, GOSH, YOU'RE MY DESERT MARILYN MONROE.

THIS IS THE EMBLEM OF THE FOREIGN LEGION. EVERY MAN WHO WEARS THIS EMBLEM HAS PLEDGED HIS HONOR AND HIS LIFE TO BRING LAW AND ORDER WHERE EVER THEY LIVE AND FIGHT!

THESE ARE THE LEGIONNAIRES, MEN WITH BODIES OF STEEL — DESERT FIGHTERS AND SHARP SHOOTERS — MEN FROM EVERY COUNTRY IN THE WORLD. THEIR BATTLE CRY IS "HONNEUR ET FIDELITÉ", WHICH MEANS "HONOR AND LOYALTY."

Pilgrim's Progress in the West

Moran's The Mountain of the Holy Cross

Linda C. Hults

Of all of the works produced by Thomas Moran (1837–1926), *The Mountain of the Holy Cross* (frontispiece) offers a particularly rich access to his approach to the western wilderness landscape—in fact, *Holy Cross* tapped American thought as thoroughly as the landscapes of Thomas Cole or Frederic Church. This evocative work illustrates not only Moran's characteristic recombination of topographic drawings and photography into aesthetically successful compositions, but also the iconological motivations underlying such recombinations. The widely exhibited *Holy Cross* and its various graphic versions echoed the intensely exhortatory tone of American nationalism in the post–Civil War era.[1] Addressing each American as a pilgrim on the rocky road toward national virtue, *Holy Cross* expressed both the rewards and the costs of keeping the American covenant.

The northernmost peak of the Sawatch Range, Holy Cross itself has a fascinating history that reveals a mythic dimension. With an elevation of about fourteen thousand feet, the mountain is an impressive geological sight. But it was the freakish marking of its northeastern face that sealed its destiny as an American symbol. In late summer, when filled with the winter's remaining snow, two perpendicular ravines formed a Latin cross about eleven hundred feet tall. One of the first white men to note the emblem was William H. Brewer in 1869, but legends—deemed credible in an early review of Moran's painting—pushed the cross's

debut back to the time of the early Spanish explorers of North America. These stories, embellished with reports of dramatic spiritual redemptions and meteorological disturbances, carried a subtext of Christian imperialism and implied the tacit assent of the Indians to white conquest of the West.[2]

The location of the mountain—fourteen miles from the Continental Divide and about one hundred miles west of Denver, at a crucial point between the thirty-ninth and fortieth degrees of latitude—enhanced its potential as a symbol of Manifest Destiny. In 1870 William Jackson Palmer organized the Denver and Rio Grande Railway with the hopes of traversing the Rockies by rail. By 1881, tracks were laid over Tennessee Pass near Holy Cross as part of a network of Colorado railroads constructed between 1878 and 1883. Palmer's vision was social and linked to that of his contemporary William Gilpin, whose theory of world empires and American hegemony, republished in 1873 from his 1860 book, put the Colorado Territory (to become a state in 1876) at the heart of the world and at the turning point in world history.[3] The connection of Moran's canvas to railroad development was ultimately fused when the vice president of the Denver and Rio Grande, William A. Bell, purchased the painting in 1880. According to Colonel Henry Dudley Teetor, who wrote two nearly identical articles on Moran's painting in 1889 and 1890, Bell associated it with the

Thomas Moran, *The Mountain of the Holy Cross*, 1875. Oil on canvas, 83 1/2 x 63 1/2 in. Gene Autry Western Heritage Museum, Los Angeles

1 William Henry Jackson, *Mountain of the Holy Cross*, 1873 (retouched version). Silver albumen print, 7 x 5 in. Denver Public Library, Western History Department

"herculean efforts of his road to penetrate these Rocky Mountain fastnesses" and with a recent Supreme Court victory over the Atchison, Topeka and Santa Fe Railroad for control of the valley of the upper Arkansas River—again, in the vicinity of Holy Cross.[4]

The most strident part of Teetor's articles is a purple passage in which he associated the snowy cross with the red cross of the pagan-chasing Crusaders (clearly the pagans were now the Indians). The Crusaders' red cross suggested violence, whereas the white cross, which had been put in place by God's "unmailed" hand, symbolized peace. Teetor also stressed the antiquity of the cross and the timelessness of Manifest Destiny by asserting that the rock of the

mountain was the same as that of the Grand Canyon. There was no contradiction in Teetor's mind between the railroad and the wilderness it invaded; indeed, the train he rode seemed to obey the commands of this "American Sinai."[5]

But there was a conflict between the sanctity of the wilderness cross and the settlement of the Rocky Mountain region. This conflict is evident in another category of Holy Cross legends of indeterminate age concerning miners who dared to lay a pickax to the stem of the cross, which reputedly held a rich vein of gold.[6] These "curse of the cross" legends dealt with God's retribution on those who would plunder the cross. They implied a clear paradox: although the cross was God's "stamp of approval" for white,

Christian occupation of the West, it was also a dangerously numinous object, like the Ark of the Covenant. Those faithless, greedy members of the new chosen people who violated the new covenant represented by the cross were doomed.

Moran also suggested, through the pictorial structure of his canvas—his juxtaposition of the images of a remote emblem and a compelling but forbidding path—that a rigorous morality was a prerequisite to the settlement of the West and the fulfillment of American destiny. In doing so, he echoed cries against American materialism and moral decadence that appeared in popular literature around the time of the Centennial. On the one hand, *Holy Cross* expressed Moran's connection to the U.S. Geological Surveys—especially Ferdinand V. Hayden's, which had brought the mountain to the attention of the American public—and served as a testimony of faith in western exploration and settlement. On the other hand, the painting also embodied the modifications of Manifest Destiny imposed by an anxious, postwar America. *Holy Cross* was a call to rethink American destiny in terms of individual stewardship. It was an image of faith in America's future, but it was also an image imbued with all the urgent apprehension that faith had to overcome in the mid 1870s.

The first images of Holy Cross date from 1873, when it was photographed by William Henry Jackson on an expedition into Colorado by the U.S. Geological Survey under Hayden (fig. 1). Also on this survey were William Rideing, a reporter for the *New York Tribune*, and the artist-geologist William Henry Holmes. Moran was unable to accompany Hayden because of his commitment to John Wesley Powell's expedition on the Colorado River.[7] The rivalry between Hayden and Powell, both of whom were important to Moran's career, was to also play a role in Moran's choice of imagery in *Holy Cross*.

Late in 1873, when Moran was

commissioned to design wood engravings, including one of Holy Cross, for the second volume of *Picturesque America*, he referred to Jackson's photograph and perhaps to Holmes's watercolor (fig. 2) and Rideing's description (the reporter wrote the Rocky Mountain section of *Picturesque America*). Moran vowed to see the site himself, however, and did so in August 1874 with a Hayden-sponsored party led by James Stevenson.[8]

Jackson's photograph, seen here in its retouched version, was taken from Notch Mountain, a peak that blocks the view of Holy Cross from the east but whose summit offers the best view of the cross. The photograph is a grand but understated image. Holmes, however, was more dramatic in his approach to the snowy cross. For his watercolor, Holmes chose a vertical format in which the height of the peak and size of the cross are exaggerated. He displayed a similar sense of drama in an article he wrote in May 1875 for the *Illustrated Christian Weekly*, in which he described Jackson as "transfixed" and "amazed" at the first sighting.[9] Interestingly, the bombastic wood engraving that accompanied his article also appeared in Hayden's official report, next to dry prose about the glacial activity that had carved out the stream beds, lakes, and meadows around the mountain (fig. 3). Yet both the watercolor and the wood engraving must have been based on Jackson's photograph, for when the exploration party split into two parts, Holmes did not go with Jackson but instead accompanied Hayden up Holy Cross Mountain to the foot of the emblem itself.[10] Early on, then, depictions of Holy Cross were highly embellished.

The illustration that Moran designed for *Picturesque America*—much like his later oil painting—is also vertical with a rugged foreground filled with boulders and a turbulent sky (fig. 4). Beyond its greater realism, the chief difference between Moran's wood engraving and the one accompanying Hayden's report is the

2 William Henry Holmes, *Mountain of the Holy Cross*, 1873. Watercolor, 18 1/2 x 12 1/2 in. Collection of Carl F. Rainone, Arlington, Texas

3 After William Henry Holmes, *Mountain of the Holy Cross*, 1873. Wood engraving, 4 1/2 x 7 in. Published in Ferdinand V. Hayden, *Annual Report of the United States Geological and Geographical Survey of the Territories Embracing Colorado, Being a Report of the Progress of the Exploration for the Year 1873* (Washington, D.C.: Government Printing Office, 1874). Colorado Historical Society, Denver

emphasis on a central pathway along the obstacle-ridden shores of a cascading stream. One did indeed ascend a stream—Cross Creek or "Roches Moutonnés" Creek (named after its "sheep-back" boulders)—to reach the mountain after descending the Great Divide, but the cross was invisible from that stream. In a characteristic rearrangement of topography, Moran put the cross and stream together. His field sketch shows the reality of the terrain (fig. 5). Although Moran's account of the journey to Holy Cross suggests that he made the decision to include the stream on the way down from Notch Mountain, it seems clear that it was already a part of his

iconographic conceit when he designed the illustration for *Picturesque America*. The stream was important to Jackson as well. On the negative he used for his famous photograph, he not only high-lighted the foreground rocks and tidied up the cross itself but also added a cascade at the foot of the mountain. There were, as it turns out, good reasons for both artist and photographer to be preoccupied with the stream.[11]

Moran's emphasis on the stream that forms the central pathway balances the stress on the revealed image of the cross with an equal insistence on the journey *to* that cross. These qualities are enhanced in his 1875 oil, in which the cross is seen as

4 Thomas Moran, *Mountain of the Holy Cross*, 1874. Wood engraving, 4 1/4 x 6 1/4 in. Published in William Cullen Bryant, ed., *Picturesque America*, 2 vols. (New York: D. Appleton, 1872–1874)

the devotional focus of the pilgrim-heroes of the U.S. Geological Surveys (especially Hayden's), including the artist-explorers who accompanied these expeditions. These pilgrim-heroes were on an urgent mission to bring both scientific and aesthetic knowledge to the attention of the American public, attention that would in turn provide new pilgrims to settle the West. As Hayden wrote in his annual report of 1873, the "prospect of [the rapid development of the eastern Rockies] within the next five years, by some of the most important railroads in the West, renders it very desireable that its resources be made known to the world at as early a date as possible."[12] The ascent in Moran's painting is a Hill of Calvary for the pilgrim-explorers, and the cross the numinous emblem of their mission, as well as of God's sanction of and call to future pilgrims. Moran expressed the relentlessness of settlement spatially: the pathway pulls us up and toward the mountain that lies immediately to the west of the Great Divide, soon to be traversed by rail.

Moran's biographer, Thurman Wilkins, suggests that Hayden approved a second expedition to Holy Cross in 1874 because he realized the publicity value of a painting by Moran. This suggestion is supported by the fact that, in the spring of 1874, the congressional Committee on Public Lands held hearings on the four independent surveys competing for government funds. The hearings were provoked by a clash between the Hayden and Wheeler expeditions into Colorado in the summer of 1873.[13] During this period of intense rivalry, when the consolidation of the surveys was being considered, Moran's well-traveled painting could not have been more timely.

In addition to promoting Hayden, *Holy Cross* also advanced Moran as the successor of Frederic Church. At the Corcoran, *Holy Cross* begged comparison to *Niagara* (1857, Corcoran Gallery of Art, Washington, D.C.), and, in Philadelphia, to Church's great South American mountain picture *Chimborazo* (1864, Museum of Fine Arts, Boston), which had been coolly received by the Centennial audience. Unlike *Chimborazo*, whose cosmic breadth and naturalistic display were out of fashion, Moran's canvas was read in terms of the specific hopes and anxieties of 1876.[14]

Contemporary Americans saw Moran's painting as a renewed call to take up the challenge of their covenant with God and live up to the burden of being his new "chosen" people. America's vision of itself as the "redeemer-nation" that would usher in the millennium did not die out after the Civil War, despite the disillusionment of the postwar era, with its political scandals, corporate exploitation, and other widely perceived signs of moral decay. Rather, the war could be understood as God's visitation of wrath upon his chosen people for their faithlessness. It was a purgation that prepared America for the golden millennial age to come, when the nation would fulfill its destiny as the embodiment of peace, justice, freedom, and prosperity. In this paradoxical era of hope and anxiety, Moran's painting must have appeared as an image of unity and reconciliation, in the spirit of the Gettysburg Address, and as a confirmation that God had always directed American destiny, as in the apocalyptic strains of Julia Ward Howe's *Battle Hymn of the Republic*.[15] But it also gave visual form to the sentiment, frequently encountered in the popular literature of the day, that America's fulfillment of its destiny could only be accomplished by a reassertion of virtue and restraint on the part of individual Americans. Although modified by this apprehensive call for individual stewardship, an American sense of a world-redeeming mission was still very much alive.

It was in this atmosphere that Gilpin published *Mission of the North American People*, a revision of an 1860 collection of public addresses entitled *The Central Gold Region*. Gilpin was a former governor of the Colorado Territory, and his view of the course of history and of Colorado's crucial place within it influenced not only Moran but also the public's reception to his painting. Gilpin believed in a succession of world empires, culminating in the republican empire of the United States. With every westward thrust, this empire moved to a higher spiritual and moral plane.[16]

In Gilpin's judgment, history was closely linked to topography. Borrowing

the idea of an isothermal zodiac from Alexander von Humboldt, he asserted that the great empires developed along a zone that snaked around the Northern Hemisphere above and below the fortieth degree of latitude, the same zone occupied by Holy Cross. Whereas all previous empires were doomed to fail, the American empire was destined to enjoy peace and unity because of its topography. Bounded at the east and west by mountains, the American interior was a great bowl, unified by its river systems. Colorado, centered on the fortieth degree of latitude, was also where the Pacific and Atlantic worlds met. Denver was the city where "the zodiac of nations closes its circle" and which, with the help of the railroads, would become the true crossroads of the globe—the "focal point of impregnable power in the topographical configuration of the continent."[17]

Gilpin's expansionism implied a weighty responsibility. Americans were not only to subdue a continent but to establish a New Jerusalem and transform, by their example, all people into paragons of virtue, peacefulness, and scientific acumen. Yet on the eve of the Centennial it was not at all obvious that Americans were up to this challenge. In *Democratic Vistas* (1868), Walt Whitman had written that the major lacuna in the American character was "conscience, the primary moral element." Its lack was "grounds of the darkest dread, respecting the America of our hopes." Greed, the sin of the hapless Holy Cross miners, seemed ubiquitous after the war, underlining a materialistic trait in the American character that disturbed many citizens. The anonymous writer of the Centennial article "What is an American?" in the *Atlantic Monthly* stridently stated this moral decline:

Ten years ago we had wrung from the world an amazed respect and admiration for our courage, our constancy, our unlimited power of self-devotion and sacrifice. What have we added to ourselves in these ten years? Several new varieties of infamy. What is the name of the American in Europe? A synonym for low rascality.

America was in danger of becoming a "deplorable spectacle of a country without solidarity, without a soul; an accidental conglomerate of uncongenial particles, a population of immigrants, a base mart."[18]

Yet there is an assertion of hope at the center of this author's despair, for with repentance comes redemption. The anonymous Philadelphian who composed this jeremiad saw the Centennial as just such an opportunity—it was a chance that Americans could not afford to lose. The moment for action had arrived. The author hoped that the "supreme occasion of rekindling fires of enthusiasm at hallowed altars, or refreshing languid faith at pure springs . . . of making solemn pledges to ourselves and to one another for a future which shall redeem the present and be worthy of the past" would

not send Americans "forward in the slippery track of material prosperity, *but upward along the path traced for us a century ago by men of clean hands and single minds*" [italics added].[19]

This is exactly the mood conveyed by Moran's painting, which combines compelling spatial movement along a rugged path with a radiant but remote promise embodied in a snowy cross. The upward path recalls fifteenth-century devotional images of the "mountain of virtue" one must ascend before reaching God, or—closer to home—the frontispiece of the 1844 American edition of John Bunyan's Puritan allegory, *The Pilgrim's Progress* (fig. 6).[20] Here, the New Jerusalem hovers above a shining cross in a mountainous landscape with a central stream. Moran's canvas visualized the rigorous morality and return to national principles that the author of the *Atlantic Monthly* essay hoped would occur.

In contrast to earlier ideas of an inexorable, coherent national will—a divine destiny sweeping each citizen along—there was a distinctly individualized, intensely exhortatory cast to this notion in the 1870s. Manifest Destiny was made conditional upon the virtue of individual Americans. In contrast to Church's *Niagara*, a pictorial symbol of Manifest Destiny, Moran's *Holy Cross* posits a definite pathway and invites each viewer to scale its difficult length to the beckoning cross beyond. The individualized, up-and-over spatial dynamic of Moran's composition modifies the sweeping, impersonal right-to-left movement of Church's waterfall in the same way that postwar rhetoric modified older ideas about America's divine destiny. Moran's choice of a vertical format, rather than the more spacious horizontal panorama, reinforced the moral imperative he wanted his Centennial picture to embody. As the *Atlantic Monthly* author expressed it, "We forget that bigness is not greatness; in the spaciousness of our

7   Joseph Anton Koch, *Der Schmadribachfall*, 1823. Oil on canvas, 50 5/8 x 42 5/16 in. Neue Pinakothek, Bayerische Staatsgemäldesammlungen, Munich

8   *(overleaf)* Thomas Moran, *Mountain of the Holy Cross*, 1888. Etching, 30 5/8 x 21 3/4 in. Jefferson National Expansion Historical Association/National Park Service, St. Louis

9   *(overleaf)* Thomas Moran, *Mountain of the Holy Cross*, 1894. Pencil and watercolor, 19 1/2 x 14 in. Denver Art Museum

land we overlook its [moral] emptiness."[21]

The urgency of this imperative, coming from the fear that the opportunity presented by the restoration of the Union would be lost, explains the tension between the inexorable spatial movement of Moran's composition and the remoteness of the cross. The promise of the cross is accessible only by taking a hard, lonely journey, but take it Americans must. It was a common postwar message. Prominent citizens—the Congregational

minister Henry Ward Beecher, the political leader Carl Schurz, the editor Edwin L. Godkin, for example—called for an abandonment of collective certainty in favor of individual responsibility and a return to the virtues of the earliest pioneers.[22] This exhortatory tone is found throughout the wide range of Centennial addresses published in an anthology volume in 1893.[23]

The author of the *Atlantic Monthly* article identified, out of all Americans, the

"brave and patient pioneers of Colorado and Nevada, who live and toil for the future," as possessing the virtues required for national renewal.

They wage valiant warfare with the wilderness and the savage, to win new realms for civilization from barbarism and the hostile elements. They are our inland colonists, the pilgrim fathers of our western coasts. . . . They carry on the traditions of the settlers of our soil; they are the parents of the broader land.[24]

This notion that it was in the West that America could fulfill its true destiny and where American virtue would be realized is central to Moran's painting. Whitman understood the West as a new "dominion-heart" that would "compact and settle the traits of America, with all the old retained, but more expanded, grafted on newer, hardier, purely native stock." It was a merging of western individuality ("solid personality, with blood and brawn and the deep quality of all-accepting fusion") with older American characteristics that would create a new aggregate entity—a new American nationality.[25]

The old Puritan notions of the wilderness as an enemy to be conquered and as a test of moral character still operated in the nineteenth century when the West was being settled. Although Moran certainly glorified the magnificence of the wilderness in *Holy Cross*, the painting's pictorial structure also suggested a moral allegory—a "Pilgrim's Progress" in which God is the end of an uphill battle against chaos and evil, symbolized by wild nature. It is in this moral realm that the link between the painting's functions as a Centennial jeremiad and as a monument to the surveys becomes evident.[26] Without the explorers, the new pioneers—the hope of America and of humanity in general— were doomed to fail.

The one element of vital importance

to the survival of these western pioneers in the 1870s was water. At the time of Moran's journeys with Powell and Hayden, the Homestead Act of 1862 was being seriously questioned. Could the 160-acre farms allotted under the Homestead Act be sustained in the drier areas west of the 100th meridian? Several important American thinkers, Hayden prominent among them, insisted that rain would follow the plow—that settlement by small yeomen farmers, forestation, and even the presence of railroads and telegraph lines would actually increase precipitation.[27] In 1867, Hayden claimed that precipitation had increased in Nebraska because of settlement. "I am confident," he asserted, "that this change will continue to extend across the dry belt to the foot of the Rocky Mountains. Moreover, according to Hayden, it was the eastern slopes of the Rockies that should be settled first, thus utilizing the water from streams formed from mountain snows and creating more precipitation for the plains to the east. "Let the population gather around the points where these [mountain streams] burst from the mountains, and as it increases pushing out on the plains eastward, and I believe the supply of water will accompany it."[28] Hayden's theory is reflected in the point of view Moran chose to use, which suggests westward expansion over the Rockies as well as the flow of water eastward from mountain snows.

Powell's was the most important dissenting voice amid the optimism. In the congressional hearings on public lands in the spring of 1874, he introduced his ideas on the settlement of lands west of the 100th meridian. These ideas would preoccupy him for the rest of the decade and lead to the publication of his *Report on the Lands of the Arid Region* in 1878. At the congressional hearings, Powell claimed that few western lands could be cultivated except by irrigation and that the chief job of the surveys should be to search for irrigable land in anticipation of the inevitable waves of settlers.[29] It is important to note that, despite Powell's greater pessimism, his motives were like Hayden's—he simply wanted to find the best way to accommodate settlement.

In *Report on the Lands of the Arid Region*, Powell boldy and logically insisted that the small farms of the Homestead Act would not work in the West—tracts of land must be larger and division of land must take into account sources for irrigation.[30] Powell made sense, but since his views directly countered the myth of the West as a paradise populated by yeomen farmers, they fell largely on deaf ears.

We are now in a better position to understand why the pilgrims' pathway in Moran's painting ascends along a gushing stream. Along with the moisture-laden clouds, it would seem to confirm Hayden's optimism about water in the West. Indeed, the relationship of the painting to the question of water may also help to explain Moran's choice of a vertical format instead of the panoramic view of Jackson's photograph or Albert Bierstadt's *Rocky Mountains* (1863, Metropolitan Museum of Art), which also contained (albeit less emphatically) a central, descending stream. The composition of *Holy Cross* is reminiscent of such European works as Joseph Anton Koch's *Der Schmadribachfall*, which has recently been described as a picture of the birth of a mountain stream, related to geological ideas about the crucial role of mountains as sources of melting snow and as points where water vapor condenses in the water cycle (fig. 7). In a series entitled "Studies of Mountains," published in 1888, the journalist Ernest Ingersoll, with whom Moran was acquainted, summarized the late-nineteenth-century understanding of the role of mountains in determining climate, proclaiming that North America was ideal in its mountainous configurations and, more important, in the human

progress it exemplified. The experience of mountains was fundamental for the development of individualism and "the stirring of a desire to explore and possess [the spaciousness of the earth]." Ingersoll felt that this notion particularly applied to the Aryan race and to the victorious side in the Civil War ("that half of the country which had the mountains").[31]

Moran's letters to Hayden and Powell in the 1870s reveal a polite deference to both men (even when Powell was terribly late with a payment) but a distinctly warmer relationship with Hayden. In a letter to Powell in May 1875, Moran expressed his awareness that *Holy Cross*, as a picture glorifying Hayden's triumph, might be a sore point with Powell:

The Mountain of the Holy Cross *has been on exhibition for some time and has received the highest praise from the artists and the public with a fair share of newspaper laudation. I know you have no interest in the subject for a picture, I have therefore made no reports during its progress.*[32]

Moran could not afford to offend Powell, who was also one of his major benefactors, so *Holy Cross* covered all bases with respect to water in the West. Powell firmly believed that irrigation would transform the West's Arid Region and prevent hapless settlers from being subject to the vicissitudes of fluctuating rainfall. Indeed, in accounts of Colorado during the late 1860s and early 1870s— for example, *Colorado: A Summer Trip* (1867) by the poet Bayard Taylor— irrigation figured prominently in the agriculturally optimistic assessment the state typically received. For Powell, the mountain streams of the Rockies would be primary sources of irrigation.[33] Moran's emphasis on this pictorial element would probably have rung true to Powell.

Indians, of course, also presented an obstacle to western settlement by white

Christians. In *Three Thousand Miles through the Rocky Mountains* (1869), the journalist Alexander McClure discussed the Indian question extensively. His racism was bound up with an optimistic expansionism that encompassed both the ideas of the plenitude of water and the connection of the Atlantic and Pacific by rail—two notions embodied in Moran's painting. McClure believed that irrigation in Colorado would create precipitation, precluding the need for further irrigation and ensuring the success of farming. Because the Indian would not "civilize," McClure asked impatiently, "Must all civilization therefore be arrested in the heart of the continent?"[34]

Despite its moral exhortation to Americans and its portrayal of wilderness grandeur, Moran's painting of the "heart of the continent" ultimately ordained a Christian hegemony in the West. With its gleaming cross, moisture-laden clouds, and central, gushing stream, *Holy Cross* affirmed the wisdom of God's plan for the American continent. No wonder it inspired the wood engravings that illustrated the first western travel books lauding the prosperity awaiting all future settlers. In the rosy prose of such publications, the warning implied by Moran's Calvary path faded. The public was still unwilling to face the ironies of civilization's march; in fact, a generally glowing review in the *Aldine* complained of Moran's pictorial "belittling" of the mountain, as though it were not exalted enough.[35]

Moran's composition apparently maintained its significance into the 1880s—witness his dynamic etching of 1888—although the softened, floating versions from the 1890s suggest a melancholy nostalgia for a past heroic era (figs. 8, 9).[36] A wood engraving based on Moran's design also decorated William Thayer's *Marvels of the New West*, which synthesized, as late as 1887, the components of the postwar ideology of Manifest Destiny, now depen-

dent on the moral superiority of western pioneers. Immersed in the ideology's optimism, Thayer exalted irrigation while also claiming that forestation projects would increase western rainfall. He drew upon theories of the racial superiority of the Anglo-Saxons, "who now control the destiny of the human family." The consummation of history will occur, Thayer claimed, when "Anglo-Saxon Supremacy over the New West shall bring its multiform elements into complete accord for the Union, and the Christian religion shall control the whole for humanity and for God." Yet permeating such expressions of supremacy was anxiety. All depended upon the western pioneers living up to their image: "If the New West shall fail of the achievements predicted, the Republic will fail to maintain its advanced rank among the nations; and if the Republic fails, mankind will fail also."[37]

The presence of the Holy Cross engraving in Thayer's book reveals more than the desire to give geographical information. Such an explicitly Christian image conveyed not only an implicit racism but also a moral exhortation, just as Moran's canvas did in the 1870s. *The Mountain of the Holy Cross*—and all of its versions before and after the painting—was double edged. It confirmed what white Christian Americans wanted to believe, but it also saddled them with the fate of the world. It functioned as Cole's *The Oxbow* (fig. 10), whose religious iconography—a central hill marked with the Hebrew word for the Almighty, *Shaddai* (read inversely as "Noah")—was intended as a means of encouraging the American people to preserve the covenant. Of particular concern to Cole was Americans' accumulation of wealth for its own sake and the resultant moral and social decay. *The Oxbow* expresses an ideal pastoral state, a compromise between wilderness and civilization, that can be achieved by a restrained and virtuous populace.[38]

10 Thomas Cole, *The Oxbow*, 1836.
Oil on canvas, 51 1/2 x 76 in. The
Metropolitan Museum of Art, Gift
of Mrs. Russell Sage

By contrast, *Holy Cross* projects a
tension between possibilities and realities,
salvation and purgation, renewal and
sacrifice. Rather than picture utopia as
a way of urging Americans to attain it,
Moran took a more urgent, questioning
tone: Would Americans take the upward
path? Any harmony of wilderness and
civilization was derived not from the
painting's imagery but from the

audience's answer. In the postwar era,
as the sweep of Manifest Destiny was
modified by an increased emphasis on
individual stewardship, the promise of the
snowy cross—the fulfillment of the
American covenant and, by extension, the
regeneration of mankind—was possible
only through the morality of individual
Americans, especially the pioneers of the
New West.

Notes

For another discussion of *The Mountain of the Holy Cross*, see Joni L. Kinsey, "Creating a Sense of Place: Thomas Moran and the Surveying of the American West" (Ph.D. diss., Washington University, St. Louis, 1989), 2:381–468. Dr. Kinsey's research, done simultaneously with my own, focuses on the subsequent reception and social significance of Moran's painting.

1   Moran's painting was exhibited in New York City, Washington, D.C., Boston (where Henry Wadsworth Longfellow saw it and was inspired to write a poem), Philadelphia (at the Centennial Exhibition, where it won a gold medal), and finally in London (where Mrs. William A. Bell saw it and urged her husband to purchase it). See Thurman Wilkins, *Thomas Moran: Artist of the Mountains* (Norman: University of Oklahoma Press, 1966), pp. 101–3.

2   William H. Brewer, *Rocky Mountain Letters 1869: A Journal of an Early Geological Expedition to the Colorado Rockies*, edited and annotated by Edmund B. Rogers, supplement to *Trail and Timberline*, May 1930, p. 49. Also see Brewer, "Explorations in the Rocky Mountains and the High Peaks of Colorado," *Journal of the American Geographical Society of New York* 3 (1873): 214. The review is "Moran's 'Mountain of the Holy Cross,' " *Aldine* 7 (July 1875): 379–80. The ethos of the early legends is summarized in Eugene Field's anti-Semitic short story, "The Holy Cross," in *The Holy Cross and Other Tales* (New York: Scribner's, 1896), pp. 3–23. Many of these legends are found in newspaper stories in the clippings file, Western History Division, Denver Public Library.

3   William Gilpin, *Mission of the North American People: Geographical, Social and Political* (Philadelphia: Lippincott and Company, 1873). See also William Jackson Palmer, *The Westward Current of Population in the United States* (London: Chapman and Hall, 1874). On railroad development in Colorado and the relationship between Palmer and Gilpin, see Carl Abbott, *Colorado: A History of the Centennial State* (Boulder: Colorado

Associated University Press, 1976), pp. 82–83, 88–93.

4   Henry Dudley Teetor, "The Mountain of the Holy Cross: Study of a Historical Painting," *Magazine of Western History* 11 (November 1889): 4–8, and Henry Dudley Teetor, "Mountain of the Holy Cross," *The Great Divide* 2 (February 1890): 193.

5   Teetor, "Study of a Historical Painting," pp. 7–8.

6   See Al G. Birch, "Mining Men Declare Spirit of God Hovers over Shrine," *Denver Post*, 16 June 1929, p. 10. Gold, of course, was one of the most important resources of the Colorado Territory: Gilpin, p. 96, emphasizes gold as the source of sound money, part of the foundation of the American empire. If Moran were aware of the legends of the gold vein in the cross, it would surely magnify the moralistic implications of his canvas—i.e., material wealth must be earned by taking the hard, upward path.

7   Among the accounts of the expedition are Ferdinand V. Hayden, *Annual Report of the United States Geological and Geographical Survey of the Territories Embracing Colorado, Being a Report of the Progress of the Exploration for the Year 1873* (Washington, D.C.: Government Printing Office, 1874), pp. 73–74; William H. Holmes, "The Mountain of the Holy Cross," *The Illustrated Christian Weekly*, 1 May 1875, pp. 209–10; and William Henry Jackson, *Time Exposure: The Autobiography of William Henry Jackson* (New York: G. P. Putnam's Sons, 1940), pp. 214–18. In a letter of 28 June 1873, Moran apologized to Hayden for being unable to attend; see Moran Papers, East Hampton Free Library, East Hampton, New York.

8   William Cullen Bryant, ed., *Picturesque America*, vol. 2 (New York: D. Appleton, 1874); for accounts of Moran's journey, see Fritiof Fryxell, "Thomas Moran's Journey to the Mount of the Holy Cross," *Trail and Timberline* 203 (September 1935): 103–5; Wilkins, pp. 95–107; Thomas S. Fern, *The Drawings*

and Watercolors of Thomas Moran (Notre Dame, Ind.: The Art Gallery, University of Notre Dame, 1976), pp. 48–61; and Patricia Trenton and Peter H. Hassrick, *The Rocky Mountains: A Vision for Artists in the Nineteenth Century* (Norman: University of Oklahoma Press, 1983), pp. 197–203. Moran's letters to his wife from the journey are published in Amy O. Bassford, ed., *Home-Thoughts from Afar: Letters of Thomas Moran to Mary Nimmo Moran* (East Hampton, N.Y.: East Hampton Free Library, 1967), pp. 43–57.

9   Holmes, p. 210. Contrast this description with Jackson's own account, p. 217, in which the cross's grandeur is upstaged by the photographer's hunger. It is interesting that Jackson's son Clarence also exaggerated the emotional impact of the cross on his father; see Clarence S. Jackson and Lawrence W. Marshall, *Quest of the Snowy Cross* (Denver: University of Denver Press, 1952), pp. 131–32. Clarence even produced a composite photograph (opposite p. 129) in which his father's image of Holy Cross is seen through parting clouds.

10 Hayden, fig. 18, opposite p. 74. On Holmes's watercolor, see Trenton and Hassrick, pp. 168–69, plate 59.

11 On Moran's decision to include the stream, see his letter of 24 August 1874 in Bassford, pp. 51–57. On Jackson's alterations of the photograph, see Zeke Scher, "How They Promoted the Mount of the Holy Cross," *Empire Magazine*, 19 December 1976, pp. 10–11.

12 Hayden, p. 1.

13 Wilkins, p. 96. On the clash between the Hayden and Wheeler expeditions, see Henry Nash Smith, "Clarence King, John Wesley Powell, and the Establishment of the United States Geological Survey," *Mississippi Valley Historical Review* 34 (June 1947): 37–58.

14 See David C. Huntington, *The Landscapes of Frederic Edwin Church: Vision of an American Era* (New York: George Braziller, 1966), pp. 53–54, 64–71;

David C. Huntington, "Frederic Church's *Niagara*: Nature and the Nation's Type," *Texas Studies of Literature and Language* 25 (Spring 1983): 100–38; and Jeremy Adamson, *Niagara: Two Centuries of Changing Attitudes* (Washington, D.C.: Corcoran Gallery of Art, 1985).

15 See Ernest Lee Tuveson, *Redeemer Nation: The Idea of America's Millennial Role* (Chicago: University of Chicago Press, 1968), pp. 187–214.

16 Gilpin, pp. 99–124.

17 Ibid., pp. 114, 121.

18 Ibid., p. 124; Walt Whitman, *Democratic Vistas* (New York: Liberal Arts Press, 1949), p. 38; "What is an American?" *Atlantic Monthly* 25 (May 1875): 561–67.

19 "What is an American?" p. 567. Paul C. Nagel, in his analysis of this article in *This Sacred Trust: American Nationality 1798–1898* (New York: Oxford University Press, 1971), pp. 231–32, de-emphasizes the implied hope.

20 John Bunyan, *The Pilgrim's Progress* (Philadelphia: Presbyterian Board of Publication, 1844).

21 "What is an American?" p. 563.

22 See Nagel, pp. 218, 232, 234–35.

23 Frederick Saunders, ed., *Addresses, Historical and Patriotic, Centennial and Quadrennial, Delivered in the Several States of the Union, July 4th, 1876–1883, Including Addresses Commemorative of the Four Hundredth Anniversary of the Discovery of America, 1892–1893* (New York: E. B. Treat, 1893). See especially pp. 375–80, 398–409.

24 "What is an American?" p. 566.

25 Whitman, p. 25.

26 On Puritan notions, see Roderick Nash, *Wilderness and the American Mind* (New Haven, Conn.: Yale University Press, 1982), pp. 34–43. Patrick Daryl notes that the explorers' struggle against nature was an important part of the content of the images of the West by Moran and other artists; see his "The Iconological Significance of Selected Western Subjects Painted by Thomas Moran" (Ph.D. diss., North Texas State University, Denton, 1978), p. 135.

27 On the controversy about rainfall west of the 100th meridian, see Walter Prescott Webb, *The Great Plains* (New York: Ginn and Company, 1931), pp. 319–452; Henry Nash Smith, "Rain Follows the Plow: The Notion of Increased Rainfall for the Great Plains," *Huntington Library Quarterly* 10 (February 1947): 169–187; and William Culp Darrah, *Powell of the Colorado* (Princeton, New Jersey: Princeton University Press, 1951), pp. 221–36.

28 Ferdinand V. Hayden, *First, Second and Third Annual Reports of the United States Geological Survey of the Territories for the Years 1867, 1868 and 1869, under the Department of the Interior* (Washington, D.C.: Government Printing Office, 1873), p. 14, 237.

29 See Smith, "Clarence King," p. 39, and Darrah, p. 222.

30 John Wesley Powell, *Report on the Lands of the Arid Region of the United States with a More Detailed Account of the Lands of Utah* Washington, D.C.: Government Printing Office, 1879).

31 Ernest Ingersoll, "Studies of Mountains," *Chatauquan* 7 (1888): 203–4, 456–58, 521–23. On Koch's painting see Timothy Mitchell, "Caspar David Friedrich's *Der Watzmann*: German Romantic Landscape Painting and Historical Geology," *Art Bulletin* 66 (September 1984): 456–57.

32 Letter of 10 May 1875, Moran Papers.

33 Powell, pp. 10–13; Bayard Taylor, *Colorado: A Summer Trip* (New York: G. P. Putnam and Son, 1867), pp. 41–48.

34 Alexander McClure, *Three Thousand Miles through the Rocky Mountains* (Philadelphia: J. B. Lippincott, 1869), p. 360. Powell, too, noted the need to "remove" the Indians from the Rockies because they started fires for hunting purposes and depleted the timber needed by the lumber industry. In his account of the journey to Holy Cross, Moran mentioned having to climb over "burnt and fallen timber" (Bassford, pp. 51–57). One wonders if the painting's emphasis on fallen timber refers to this concern or rather to the concern for the excesses of lumbering, which were widely acknowledged; see Barbara Novak, *Nature and Culture: American Landscape and Painting 1825–1875* (New York: Oxford University Press, 1980), pp. 157–66, on the axe and tree stump as symbols of progress and destruction. If Moran intended the fallen trees to refer to the axe's destructiveness, this would increase the ironic and cautionary content of his painting.

35 "Moran's 'Mountain of the Holy Cross,'" p. 380.

36 On the etching, see Fern, p. 56, no. 42. There is also a late oil painting, circa 1892, in the Denver Public Library.

37 William M. Thayer, *Marvels of the New West: A Vivid Portrayal of the Stupendous Marvels in the Vast Wonderland West of the Missouri River* (Norwich, Conn.: Henry Bill Publishing Company, 1890), pp. 16–17, 658, 702–7, 715.

38 See Matthew Baigell and Allen Kaufman, "Thomas Cole's 'The Oxbow': A Critique of American Civilization," *Arts Magazine* 55 (January 1981): 136–39.

"Who Will Paint New York?"

"The World's New Art Center" and the Skyscraper Paintings of Georgia O'Keeffe

Anna C. Chave

"For the First Time Europe Seeks Inspiration at Our Shores in the Persons of a Group of Modernist French Artists, Who Find Europe Impossible Because of Its War-Drenched Atmosphere— Macmonnies Predicts that the Effect of this Migration will be Far-Reaching on Art of America and the Older Continent" proclaimed a long headline in the *New York Tribune* in October 1915. The French artists in question concurred that New York was "destined to become the artistic centre of the world," and not only because of the war. Albert Gleizes averred that New York's skyscrapers were "works of art . . . which equal the most admired old world creations" and that "the genius who built the Brooklyn Bridge is to be classed alongside the genius who built Notre Dame de Paris." Francis Picabia argued, "Since machinery is the soul of the modern world, and since the genius of machinery attains its highest expression in America, why is it not reasonable to believe that in America the art of the future will flower most brilliantly?" Jean Crotti predicted that "New York will come to be looked upon as the cradle of art, usurping the proud place enjoyed so long by Paris and other important European cities. . . . Americans have come over to us. Now we are coming over to you." That same year, Marcel Duchamp complained, "If only America would realize that the art of Europe is finished— dead—and that America is the country of the art of the future, instead of trying to base everything she does on European

traditions!" He continued, "And yet in spite of it, try as she will, she gets beyond these traditions even in dimension alone," alluding to the city's great skyscrapers.[1]

Though they had sought out New York as a remote haven during wartime, these vanguard Parisians found they had landed not at the peripheries of modern culture, but at something like its very center. "The Great War . . . hastened what prophets regarded as inevitable," Frederick James Gregg announced in *Vanity Fair* in January 1915. "New York is now, for the time being at least, the art capital of the world, that is to say the commercial art centre, where paintings and sculptures are viewed, discussed, purchased and exchanged." The momentous declaration of Gregg's headline— that New York had become "The World's New Art Center"—was not the last of its kind. The same claim was made in the late 1920s by the critic Henry McBride and again by Clement Greenberg in 1948, but only Greenberg's statement would lodge in the standard narratives of modern art: "Now when it comes to the Zeitgeist, we Americans are the most advanced people on earth, if only because we are the most industrialized." That the "most advanced people" should start producing the most "advanced" art in the world's most "advanced" city seems consistent enough, though Greenberg described himself as startled by the realization that "the main premises of Western art have at last migrated to the United States, along with the center of gravity of industrial production and political power. . . . It is not beyond possibility that the cubist tradition may enjoy a new efflorescence in this country." For Greenberg, then (in contrast to the prognostication of the American sculptor Frederick Macmonnies), the migration of influences was to travel one way only. Because he viewed Cubism—as most modern art historians have ever since—as the source of all legitimate modern visual languages, he lauded only those artists who had drunk deep from that fountain-head of modern art, artists such as Jackson Pollock (whose work largely prompted this claim of American dominance). The pivotal, global shifts in economic and political power to which Greenberg alluded occurred, however, not after the Second World War when Pollock hit his stride, but following the first. In the decade after World War I, New York replaced London as the financial capital of the world, while the United States as a whole became "incomparably the greatest economic power in the world."[2]

The newfound affluence of the United States was expressed most visibly in a construction boom, and extensive building was necessary to accommodate the flow of people from rural areas to the city. In the 1920s the population of urban America grew by 27 percent, as the nation became for the first time predominantly urban. New York "got a brand new skyline," with the area around Grand Central Station, in particular, almost totally rebuilt with the tall buildings that were increasingly greeted as the symbol of a new architectural era. The American architectural theorist Claude Bragdon observed in 1925:

Eminent European critics, visiting these shores, are in the habit of declaring that the American Spirit expresses itself most eloquently in jazz music and in the skyscraper. . . . Not only is the skyscraper a symbol of

the American Spirit—restless, centrifugal, perilously poised—but it is the only truly original development in the field of architecture to which we can lay unchallenged claim.

Bragdon made these observations in an essay on the newly completed Shelton Hotel, then the most celebrated feature of the new skyline near Grand Central.[3]

As it happened, Bragdon lived in an apartment in the Shelton close to that of Georgia O'Keeffe (1887–1986) and her husband, Alfred Stieglitz, and it was just this manifestation of the "American Spirit"—the Shelton Hotel (fig. 1) and other skyscrapers from the same burgeoning Manhattan neighborhood—that O'Keeffe would capture in a remarkable series of urban landscapes painted between 1925 and 1930. Evincing a forthright pragmatism unashamedly overtaken by a visionary romanticism, O'Keeffe's skyscraper paintings glorified that phenomenon that—as the first artifact of American culture to attract sustained international attention—had unexpectedly succeeded in giving New York City a unique, global identity.

"Paris is no longer the capital of Cosmopolis. . . . New York . . . has become the battleground of modern civilization," declared Henry McBride in 1929. American artists who persisted in traveling abroad to work were "jeopardizing their careers for the dubious consommations [*sic*] of the Café de la Rotunde."[4] McBride's counsel was wasted on Georgia O'Keeffe, who spurned the European capitals until her old age, but others were less receptive to such tidings, even those living in Paris at the time.[5] Writing from Paris in 1921, a puzzled Charles Demuth noted how interested the French avant-garde was in events in New York: "Sometimes it seems impossible to come back— we are so out of it," he wrote. "Then one sees Marcel [Duchamp] or Gleizes and they will say, 'Oh! Paris. New York is the place,—there are the modern ideas,—

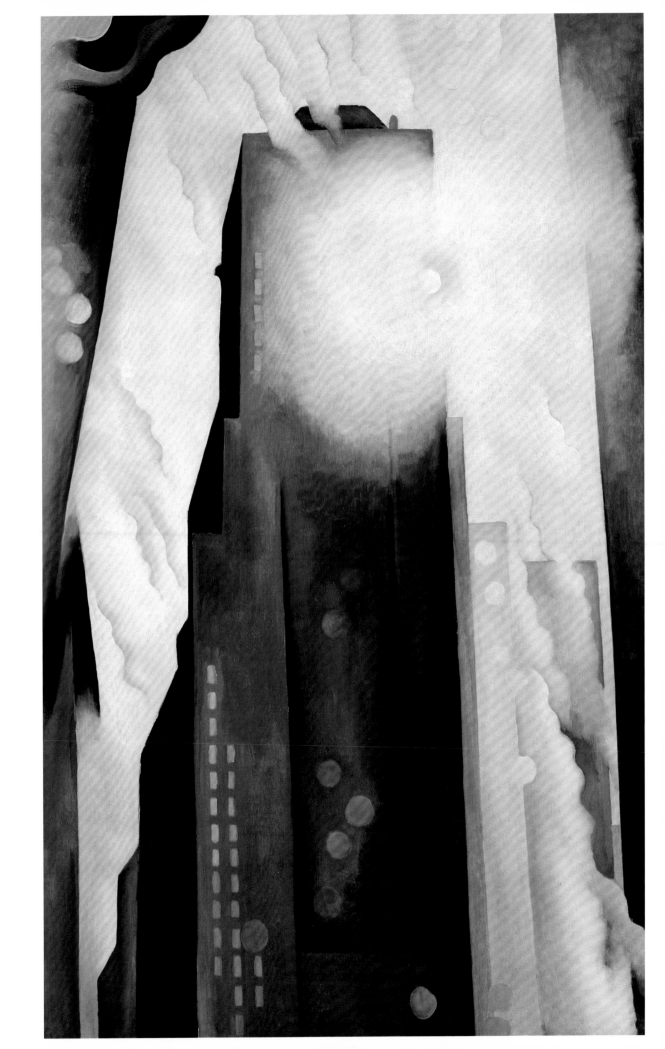

Europe is finished.' " Even so, the problem for American artists was that "our art is, as yet, outside of our art world," as Robert J. Coady put it in 1917, citing the skyscraper, the steam shovel, and Charlie Chaplin, among other examples. To Duchamp, this was no problem: "New York itself is a work of art, a complete work of art," he proclaimed in 1915, and he proposed to designate Cass Gilbert's Woolworth tower, the architectural sensation of the day, as one of his "ready-mades." Duchamp saw no reason to use an antiquated medium such as painting to represent New York. But photography was another matter. "I would like to see it make people despise painting until something else will make photography unbearable," Duchamp wrote to Alfred Stieglitz in 1922. For that matter, New York proved from the outset to be a less tractable subject for painters (or sculptors) than for photographers, such as Stieglitz or Berenice Abbott, who could turn their machines on a machine-made subject. But

Coady believed that an authoritative image of New York would have to be a painted image because painting was historically the authoritative medium.[6]

"Who will paint New York? Who?" Coady asked again and again in the first issue of *Soil*, published in 1916. Henry Tyrrell echoed this cry in the *New York World* in 1923:

New York, grandiose and glittering—the modern Wonder City of dynamic pulses, wireless, magnetism, electricity and tempered steel, of piled-up architecture like magic pinnacles of Alpine ice. . . . There she stands, matchless and overwhelming. Who shall paint her portrait? This to modern art is the flaming cynosure, this to modern artists the task that beckons with the fatalistic fascination of the unattainable.[7]

As Coady and Tyrrell saw it, attempts at painting the city made by artists like Abraham Walkowitz (fig. 2) and Joseph Stella did not solve the problem, for these artists pictured New York more or less as Fernand Léger and Robert Delaunay had pictured Paris: in a Cubist vernacular. That New York was intrinsically "the Cubist city, the Futurist city" had been decreed by Francis Picabia the moment he arrived there. Fresh from Paris, he claimed that he saw "much, much more" in New York "than you who are used to see[ing] it" and that he could show Americans how to describe New York most effectively—with the fractured idiom then current in Paris. Cubism helped to stress the disjunctiveness of lives lived at quickening tempos in Paris's ever more crowded surroundings, where artifacts of new regimes abruptly insinuated themselves amid the pervasive artifacts of old regimes and of a pretechnological order. But to paint New York, where the new was fairly continuous with the old (which was not so old in any case) and where the new looked newer than anywhere else, posed a

different problem. Solving that problem implied solving the greatest problem of all for American artists: that of formulating an indigenous mode of expression, a new art for the New World.[8]

Cubism undertook "the task of [the] revaluation of old values in Art and . . . perform[ed] it with violence," Naum Gabo once wrote. Cubist paintings are "like a heap of shards from a vessel exploded from within." The Futurists seized on Cubism's violence from the first, stressing that artists had to destroy the preexisting visual order to recover space for their own visions. Making room for new structures by demolishing old ones was a radical proposition to the Italians and the French, but it was a routine practice in an American city like New York. While European artists had liberating dreams of a tabula rasa, the specter of a cultural void was a terrifying, all too real prospect to American artists. What history they had was secondhand—rootless, eclectic, and reimagined—and that was the kind of history they often endeavored not to eradicate, but to recuperate and integrate into their work. Using remnants of European culture to help piece together their own self-image, Americans articulated their identity as ex-colonies. The skyscraper Duchamp wanted to designate a ready-made, for example—the Woolworth building—was an ornate, ersatz, Neo-Gothic cathedral built by a dimestore magnate.[9]

"Look at the sky-scrapers!" Duchamp exulted. "Has Europe anything to show more beautiful than these?" No matter how ornate and Europeanized the Woolworth building was—and Duchamp regretted that aspect of the building—no one could envision such an illimitable structure in Europe. The skyscraper appeared at once tellingly American and distinctly modern—a persuasive answer to that pressing question: "What will the building of the twentieth century look like?" The American critic Charles

Downing Lay observed in 1923, "Like all great art [New York's architecture] has grown from the conditions of our life . . . as an expression of our composite genius," while singling out the Shelton Hotel for his praise. But those huge, ornamented, masonry structures, such as the Woolworth building and the Shelton, which were seen as exemplary by critics in their day, are generally downplayed by historians today in favor of those (less representative) buildings that can be seen as foreshadowing the sleek, modernist vision of the Bauhaus or the International Style. By the early 1920s European architects such as Ludwig Mies van der Rohe were applying Bauhaus principles to skyscraper design, picturing an ideal modern tower—a geometric volume cleansed of ornament and historical referents—made possible by new building technologies (fig. 3). There was no call in Europe for such structures, so these architects looked hopefully instead to the United States for opportunities to realize their visions, perceiving it as a country that had "escaped Europe and its history willfully, in order to create a new universe and to initiate a new time," as Thomas van Leeuwen has expressed it.[10]

The European fascination with the skyscraper was connected with "the appeal America exercised as the ideological reflection of anything inadmissible in ancien regime Europe," Van Leeuwen has written.

America was free, it was unlimited in space, it abounded in natural resources and in money. It knew no tradition, it had no history.

From this perspective, the fact that American architects and artists persisted in following the precepts of tradition was baffling and even unforgivable. Many Europeans became convinced that they had a clearer vision of the new art and architecture that belonged in the New World than those who lived there, and they remonstrated with Americans to address their lack of self-perception. "The American character contains the elements of an extraordinary art," because American life is "abstract," "scientific," and "cold" like the twentieth century itself, Duchamp reasoned in 1915, but "the traditions weigh too heavily upon you, turn you into a sort of religious fanatics [*sic*] as little yourselves as possible." For Duchamp as for Mies, the advent of the skyscraper signaled "the call of utility." Americans, however, saw their "cathedrals of commerce" not only as models of efficiency but also as magic mountains of steel and stone, signifying both their material and spiritual ambitions. And while some of Mies's pristine towers were eventually built in the United States, they would never capture the public imagination as did those American-designed, tall buildings that evoked great historical and natural monuments.[11]

"The major formal and theoretical changes in skyscraper design began in the early 1920s with the work of Ferriss, Goodhue, Hood, and others," the architectural historian Carol Willis has written. "The characteristics of this new aesthetic were an emphasis on formal values of mass and silhouette with a subordination of ornament."[12] The identifiable buildings painted by O'Keeffe all dated from this period and were all located in the city's second great outcropping of skyscrapers. Ignoring the downtown skyscrapers rendered by artists before her—the tall buildings packed along the narrow lanes of the Wall Street area, which Joseph Pennell had etched; the famed Flat Iron Building, which Stieglitz had photographed; the ornate Woolworth and Municipal buildings, painted in watercolor by John Marin; even the low-rise, bohemian district of Greenwich Village, depicted by John Sloan—O'Keeffe made her own the stately skyscrapers rising along the broad avenues of her midtown neighborhood. This area boasted fashionable shops, galleries, offices (including the celebrated Radiator Building, designed by Raymond Hood; fig. 4), and, her preferred subject, upscale residential hotels—the Shelton, the Berkley (fig. 5), and the Ritz Tower. Taking some cues on visual poetics from the dark, theatrical drawings of the visionary architectural draftsman Hugh Ferriss (fig. 6) and some on composition, perhaps, from the cleanly composed architectural photographs of Charles Sheeler (fig. 7), O'Keeffe contrived her own ravishing vision of New York as a city awash in sunlight, moonglow, or the dazzling aura of an artificial firmament.[13]

It is difficult now, except in O'Keeffe's pictures of it, to see the appeal of the Shelton Hotel—her favorite architectural subject—which exemplified a vital turning point in skyscraper design. But to critics of the day this mammoth, austere structure was a revelation; it was "not a tower on a building, but it is itself a tower and . . . a really thrilling example of

5 *New York, Night*, 1929. Oil on canvas, 40 1/8 x 19 1/8 in. Nebraska Art Association, Thomas C. Woods Memorial Collection, Sheldon Memorial Art Gallery, University of Nebraska-Lincoln

6 Hugh Ferriss, *The Shelton Hotel*, 1927. Published in Ferriss, *The Metropolis of Tomorrow* (1929; reprint, Princeton, N.J.: Princeton Architectural Press, 1986)

7 Charles Sheeler, *The Shelton*. Photograph published in *The Arts* 4 (August 1923)

vertical movement in composition. . . . No one, I believe, can look on the Shelton from near or far without some lifting of the spirit."[14] The hotel O'Keeffe chose to live in was the center of interest in architectural circles for technical reasons as well. As one of the first major buildings to make effective use of the so-called setback mode necessitated by a 1916 zoning law (enacted to ensure that tall buildings not prevent sunlight from reaching the streets), the Shelton proved highly influential. Ferriss had executed a series of studies of architectural solutions to the law's stipulations, and, in designing the Shelton, Arthur Loomis Harmon followed his basic dictum that the setbacks be boldly articulated in architectural

form, not camouflaged by ornamentation. Ferriss's renderings of the Shelton shared with O'Keeffe's (fig. 8) an emphasis on its stepped, massive, zigguratlike silhouette. Historically, the ziggurat was a "cosmic mountain," a symbolic image of the cosmos, and both artists rendered the atmosphere enveloping the building in dramatic ways, suggesting cosmic or visionary overtones.

To Hugh Ferriss, there was in the Shelton "something reminiscent of the mountain. Many people choose it as a residence, or frequent its upper terraces, because . . . it evokes that undefinable sense of satisfaction which man ever finds on the slope of the pyramid or the mountainside." O'Keeffe and Stieglitz

New York—nor of anywhere. We live high up in the Shelton Hotel. . . . We feel as if we were out at midocean—All is so quiet except the wind—& the trembling shaking hulk of steel in which we live—It's a wonderful place.[15]

O'Keeffe's vision of the Shelton stressed its natural aspect, likening it to an architectural mountain faced by a sheer cliff. To her and Ferriss both, the experience of the skyscrapers was one of sublimity, and by omitting human figures (surrogate viewers) within the image itself, they offered an unmediated access to that experience, picturing a New York viewed from too high up or with the head tilted too far back to admit the presence of others.

When asked about his interest in the vaunted architectural traditions of the École des Beaux-Arts, Ferriss replied that he preferred "to seek the masses of the Grand Canyon and the peaks and spaces of southern California for inspiration rather than the past of Europe" because "they are more truly American." The perceived naturalness and Americanness of O'Keeffe's vision was likewise a factor in the reception of her work. "O'Keeffe is America's. Its own exclusive product," Frances O'Brien wrote in the *Nation* in 1927. "It is refreshing to realize that she has never been to Europe. More refreshing still that she has no ambition to go there. . . . In her painting as in herself is the scattered soul of America come into kingdom." What was so American about O'Keeffe's art was not only that she painted, and painted in, a skyscraper, but also that she painted with clarity and directness. "Having purged herself of New York's borrowed art theories" during her sojourns west of the Hudson, as O'Brien saw it, she had become "of all our modern painters . . . the least influenced by any of the . . . aesthetic fashions of the time." Others also saw O'Keeffe as refusing the abstruse and dissembling ways of the Continent for a mode of visualization founded squarely on perception and

8 *The Shelton Hotel at Night.*
Present whereabouts unknown.
Reproduced in *Arts and Decoration*
26 (March 1927)

regarded their lofty quarters as just such a refuge. Stieglitz wrote to his friend Sherwood Anderson:

New York is madder than ever. . . . But Georgia and I somehow don't seem to be of

resemblance. "O'Keeffe's pictures are the clean-cut result of an intensely passionate apprehension of things," wrote Virgil Barker in 1924, and in 1927 McBride praised one of her aerial views of New York as "a sufficiently literal rendering of one of the most amazing scenes on earth. . . . The mere facts are overpowering without any mysticism."[16]

McBride also perceptively praised O'Keeffe for painting the skyscrapers "as though their largeness was their main attraction—as it probably is." Eschewing the splintering effects of Cubism, O'Keeffe pictured the midtown towers as virtually whole, sometimes isolated icons of modernity, perceived from the unobstructed viewpoints the New York of her day sometimes afforded. Constructing her portraits of skyscrapers with a few bold, vertical shapes (sometimes punctuated by rows of minuscule windows), O'Keeffe formulated a vision of the tall building that accorded with the architects' own. Louis Sullivan identified "the dominant characteristic of the tall office building" as "its tallness: the force of altitude must be in it. Let it be therefore 'a proud and soaring thing, without a dissenting line from bottom to top.'" O'Keeffe's acute sense of the skyscraper's height was undoubtedly enhanced by her living and working in one, as she was the first artist—and among the first people ever—to reside in a skyscraper. She was able to find an apartment atop a tall building in 1925, whereas Duchamp had failed in his efforts to do so a decade earlier. The building codes had changed in the interim, allowing not only office buildings but also residential hotels (though not, as yet, apartment houses) to take the form of towers.[17]

For O'Keeffe, the prospect of living in a skyscraper prompted the idea of painting New York:

When I was looking for a place to live, I decided to try the Shelton. I was shown two rooms on the 30th floor. I had never lived up so high before and was so excited that I began talking about trying to paint New York. Of course, I was told that it was an impossible idea—even the men hadn't done too well with it.

New York was seen as a man's subject, no doubt because of the skyscrapers' priapic forms, because rendering the city meant taking the kind of commanding perspective that men alone were ordinarily socialized to assume, and because men controlled the civic space.[18] O'Keeffe knew well that New York was Stieglitz's milieu more than her own. In her picture of the Radiator Building she inscribed "ALFRED STIEGLITZ" on a brilliant red sign atop an adjacent building (see fig. 4), thereby imagining her dealer-husband effectively advertising his gallery as he, in fact, had refused to do. Moving to the Shelton eased that feeling for a time, as she became attuned to the city's poetry and found ways of articulating it. Many of her New York pictures offer relatively intimate views of one or two buildings, and she often focused on the open spaces between or over buildings, emphasizing the void as much as, or more than, the skyscrapers' phallic forms. "I saw a sky shape near the Chatham Hotel where buildings were going up," O'Keeffe recalled. "It was the buildings that made this fine shape, so I sketched it and then painted it. This was in the early twenties and was my first New York painting" (fig. 9).[19] Some subsequent paintings emphasized the slitlike canyons between rows of tall buildings facing each other along an avenue.

To work and live atop a skyscraper was to realize a peculiarly modern and American vision of success and emancipation—one not commonly identified with women. Once she started realizing some income from her art, O'Keeffe's ideal urban home became a corner suite (without a kitchen) on an upper floor of a stylish residential hotel initially designed for bachelors. "Miss O'Keeffe lives there [at the Shelton]—by choice," McBride informed his readers in 1928.

It has long lines, long surfaces—it has everything. At night it looks as though it reached to the stars, and the searchlights that cut across the sky back of it do appear to carry messages to other worlds.

Although none of her biographers have noted it, late in 1927 O'Keeffe evidently moved within the Shelton from the twenty-eighth to the thirtieth floor (of a thirty-three story building), probably to improve her view. A letter to her sister in December 1926 describes two rooms on the twenty-eighth floor with views facing north, east, and south. After January 1928 visitors described going to the thirtieth floor, to a suite with views in every direction. "I am going to live as high as I can this year," O'Keeffe said, after she had moved to her new apartment.[20]

"I realize it's unusual for an artist to work way up near the roof of a big hotel in the heart of the roaring city," O'Keeffe told a critic in 1928, "but I think that's just what the artist of today needs for stimulus. He has to have a place where he can behold the city as a unit before his eyes." Gazing east from the Shelton in the late mornings or through the late afternoon haze, O'Keeffe could render one of those spectacular, urban vistas—across the river to the industrial districts of Queens (fig. 10)—which constitute a uniquely modern vision. Looking north from her corner aerie in the evening, she could capture the whimsical, pagoda-roofed tower of the nearby Berkley Hotel and the bright stream of headlights coursing down Lexington Avenue into the stoplight- and neon-lit well at the base of her building. Most impressive of all were her awesome views of the towers seen from street level: the Shelton, illuminated by the sun and the moon; the black and silvery Radiator

Building, lit up like a colossal Christmas tree; as well as anonymous structures (fig. 11). In a subtly abstracted way, O'Keeffe limned the flat, continuous shapes the tall buildings carved into the sky. In her nocturnal views of the Radiator Building and the Berkley Hotel, she similarly depicted the fantastic ornamentation of the buildings' crowns and the complex patterns created by the extravagant displays of artificial light from within and without. O'Keeffe captured New York's spellbinding theater both in its epic and in its vaudevillian aspects: "Her summation of Manhattan, unequalled in painting, has the rude thrust as well as the delicacy and glitter that distinguishes the city of America," pronounced Herbert Seligmann.[21]

O'Keeffe painted more than twenty New York scenes between 1925 and 1930, and while her own recollections do not comprise a seamless account of the course of events, she evidently painted her first city picture—*New York at Night with Moon*—early in 1925, when she lived in an apartment at 35 East 58th Street. Probably in March of that year (not the fall as she recalled), she urged Stieglitz to exhibit the picture in a group show he was organizing at the Anderson Galleries, but, anxious about premiering her outsized flower paintings at the same show, Stieglitz refused. Her city paintings had their debut instead in her solo show in February and March of 1926. *New York at Night with Moon* was the first painting to sell, by her account, on the day the show opened. "No one ever objected to my painting New York after that," she wryly remembered.[22] O'Keeffe and Stieglitz had moved to the Shelton in November of 1925, and during the few months remaining before her 1926 show she seems to have painted three detailed panoramas of the view east from her window. Given that she credited the building with inspiring her to paint the city, however, she may have been shown

9 *New York at Night with Moon,*
1925. Oil on canvas, 48 x 30 5/16 in.
Thyssen-Bornemisza Collection,
Lugano, Switzerland

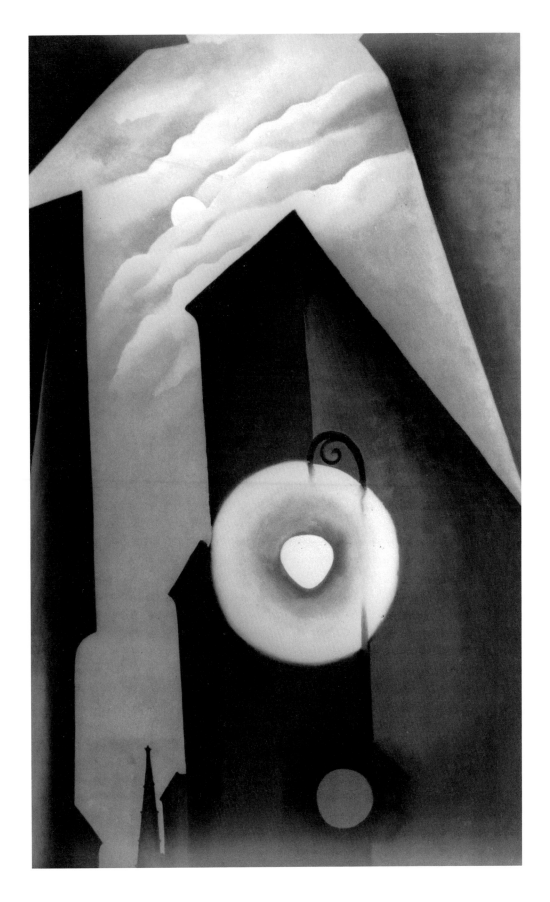

10 *East River from the Shelton*, 1927–28. Oil on canvas, 25 1/16 x 21 15/16 in. New Jersey State Museum, Trenton, Purchased by the Association for the Arts of the New Jersey State Museum with a gift from Mary Lea Johnson

11 *City Night*, 1926. Oil on canvas, 48 x 30 in. The Minneapolis Institute of Fine Arts, Gift of the Regis Corporation, Mr. and Mrs. W. John Driscoll, the Beim Foundation, the Larsen Fund, and by public subscription

the apartment before painting *New York at Night with Moon*, that is, in January or February of 1925, and she probably painted some or all of the four images of the building's facade that were in the 1926 exhibition before moving in.

Nine New York paintings led off the list for O'Keeffe's 1926 exhibition, which the *New Yorker* described as a "marvelous show of a genius which it would be foolish to miss." Six New York pictures topped the list of works at her annual show in 1927, and three city paintings headed the list the following year. These New York paintings drew some special mention in the press, but several of O'Keeffe's regular supporters—Paul Rosenfeld, Waldo Frank, Paul Strand,

and Lewis Mumford, who had been principally attracted by the organic quality of her art—disapproved of the skyscraper, complaining of its dehumanizing effects.[23] What influenced O'Keeffe to quit painting New York, however (as she did in 1930, with two exceptions), was probably less the uninterest of those critics in her city pictures than the fact that the newfound spirit of American cultural pride that had permeated her New York pictures collapsed in October 1929 with the stock market crash. (It may be a factor as well that Stieglitz resumed photographing the city at this time, capturing the view west from the Shelton of the construction of Rockefeller Center, for O'Keeffe disliked sharing subjects with him.)

O'Keeffe's last painting of New York, executed in the 1940s, was a rather dry and rigid image of the Brooklyn Bridge (1948, Brooklyn Museum). Her other late painting of the city was a failed but telling experiment: a triptych showing a panorama of Manhattan rendered in a Cubist syntax and dotted with her trademark flowers (fig. 12).[24] O'Keeffe contrived this awkward work for an invitational exhibition of mural proposals by American artists. Organized by the Museum of Modern Art in 1932, the show was meant to convince the designers of Radio City Music Hall that they should not look exclusively abroad for talent to decorate the building. The show's premise and the Eurocentric bias of the Museum of Modern Art must have influenced O'Keeffe in an exceptional (perhaps unique?) attempt to demonstrate her command of the dominant modernist language. Betraying her indifference to Cubism's dire report on the fragmentation of the modern subject would have, in this context, simply stigmatized her as parochial. Her shrewd entry to the exhibition, however, brought the desired outcome, a chance to decorate the women's powder room at Radio City,

12 *Manhattan*, 1932. Oil on canvas
triptych, each panel 48 x 21 in.
Present whereabouts unknown.
Reproduced in *Murals by American
Painters and Photographers* (New
York: Museum of Modern Art, 1932)

but Stieglitz interfered, and O'Keeffe
withdrew from the project.[25]

Stieglitz was ambivalent about pub-
licizing O'Keeffe's work within the
United States, and he declined to promote her career abroad: "I have been
asked to let this work go to Europe,"
he said of the show in which the city
paintings premiered. "But they do not
take the Woolworth Tower to Europe.
And this work here is as American as
the Woolworth Tower." European van-
guardists might not have recognized in
O'Keeffe's pictures their image of the
New World's new art or architecture, in
any case, for they generally perceived as

truly modern only that art which con-
formed to their own visions of the new
visual order. They widely intimated that
Americans did not yet know themselves—
at least not as well as the Europeans knew
them. "When the Americans have traveled
sufficiently across the old world to
perceive their own richness, they will be
able to see their own country for what it
is," said a paternalistic Henri Matisse
in 1930. While Matisse regarded Americans
as cultural "primitives," however, no
paintings come so close as O'Keeffe's
Radiator Building, Shelton with Sunspots,
or *City Night* to capturing the exhilarating
experience of New York as Matisse

the leading sculptor of the Paris avant-garde. An awed Constantin Brancusi discovered in New York in 1926

a great new poetry seeking its peculiar expression. In architecture you have found it already in the great skyscrapers. We in Europe are far behind you in this field.

Faced with O'Keeffe's paintings of the city on a visit to Stieglitz's gallery, Brancusi said admiringly, "There is no imitation of Europe here. . . . It is a force, a liberating free force." A sense of liberation was what Brancusi sought in his own work too, and he reveled in the relation of his soaring *Birds in Space* series (1923–40) to the "wonderful, inspiring flight heavenward" of the city's skyscrapers. Piet Mondrian, arriving in New York in the early 1940s, likewise perceived a profound affinity between his art and the architecture of the city, particularly as it was laid out on the clear grid of streets in the midtown area. In New York, Mondrian painted the most ambitious pictures of his career—*Broadway Boogie-Woogie* (1942–43, Museum of Modern Art) and the unfinished *Victory Boogie-Woogie* (1943–44)—and he found a circle of devotees there, as well as entrées to the market and the public. In fact, the first and only solo show Mondrian had in his lifetime was held in New York (no dealer had offered to represent him during the more twenty years he lived in Paris).[27]

To a steady stream of European, avant-garde artists who traveled to New York between the first and fifth decades of the twentieth century, then, the city's great new skyscrapers were more than architectural marvels: they were the true beacons of and for the new art. New York's "skyscrapers . . . say that the country understands art," decreed Brancusi, who had reason to deem Americans "best qualified to speak authoritatively of modern art." All of Brancusi's major patrons were Americans, and all of his

himself described it (while comparing the city favorably both to Paris and to the Swiss Alps): "The first time that I saw America, I mean New York, at seven o'clock in the evening, this gold and black block in the night, reflected in the water, I was in complete ecstasy. . . . New York seemed to me like a gold nugget." Strolling down the "grand avenues" of the midtown area O'Keeffe had painted, Matisse was "truly electrified" to discover that the skyscrapers created "a feeling of lightness . . . [and] of liberty through the possession of a larger space."[26]

The same New York that so inspired both O'Keeffe and Matisse also inspired

solo exhibitions until the year before he died occurred in the United States, beginning with a show at Stieglitz's "291" gallery in 1914. (O'Keeffe's first solo show took place at the same gallery in 1917.) Matisse also knew that a greater public for modern art existed among Americans than among the French, as his most devoted patrons were nearly all American. Matisse had the first showing of his sculpture at "291" in 1912. He conjectured that "Americans are interested in modern painting because of its immediate translation of feeling. . . . It is more in rapport with the activity of their spirit." As for Duchamp, who would make a home in New York and eventually become an American citizen, it was in America and not in France where he was treated, from the time of the Armory Show, as a celebrity and an authority: he had both his first solo show and his first major retrospective in the United States.[28]

In short, many of those pivotal figures who are ordinarily credited with making Paris the world's art center saw New York in that role instead well before the end of the Second World War. After World War I, New York generally provided artists with better opportunities for showing and selling modern art, and zealous American collectors were working to make modern art publicly accessible in New York in a way it was not in Paris. Stieglitz's highly subsidized "291" gallery was the prelude to Katherine Dreier's nonprofit Société Anonyme gallery, which opened in a New York brownstone in 1920, and A. E. Gallatin's Gallery of Living Art, which opened at New York University in 1927. Two years later the Museum of Modern Art, the brainstorm of a cartel of society women, opened to the public. The Whitney Museum of American Art began operations in 1931, financed by the wealthy sculptor Gertrude Vanderbilt Whitney, and Solomon R. Guggenheim made his collection public in the Museum of Non-Objective Art in 1939.

The sense that Paris had become an "onlooker" to New York dawned on different observers at different moments. In a 1931 essay on the "most beautiful spectacle in the world," Fernand Léger exclaimed how that "daring vertical new continent," Manhattan, prefigured a whole new egalitarian world marked by a "new religion" consecrated to business and technology. "New York and the telephone came into the world on the same day, on the same boat, to conquer the world. Mechanical life is at its apogee here." Picturing the mechanical was Léger's forte, but he could not believe that any artist would ever successfully describe New York: "It is madness to think of employing such a subject artistically. One admires it humbly, and that's all."[29]

So who would dare to paint New York? Léger and Matisse would not even try it, and Mondrian's vision of the city, however compelling, was continuous with his vision of Paris and London. It was Georgia O'Keeffe who would paint New York, depicting its towering buildings in a legible, lyrical way that reciprocated the democratized aspect of the city while evincing the limitless aspirations embodied in its newfound imago: the skyscraper. O'Keeffe believed that her images of the city included "probably my best paintings," and she hoped that they would "turn the world over," as the buildings she was painting were very nearly doing.[30] That she pictured "the world's new art center" never did earn O'Keeffe her due, however, for in the standard, Eurocentric narratives of the history of modern art, New York was not the world's art center at the time she portrayed it—no matter who thought so—and O'Keeffe was not a world-wise artist.

The best answer to the question "Who will paint New York?" then, may well be a second question: "Who will get to say when New York has been painted?" From an American vantage point, the most obvious answer to the latter query is

Clement Greenberg, who would most likely have chosen his protégé, Jackson Pollock. Pollock did not paint New York in a literal way, of course—no one asked that anymore by the end of the Second World War—but to Greenberg's eye his art represented "an attempt to cope with urban life; it dwells entirely in the lonely jungle of immediate sensations, impulses and notions, therefore is positivist, concrete"—notwithstanding the fact that the famed poured paintings were made in a barn on a Long Island farm. In the standard art historical narratives, Pollock gets most of the credit for precipitating the shift in the art world's center from Paris to New York, or for "turning the world over."[31] Yet, in a sense, Pollock's art spells the triumph of the Old World's vision of the New World as unlimited in space and energy and innocent of culture. Erasing the colonial past, Pollock invented that much-anticipated art without history. If Pollock found a way to picture America's stark, cultural nakedness, it was Georgia O'Keeffe who first pictured the world's new art center in all its awesome cultural finery.

Notes

I am very grateful to Calvin Brown and Carol Willis for their help with this essay.

1 *New York Tribune*, quoted in Rudolf E. Kuenzli, ed., *New York Dada* (New York: Willis Locker and Owens, 1986), pp. 130–33; Marcel Duchamp, quoted in "The Iconoclastic Opinions of M. Marcel Duchamps [*sic*] Concerning Art and America," *Current Opinion* 59 (November 1915): 346.

2 F. J. G. [Frederick James Gregg], "The World's New Art Centre," *Vanity Fair* 5 (January 1915): 31; Clement Greenberg, quoted in John O'Brian, ed., *Clement Greenberg: The Collected Essays and Criticism* (Chicago: University of Chicago Press, 1986), vol. 2, *Arrogant Purpose, 1945–1949*, pp. 193, 215.
   According to William E. Leuchtenberg, "In 1914 the United States was a debtor nation; American citizens owed foreign investors three billion dollars. By the end of 1919 the United States was a creditor nation, with foreigners owing American investors nearly three billion dollars. In addition, the United States had loaned over ten billion dollars to foreign countries, mostly to carry on the war, in part for postwar reconstruction. These figures represent one of those great shifts of power that occurs but rarely in the history of nations"; Leuchtenberg, *The Perils of Prosperity: 1914–1932* (Chicago: University of Chicago Press, 1958), pp. 108, 225–26.

3 Leuchtenberg, pp. 182, 227; Claude Bragdon, "The Shelton Hotel, New York," *Architectural Record* 58 (July 1925): 1. The Shelton Hotel (now the Halloran House) is on the east side of Lexington Avenue between 48th and 49th Streets.

4 Henry McBride, quoted in Daniel Catton Rich, ed., *The Flow of Art: Essays and Criticisms of Henry McBride* (New York: Atheneum, 1975), p. 256.

5 Once O'Keeffe finally traveled to the cities of Europe, she found they didn't compare: "My ideal city is New York. European cities seem villages in comparison"; quoted in Thomas Lask, "Publishing: Georgia O'Keeffe," *New York Times*, 25 June 1976. (O'Keeffe made her first trip to Europe in 1953.)

6 Charles Demuth, quoted in Joshua C. Taylor, *America as Art* (New York: Harper and Row, 1976), p. 190; R. J. Coady, "American Art," *Soil* 2 (January 1917): 55, and 1 (December 1916): 3; "A Complete Reversal of Art Opinions by Marcel Duchamp, Iconoclast," *Arts and Decoration* 5 (September 1915): 428; Marcel Duchamp, quoted in "Can a Photograph Have the Significance of Art?" *Manuscripts* 4 (December 1922): 2. On the Woolworth tower as a "ready-made," see Merrill Schleier, *The Skyscraper in American Art, 1890–1931* (Ann Arbor, Mich.: U.M.I. Research Press, 1986), p. 55. Abbott conceived the idea of compiling an intensive photographic record of New York (such as Eugène Atget had done of Paris) in 1929, and she left Paris for Manhattan that year, before the October crash, to begin her first major photographic project, *Changing New York*.

7 Coady, *Soil* 1 (December 1916): 3; Henry Tyrrell, *New York World*, 21 January 1923.

8 Francis Picabia, quoted in Jean-Luc Daval, *Avant-Garde Art, 1914–1939* (New York: Rizzoli, 1980), p. 17, in Schleier, p. 65, and in "Picabia, Art Rebel, Here to Teach a New Movement," *New York Times*, 16 February 1913, p. 9. After years of exhibiting European modernists, by the 1920s Stieglitz was showing only American artists and stressing to them the importance of developing a native vision. But O'Keeffe observed of the Stieglitz circle: "I knew that at that time almost any one of those great minds would have been living in Europe if it had been possible for them. They didn't even want

to live in New York—how was the Great American Thing going to happen?"; O'Keeffe, *Georgia O'Keeffe* (New York: Viking, 1976), n.p.

9 Naum Gabo, "The Constructive Idea in Art," in *Circle: International Survey of Constructive Art*, ed. J. L. Martin, Ben Nicholson, Gabo (1937; reprint, New York: Praeger, 1971), pp. 3–4. Said Duchamp on destroying the old: "I believe that your idea of demolishing old buildings, old souvenirs, is fine. It is in line with that so much misunderstood manifesto issued by the Italian Futurists. . . . The dead should not be permitted to be so much stronger than the living. We must learn to forget the past, to live our own lives in our own time"; "A Complete Reversal," p. 428.

10 Duchamp, quoted in "Iconoclastic Opinions," p. 346 (in the same interview Duchamp described American architecture as "the only architecture"); Charles Downing Lay, "New Architecture in New York," *The Arts* 4 (August 1923): 67; Thomas A. P. van Leeuwen, *The Skyward Trend of Thought: The Metaphysics of the American Skyscraper* (Cambridge, Mass.: M.I.T. Press, 1988), pp. 3, 22–25. According to Van Leeuwen, as the skyscraper's story is usually told, Louis Sullivan emerges as its father, Chicago as its birthplace, but the Sullivan given that role is a man most unlike himself, one who spurned ornament and placed function above all else.

11 Van Leeuwen, p. 3; Duchamp, quoted in "A Complete Reversal," p. 428.

12 Carol Willis, "Drawing Towards Metropolis," in Hugh Ferriss, *Metropolis of Tomorrow* (1929; reprint, Princeton, N.J.: Princeton Architectural Press, 1986), p. 166. The way the story is usually told, the turning point in skyscraper design occurred in 1925, when Americans looked to Paris—to the Exposition of Decorative and Industrial Arts—to formulate an Art Deco style. By Willis's account, however, the Art Deco aesthetic "was hardly more than a decorative applique."

13 Ferriss published several drawings of the Shelton in 1923 and 1924. He drew the Radiator Building circa 1925 and showed his drawing at the Anderson Galleries that April (O'Keeffe had been in a show at the same location the previous month); see Willis's Appendix 2 in Ferriss, p. 190. A photograph of the Shelton by Sheeler, who did architectural photography for a living, was published in *The Arts* 4 (August 1923): 86. His photographs of the Berkley (taken in 1920) and of the Ritz Tower hotels were reproduced in *Cahiers d'Art* 2, no. 415 (1927): 180, 182. O'Keeffe wrote admiringly of Sheeler's photography in "Can a Photograph Have the Significance of Art?" p. 17.

14 Lay, p. 68.

15 Ferriss, p. 30; Alfred Stieglitz, quoted in Sarah Greenough and Juan Hamilton, *Alfred Stieglitz: Photographs and Writings* (Washington D.C.: National Gallery of Art, n.d.), p. 214.

16 Ferriss, quoted in Willis, p. 167; Frances O'Brien, "Americans We Like: Georgia O'Keeffe," *Nation* 12 (October 1927): 361–62; Virgil Barker, quoted in Barbara Buhler Lynes, *O'Keeffe, Stieglitz and the Critics, 1916–1929* (Ann Arbor, Mich.: U.M.I. Research Press, 1989), p. 215; Henry McBride, quoted in Lynes, p. 296.

17 Henry McBride, "O'Keeffe at the Museum," *New York Sun*, 18 May 1946; Sullivan, paraphrased and quoted by Claude Bragdon, *The Secret Spring: An Autobiography* (London: Andrew Dakers, 1938), p. 147. On Duchamp's apartment search see "Iconoclastic Opinions," p. 346. O'Keeffe was emulated in 1930 by the pioneering photo-journalist, Margaret Bourke-White, who made her studio and wanted (but was not permitted) to make her home high up in the newly completed Chrysler Building, one of her favorite photographic subjects. See Vicki Goldberg, *Margaret Bourke-White: A Biography* (New York: Harper and Row, 1986), p. 115. Making their offices on the top floors of skyscrapers, preferably of their own design, was also the practice of numerous architects in this period.

18 O'Keeffe, n.p. Inevitably, some critics have intimated that O'Keeffe's gender precluded her picturing the city effectively. Of her city pictures (which are mostly painted in neutral tones and black), Milton W. Brown wrote that "her prettiness of color is an intrusion, her lack of strength obvious. Such paintings as *The Shelton* . . . and *The American Radiator Building* . . . in which she introduced irrelevant embellishments, are decorative designs no more substantial than flower petals"; Brown, *American Painting: From the Armory Show to the Depression* (Princeton, N.J.: Princeton University Press, 1955), pp. 127–28. Peter Conrad has called her views of the Shelton "tributes to the perceptual power Stieglitz exercised over the city from inside it"; in *Shelton with Sunspots*, for example, "the burning upper storeys are a camera eye seared in the stone by Stieglitz's power to see through it. . . . Stieglitz—in this painting and in his own photographs—is he who dares to affront that flaming source"; Conrad, *The Art of the City: Views and Versions of New York* (New York: Oxford University Press, 1984), p. 85.

19 O'Keeffe, quoted in Katharine Kuh, *The Artist's Voice: Talks with Seventeen Artists* (New York: Harper and Row, 1960), p. 191.

20 Henry McBride, quoted in Rich, ed., p. 236; O'Keeffe, quoted in Roxana Robinson, *Georgia O'Keeffe: A Life* (New York: Harper and Row, 1989), p. 288; O'Keeffe, quoted in Lynes, p. 290. On visitors' reports on O'Keeffe's thirtieth-floor apartment, see Lynes, pp. 280, 284–86.

21 O'Keeffe, quoted in Lynes, p. 287; Herbert J. Seligmann, quoted in James Moore, "So Clear Where the Sun Will Come . . . : Georgia O'Keeffe's *Gray Cross with Blue*," *Artspace* (Summer 1986): 35.

22 For quotes and information on O'Keeffe's first city picture, see O'Keeffe, n.p. As O'Keeffe told it, the huge buildings springing up all over the city were what impelled her to enlarge her flowers in the first place; see Kuh, p. 191. As *New York at Night with Moon* is not listed by that title in the brochure of the

1926 show, she may have exhibited it under another title.

23 "Goings On About Town," *New Yorker* 2 (13 March 1926): 5. The show was so popular that its run was extended. The 1926 show included *The Shelton—New York* (I–IV), *Street, New York* (I–II), and *East River from the Shelton* (I–III). The 1927 show included *New York Night, A Building New York-Night, The Shelton at Night*, and *East River* (Nos. 1–3). In 1928 O'Keeffe showed *East River from the Shelton* (VI–VII), and *Ritz Tower, Night*. For mention in the press, see Murdock Pemberton, "The Art Galleries: The Great Wall of Manhattan, or New York for Live New Yorkers," *New Yorker* 2 (13 March 1926): 36–37, and "The Art Galleries," *New Yorker* 3 (21 January 1928): 44.

24 Whether by intent or coincidence, the central panel of the triptych resembled one of the stage sets for John Alden Carpenter's "Skyscrapers," first performed as a ballet in 1926. A photograph of Carpenter's set was reproduced in *Theater Arts Monthly* 10 (March 1926).

O'Keeffe's painting has not been reproduced since it was first shown, and she is said to have destroyed at least part of it. Each of the triptych's panels was 48 x 21 inches, with the center panel done in a second, full-scale version, 7 x 4 feet (the dimensions were set by the museum). See *Murals by American Painters and Photographers* (New York: Museum of Modern Art, 1932), n.p.

25 Stieglitz objected to the Radio City commission because he did not believe in the "democratization" of art and because of the low fee. He told the head of design for the Music Hall, Donald Deskey, that O'Keeffe was a child and not responsible for her actions in signing the contract. Deskey and O'Keeffe were both undaunted by Stieglitz's pressure until O'Keeffe discovered that the walls she was to paint had been improperly prepared and that there was insufficient

time for her to complete the project. She then withdrew from the project and suffered a breakdown, which left her virtually unable to work for over a year. See Laurie Lisle, *Portrait of an Artist: A Biography of Georgia O'Keeffe* (New York: Washington Square Press, 1980), pp. 258–61. She never painted New York's buildings again and started to spend more time in New Mexico, where Stieglitz would not go. (O'Keeffe's ambition to work on a large scale—even to design an entire house—dated from 1926, when she first exhibited her New York paintings. See Herbert J. Seligmann, *Alfred Stieglitz Talking: Notes on Some of His Conversations, 1925–1931* (New Haven: Yale University Library, 1966), p. 60.

26 Stieglitz, quoted in Seligmann, pp. 27–28; Matisse, quoted in Jack D. Flam, ed. and trans., *Matisse on Art* (New York: E. P. Dutton, 1978), pp. 62–63. Matisse, passing through New York while en route to Tahiti, wrote to his wife, "What I find here is really and truly a new world: it's great and majestic like the sea—and on top of that one senses the human effort behind it. . . . On my way to see idle primitives, I've started out seeing active primitives—two extremes. Where do we fit in? That's the question!" quoted in Pierre Schneider, *Matisse* (New York: Rizzoli, 1984), pp. 606–7.

27 Constantin Brancusi, quoted in "Brancusi Returns Here for Display," *New York World*, 30 September 1926, in Seligmann, p. 69, and in "America Holds Future of Art, Brancusi Says," *Evening Union*, 20 December 1927. Mondrian's commercial show was at the Valentine Dudensing Gallery in 1942; the Museum of Modern Art honored him with a memorial retrospective in 1944. The same museum had acquired the first of its major collection of Mondrian paintings in 1937, whereas the Musée National d'Art Moderne in Paris did not acquire a painting by the artist until 1975.

28 Brancusi, quoted in "America Holds"; Matisse, quoted in Flam, ed., p. 63. On Duchamp see Moira Roth, "Marcel Duchamp in America: A Self Ready-Made," *Arts* 51 (May 1977): 92.

Henri Rousseau's first public solo show, a commemorative exhibition in 1910, was also held at Stieglitz's "291" gallery.

29 Fernand Léger, *Functions of Painting*, trans. Alexandra Anderson, ed. Edward F. Fry (New York: Viking, 1973), pp. 84–86, 90.

30 O'Keeffe, quoted in Jack Cowart, Juan Hamilton with Sarah Greenough, *Georgia O'Keeffe: Art and Letters* (Washington, D.C.: National Gallery of Art, 1987), pp. 179, 183. Her estimation of her city pictures and her sense that they had been unjustly treated emerged when, as an old woman, she troubled to show an interviewer an almost fifty-year-old reference in a review by McBride to "one of the best skyscraper pictures that I have seen anywhere. It combines fact and fancy admirably." She remarked pointedly, "I'd be pleased to have that said in your article"; quoted in Mary Lynn Kotz, "Georgia O'Keeffe at Ninety," *Art News* 76 (December 1977): 45.

31 Clement Greenberg, quoted in O'Brian, ed., p. 166. It took a protracted campaign by American critics, however, to persuade Europeans of the legitimacy of Pollock's vision, which bears scant trace of Cubism. The Musée National d'Art Moderne would not acquire its first Pollock until 1972. My thanks to Mary Werth for obtaining this information. Observed the sculptor Constantine Nivola, "The French would say of de Kooning, 'As painting, we can recognize this.' Of Pollock, '*This* is not painting! Only in America could it happen'"; quoted in Jeffrey Potter, *To a Violent Grave: An Oral Biography of Jackson Pollock* (Wainscott, N.Y.: Pushcart, 1985), p. 221.

Ghastly News from Epic Landscapes

Max Kozloff

Richard Misrach, *Bomb,
Destroyed Vehicle and Cone Rock*
(detail), 1987, from *Bravo 20: The
Bombing of the American West*

In recent years, an admonishing view has emerged in an ordinarily bland genre: the photography of nature. One glance at the field tells us that ecological concerns, understandably enough at this historical point, have infiltrated the medium. How can they be expressed effectively? How can they be responded to? What do they tell us about our culture?

As a craft, nature photography is specialized, requiring particular tools. Only a big-view camera, for instance, has the range to thrust deep into a landscape, restoring to a picture surface remote detail that a smaller instrument would interpret only as tone. In a grand horizon one expects both texture and tone, or rather texture *within* tone. A large-format print allows a panorama to be backed up by what seems to be an endless reserve of data. This discriminative power is just as well, for the scene is likely to be devoid of a main incident. What we generally have in landscape photography is a kind of micro-nutrition—based on diffuse vegetarian ingredients—that compensates for a lack of psychological narrative and a visual center.

Such a peaceful, almost comatose state of affairs has recently been ruffled by a wave of activism. Pictorially, the chief but also misleading forebear of this would be the French *paysage moralisé*, a landscape genre which, either by reflecting our passions or inducing some philosophical meditation on life, drives home a moral. We do not just contemplate the goodness of the place but find in it an object lesson

derived from its pictorial appearance. About Nicolas Poussin's *Et in Arcadia Ego* (ca. 1640, Louvre, Paris), a famous moralized landscape, the poet Théophile Gautier wrote, "The picture of the Shepherds of Arcady expresses with a naive melancholy the brevity of life and awakens among the young shepherds and the girl who look at the tomb they have found, the forgotten idea of death."[1] Arcadia, the ideal of the pastoral tradition, here represents that strangely lovely moment when figures in a landscape uncover evidence of an ancient happiness and a witness to our mortal destiny. Gautier could call this a "naive" melancholy because he lived in the already stressed-out, coal-blackened nineteenth century.

In a postpastoral version of that melancholy, the picture of nature today may testify to the damage men have done to their environment, a damage possibly so extreme as to hasten human and animal fate. With both the earlier moralizing tradition and the current instance of it, landscape is conceived as an artifact of culture. But unlike its predecessor, the present culture leaves new traces of disorder and anomaly within the old landscape construct. We glimpse a prelude to a future that once was inconceivable but now may not even be remote: the irrevocable extinction of certain living things. The pastoral tradition had been expressive in its awareness of the natural cycle in which death and birth replace each other. Now, instead of discovering the ephemerality of sensate life in an enduring scene of beauty, the viewer must face the fragility of the scene itself—a tableau of repulsive contingencies that do not strike us as either culture or nature.

This ambiguity, though it has quite a literary and pictorial background, is the product of something we are just beginning to recognize. Artists have always liked to depict fringes, blurred borders, and vague terrains. They may have thought of them as truly mysterious regions or unregarded banalities, but in either case the prevalence of such scenes impresses them now. In some of today's landscape photography, dubious surroundings reflect a kind of unthoughtful contemporary experience. Everything runs into everything else in a manner that exhausts anyone's power of discerning cause and effect. Put differently, a sifting occurs whereby territories come to seem palpably other than—often subtly the opposite of—what they had been. Without being to any human advantage (though activated by humans), phenomena migrate to the wrong place, as do toxic gases that escape into the air. Observing such unlikely fusions, we perceive what in information theory would be called noise and what in common terms is spoken of as dirt.

"Wrongness" on this level is obviously a relative measure. It implies a contrast to what organisms want or where they need to be to maintain the conditions, systems, and functions of life. The contrast summons up what we fear: interference to patterns of natural replenishment. Here, "wrongness" is a more difficult notion to understand than, say, *incongruity*—things going inappropriately together—a state of affairs that often describes heterogeneous arrangements, natural or cultural. Surrealism has given us a taste for some of these phenomena, which can offer surprise and therefore new information. But generally speaking, the incongruous has no fatality about it. We are accustomed to the

depiction of American townscapes or rural scenes with mildly clashing features. But we do not think of them as "wrong" in the same way that symptoms indicate something is wrong to doctors. This symptomatology has become a subject of some recent American landscape photographs.

In theory, one way to observe that subject is via aerial camera or one traveling in space. Recent NASA photography of one of Neptune's moons revealed inexplicable markings that have non-plussed science. These phenomena may have originated in events that were singular or even abnormal but were hardly unnatural. On earth, categories that define natural or unnatural exist for us as products of our own culture. Even so, at some altitude, it is still often difficult to separate human-made from natural conditions in the biosphere. For example, after many years of photographing the earth from planes, Swiss scientist Georg Gerster published the results in a book called *Grand Design* (1976). He was able to show a phenomenon like red tide in a Japanese bay without attributing it to human interference, as was obvious in his images of aluminum poisoning of Australian trees or oil and tar residues along the Ivory Coast. While the view from above certainly revealed a very dynamic and fragile ecosystem, it did not deflect Gerster from stating that "man's dilemma—to change nature or adapt himself to it—is insoluble. . . . It is Man's earth. . . . The right of codetermination for wild animals? Partnership with all creatures? . . . Fashionable models all, but foolish ones."[2]

Gerster did not then question our priority as a species, but our understanding now begins to suggest that partnership with animals is an enlightened rather than a foolish idea. Yet one would be hard-pressed to read this just from the perspective of aerial photography, for the wrong spots, when they exist and are interpret-

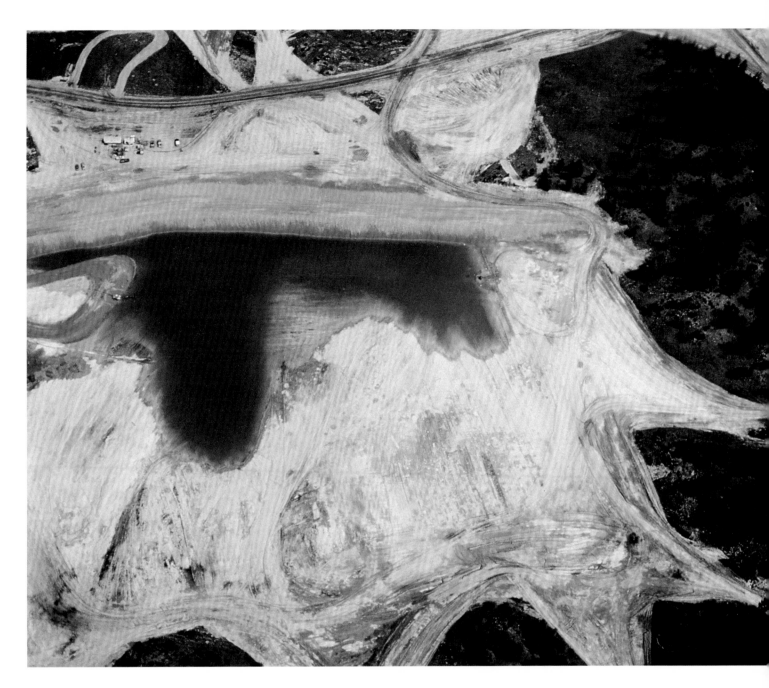

1 David T. Hanson, *Excavation, Deforestation and Waste Pond,* 1984, from the series *Colstrip, Montana,* 1982–85

able, are also coded by distance. Either specialized knowledge or explanatory texts are needed to disclose such a pathology, like that possessed by a doctor incriminating an otherwise nondescript white area in an X-ray.

A young photographer, David Taverner Hanson, has brought to his aerial photography a decidedly clinical tone that depends on a kind of color coding. He has flown repeatedly over the Montana Power plant at Colstrip and has picked out alien presences there: chemical deposits left from operations and mine tailings that show up as strident dyes draining into sandy, torn ground (fig. 1). Though these acidic hues immediately tell us that something is amiss, they are in themselves no more than splotches in an abstract topography, reminiscent of illustrations in fractal geometrics. We have to appreciate the sensory impression as an outcome of

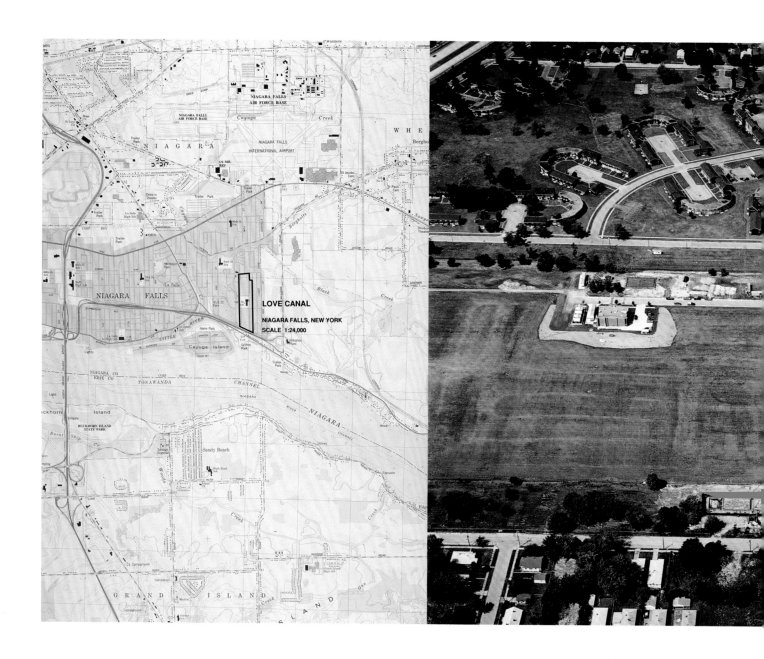

2 David T. Hanson, *Love Canal,
Niagara Falls, New York*, 1986,
from the series *Waste Land*, 1986–89

processes reported in the minerological analyses with which Hanson sometimes accompanies his pictures. Their moralizing is inevitably ex post facto. These delicately or weirdly colored photographs may have an impact, but it is delayed and finally dissociated from its cause. Such imagery works as an act of certain witness, at a remove that disconnects us from the actual hazards it describes, even as it uniquely situates them. The greater the visual perspective, the more it requires a narrative—for example, the history of a

company's failure to observe safety regulations—to account for the jumbled photographic spectacle (fig. 2). In the end, narrative tells the main story, of which the pictures are but an elegant, puzzlelike confirmation.

On the ground, the photographer may face or actually choose the problem of being too close to the wrongness of an environment and therefore resist a narrative reading. It seems unlikely that the internationally known Lewis Baltz conducted himself that way except in

LOVE CANAL
Niagara Falls, New York

Love Canal is a 16-acre landfill in the southeast corner of the city of Niagara Falls, New York, about 0.3 miles north of the Niagara River. In the 1890s, a canal was excavated to provide hydroelectric power. Instead, it was later used by Hooker Electrochemical for disposal of over 21,000 tons of various chemical wastes. Dumping ceased in 1952, and in 1953 the disposal area was covered and deeded to the Niagara Falls Board of Education. Extensive development occurred near the site, including construction of an elementary school and numerous homes.

Problems with odors and residues, first reported at the site during the 1960s, increased in the 1970s as the water table rose, bringing contaminated ground water to the surface. Studies indicate that numerous toxic chemicals have migrated into surrounding areas. Run-off drains into the Niagara River at a point 2.8 miles upstream of the intake tunnels for Niagara Falls' water treatment plant, which serves about 77,000 people. At this discharge point, the river sediment has also become contaminated.

Between 1977 and 1980, New York State and the Federal government spent about $45 million at the site: $30 million for relocation of residents and health testing, $11 million for environmental studies, and $4 million for a demonstration grant (under the Resource Conservation and Recovery Act) to build a leachate collection and treatment system.

A study completed in 1982 recommended construction of a slurry wall and cap to contain ground water in the site as the long-term solution.

In July 1982, EPA awarded a $6,995,000 Cooperative Agreement to New York for (1) construction of a slurry wall and cap, (2) four feasibility studies, and (3) a long-term monitoring study to determine seasonal variations in ground water levels and leaching. In September 1982, $892,800 was added to (1) demolish the school, (2) install a synthetic membrane over a temporary clay cap, and (3) erect a fence.

The Department of Justice, on behalf of EPA, has brought a federal civil action seeking injunctive relief against parties potentially responsible for wastes associated with the site.

long-term recoil against the prevailing sentimental or heroic genres of landscape. His two large projects along these lines are *Park City* (figs. 3, 4, 5), showing a Nevada ski resort in a stage of slipshod construction (1978–79), and *Candlestick Point* (fig. 6), the quintessential semi-urban, indeterminate, trashed, American open ground near San Francisco (1988). Though his landscape is more tractable and the abuse of it by no means as grave as Hanson's, Baltz proves to be the more pessimistic artist. The topographical view,

after all, is an attempt to map and therefore delineate earth features within a span of time and space. Topography's depiction is a pragmatic enterprise designed to inform us of differentials on our ground surface. But Baltz's precise closeups—even his horizons—are dis-informing, not only because they are nondescript but because they evince no interest in distinguishing one spiritless view, or non-view, from another. Except to notice their interchangability, Baltz is pictorially indifferent to the events that created the

3 Lewis Baltz, *Looking north from Masonic Hill toward Quarry Mountain. In foreground, new parking lots on land between West Sidewinder Drive and State High-way 248. In middle distance, from left: Park Meadows, subdivisions 1, 2, and 3; Holiday Ranchette Estates; Raquet Club Estates. At far distance on left, Parkwest Ski Area*, 1980, #1 from *Park City*

4 Lewis Baltz, *Park City, interior, 1*, 1980, #62 from *Park City*

5 Lewis Baltz, *Between West Sidewinder Drive and State Highway 248, looking Southwest, #6* from *Park City*

6 Lewis Baltz, *Candlestick Point #52*, from the series *Candlestick Point*, 1988

7   Robert Adams, *Expressway near Colton*, 1982, from the portfolio *Los Angeles Spring*. Philadelphia Museum of Art, Purchase of the Alice Newton Osborne Fund

dishevelment that seems to obsess him in a low-grade way, just as a virus drags on in an organism.

Baltz makes redundancy a principle in his photographic campaigns. Tumbleweeds, crabgrass, rusted automobile parts, snap-top beer cans, the impressions left by tracked vehicles: these proliferate in images that cover the same polemical point over and over again. His camera can never drink in enough unsightly chaff, never slake a thirst for debris and rubble. This omniverous gaze—monotonous and impassive in its spread and reiterated in serial clusters of black-and-white photographs always printed the same size—seems entirely disproportionate to the interest of its subject. In the thirties, Farm Security Administration photographs sometimes depicted automobile graveyards in rural areas; in the sixties a whole school of photographers fancied urban bushes. Baltz's program, mingling nature and culture, is different. It lacks elegy, and however deliberate, it is devoid of formalism, for he collects his dismal frames as if to show a world, perhaps *the* world, unrelieved of our forgetfulness. The sole way to drive home that prospect—of an environment consisting only of dirt—is to exclude from the visual field anything that is finished and cared for, or untouched by humans.

He leaves us to feel that this work is less worthy of being looked at than necessary to contemplate. Here are bad pictures invested with a strange psychological interest. Like ecologically minded photographers, he lets the implications sink in; unlike them, he does not suggest the value of preserving any land nor does he urge reformation of our ways. If he had any moral hopefulness, he'd have to show his denatured bits as blemish or wound and therefore as still exceptional zones that can be brought back to a state that accommodates us. In short, he'd have to convey a notion of the attractive, or at least what constitutes environmental

health. It is the absence of any sign attractive to us as social animals within an ordinary landscape of our own negligent making that distinguishes Baltz's art and gives it a terrible neutrality.

By "terrible" I mean the feeling imparted to relatively accessible vistas of a kind of ground zero, where everything resembles a mockup. Baltz shows sharply etched and summarily fabricated presences, such as unfinished condominiums, as if they were awaiting some unspeakable test. Not enough ecological hope lies in any of this material for us to interpret it as a depiction of earthly casualty or misfortune. To the contrary, the blightedness out there (which he seems to have internalized) is a given, something that preceded the photographer and will long succeed him.

On the other hand, to viewers of politically accented landscape, attraction is a very convoluted issue. Strictly speaking, whether the land seems comely or not is secondary to whether it needs to be detoxified. A conservational urgency must precede and often marginalizes an aesthetic response (otherwise social priorities would be undermined by the vagaries of taste). Still, if we do not experience some keen loss of pleasure in the wastage of the region, we are less motivated to urge measures to reclaim it. We transfer our sensitivity to injured flesh to our sense of a damaged land, provided the damage can be made evident. In these matters, the empathetic consideration is more powerful than the chemical, but less relevant to political change.

Still, merely to single out affecting landscape does not generate a very searching case for its preservation. Despite the Sierra Club's popular use of such images, which makes us want to hold on to things, gorgeous scenes hardly illumine the real jeopardy to the environment. As for Edenic nature, whether in calendar or ad, it purveys a strong cliché content,

9　Robert Adams, *On Top of the La Loma Hills, Colton*, 1983, from the portfolio *Los Angeles Spring*. Philadelphia Museum of Art, Purchase of the Alice Newton Osborne Fund

cloying rather than seductive. Far from apprising us of the dilemma of pollution, the tourist or consumer propaganda that utilizes such images tends to exploit and worsen it. Landscape photographers who want to make a statement about the deadening of the environment find that their own medium puts them into a quandary. They must steel themselves against ingratiation while somehow affirming the value of their abused subject.

In strictly *documentary* imagery, this quandary is beside the point. The act of bearing witness justifies itself quite simply as it points out such evidence as the oil-smeared wings of an egret or the balding effects of acid rain in the Black Forest. We need such witness as a palpable indictment of accident or malpractice. Nevertheless, as soon as it localizes examples of wrongness, documentary is exhausted of further meaning. It does not satisfy those who, in addition to their search for a record, look for the sounding of an attitude.

In contrast, there is a kind of picture that alerts us to the ways we ourselves remember, reflect upon, and forecast our changing situation. No matter how often

we hear of media documentary as an editorial, even as propaganda, we perceive it as a disembodied product, without any investment of the photographer's individual consciousness. Of course the image doesn't need that consciousness to make an impact upon viewers, as might the impersonal depiction of a crime that seems to implicate us all. The sight of it may or may not spur us to action, but it does not raise in us any awareness of how we ourselves process evidence. All photographs mediate reality, but instead of displaying a corporate perspective or ideological dogma external to our beings, some of them—the ones considered here—extend to us an individual regard similar to our own.

When the subject is nature, the regard tends to be solitary. Landscape seems to call upon us to be intimate with ourselves, as if to awaken in us pleasures, memories, or hopes that are not yet acculturated. The meaning of landscape is arguably bound up with an appeal to the illusion that within each of us lies something unshareable and not yet socialized. This is partly because of the ineffability of ungrasped sensation perceived in the far reaches of land under open air and partly because it still pleases North Americans to fantasize about nature not as culture and therefore not as a communal experience. Of course we know very well that the reserve into which we place our ideas of nature is a cultural reserve. But perhaps alone among the developed nations, we can still imagine our actual contact with nature to extend past that reserve, as if there were a frontier we hadn't yet transgressed. One photographer who knowingly works within that conflict between the imagined and the transgressed is Robert Adams.

Off the freeway near Colton, California, Adams climbed an eroded hillock. Fumes, haze, and effluents halate the otherwise graphically silhouetted black and white tones of photographs such as

this and others he made for his book *Los Angeles Spring* (figs. 7, 8, 9). While the effects are redundant, the compositions are individually realized, each of them variants in an expanding poetic search. What Adams achieves is a poetry of depredation. In an era of landscape color, the black and white strikes a memorial note, and a curious mournfulness pervades scenes of an otherwise humdrum brutality. It's not that Adams appears to think tenderly of these undeserving views, but that in capturing them as moments of lonely experience he projects them back into a nineteenth-century landscape tradition and perceives their horizons as seemingly deserted now as they were then. A weariness of view fuses with the freshness of radiant seeing, as if Robert Frank's vision of a fifties America had blended with the imagery of Carleton Watkins's post–Civil War Yosemite. Adams shows withered eucalyptus trees, abandoned orange groves, and bulldozed, broken stretches of earth. Having earned his attention, they stay in mind as naturalized forms, lost to a process symbolized by the road or developers' trails.[3]

In the introduction to *The American Space: Meaning in Nineteenth-Century Landscape Photography*, Adams writes, "Physically much of the land [the West] is almost as empty as it was when Jackson and Timothy O'Sullivan photographed there, but the beauty of the space—the sense that everything in it is alive and valuable—is gone." Adams considers the nineteenth-century photographers privileged because the clean skies they saw could illustrate the "opening verses of Genesis about light's part in giving form to the void."[4] Their cameras could take their fill of scenes that are now obscured or faded out by an amorphous whiteness against which the reminiscent photographer now has to struggle to describe depth.

In *Los Angeles Spring*, that description and the conventionally nostalgic desire that went with it is foiled, leaving us to judge only unkempt things in the foreground. Deep space is equated with a past we cannot restore. Consequently, these recent images evoke a regret about the wealth of information steamed out in the light. They are comparative pictures. They imaginatively comprehend a span of events in which affection for nature must be misplaced if it is to have any object at all.

On the other hand, it is possible to reposition one's attitude and enthuse over a new though sinister beauty. The ambiguous shallow space of Adams's southern California becomes very declarative in John Pfahl's *Smoke* series, begun in 1988 (fig. 10). By using a telephoto lens, Pfahl flattens the billowing, polychromed emissions from factory smokestacks. The subjects are tightly framed and very definitely brought within optical range, but at the cost of disturbing the viewer's intuitively physical relationship to their space. Telephoto's seeming intimacy is undermined by its neutralizing of vantage; we can neither establish the locale nor gauge the actual depth of the sighting. Quite aside from being the only way Pfahl could have depicted such a noxious phenomenon without choking, he clearly uses his telephoto lens to invite us in, suspend us in some unmoored place, and then disquiet us, over and over, by a study of atmosphere ecstatically befouled. During his long career, he has kept us aware of the surface of the image at the expense of its illusive depth (by disposing lines within the scene that read as two-dimensional geometric figures on the picture plane), and he has refused to ground the viewer's perspective by any kind of introductory ledge. Everything that appears in his work is perceived as if from an indefinite mental space of our own. Yet, in the end, the spectacle of the roseate benzene cloud, visualized in the melted colors of a kind of pastoral sublime, overwhelms our understanding of its evil. This work is too deliberately ingratiating to be critical, even if a critical

comment—a record of dirty clouds—defines its reason for being.

Perhaps the flaw in such a project as the *Smoke* series is its need to avoid a condemnation of the obvious. Despite having been enveloped once in benzene vapor, all the photographer has to say—all his irony will allow him to say—about such miasmas is that they're beautiful. We, the victims of such stupendous pollution, are reduced to applauding his artfulness in depicting it! Further, these clouds momentarily take heroic shapes; they belong to a stereotypical genre that celebrates the productivity of factories. Who could be blamed for imagining that Pfahl approved of it? At this particular historical moment the *Smoke* series could only be conceived in the United States, when, the general standard of living just beginning to show signs of decline, ecological consciousness is afoot yet significant environmental measures are defeated. Pfahl's blend of luxuriant aestheticism and alienated space has never proved so hollow as when it handles real debasement of the environment.

Yet it was never easy to visualize that danger. Photographers have had an aerial/abstract go at it; they have also adopted an affectless nihilism toward it. Some of them have waxed nostalgic or have been perversely engaging about our common peril. We grant them their expressive resonance. Just the same, at each turn they depended too much on their viewers to contribute their own moral earnestness to the scenography. The diffuse appearances of the terrain—whatever the state in which they were found—do not of themselves strike us with any urgency. We have been schooled to *contemplate* a pictured landscape far more than to hoot and yell in common cause to rescue the screwed-up territory it may show. We feel that landscape is "there" for us, and if for any reason we are given country that puts us off, we turn elsewhere. Arcadia, even a sad Arcadia, was inviting. But how are we

11 Joe Deal, *Backyard, Diamond Bar, California*, 1981

12 *(overleaf)* Richard Misrach, *Submerged Lamppost, Salton Sea*, 1985, from *The Flood* canto in *Desert Cantos*

to be aroused by a spectacle we reject: an American wilderness we ourselves have done in?

That kind of panorama in the West has been addressed by Richard Misrach with increasing vividness throughout the 1980s. To begin, he offers a totally convincing sense of place—the Mohave, the California inlands, the Nevada deserts, over which he has roamed repeatedly. His moment of perception is always the present, gritted in by sandy ochres and limned by sage green, mauve, and blond hues often merging into an exquisite bleached depth, though sometimes reddened by dusk or fires. Misrach lives such moments to their sensory brim without standing on any ceremony. He gives us the feeling that what happens out

there in the nominal wild happens for him and to him quite in advance of being filtered through any memory of art.

Other photographers have just as keenly possessed the land through their pictures, disclosing refuges we thought were scarce. There is something enterprising, even sporting, and yet a little sad about their project, for they bring back appetizing views as if they were trophies. Misrach works the flip side of this mode: he camps out in what passes for the remote desert only to show our unexpected hand in it everywhere. He's a specialist in transmitting drab, and finally ghastly, news from epic landscapes.

In 1983, as twilight gathered at Lake Havasu City, Arizona, Misrach evoked the distant twin arches of McDonald's as

a precious beacon in the desert. This was a sensuous epilogue to work done in the 1970s by a group of photographers that included Robert Adams, Lewis Baltz, Joe Deal, and Frank Gohlke, who showed the West as a Pop landscape in an important exhibition called "The New Topographics." Their theme, suburban development as an unexpected vernacular, disgruntled a number of viewers who were put off by the works' cool, noncommittal style (fig. 11). Actually, matters would *not* have been improved had the photographers been judgmental, for it was their very choice of such material that provoked. How eye-worthy were the ranch-style houses at the end of a new road, with their lonely tree sprigs, or the mobile-home parks and RV camps, satellite towns at some dry outskirt? Here art reckoned with the decentering caused by a shift in population to the Sunbelt. Arrangements for those middle-class folk who were passing through or who had retired had a provisional look about them— and that look was captured by the New Topographics. But the photographers concentrated so much on an atrophy of community that they didn't deal with its consequences to the land. Now, in every case their work has darkened in mood as it has explored that land. In Misrach's book *Desert Cantos*, that mood has come to flower.[5]

From the first, one gleans Misrach's intense interest in the desert as, of all things, a social phenomenon. His romanticism may have initially brought him there, but his realism takes over at the actual site. He writes, "One only needs to stand outside a 7-11 at Indio with a cherry slurpy, or dangle one's legs in a Palm Springs pool in the 105° early morning sun to know what is desert."[6] As the title *Desert Cantos* suggests, however, he transmits his realism back into a poetic framework that has Dante-esque overtones. Each of the cantos, his photographic chapters, develops a topic: *The*

Highway, The Inhabitants, Survival, The Event, The Flood, etc. Drawn in by the rocky forms and velvety tones, our normal attachments to things as they are near and distant tend to be reversed. Tiny remnants left by passersby or abandoned works are scattered everywhere and nowhere within awesome perspectives. The boxcars of a long Santa Fe freight train are reduced to lapidary points of scarlet and gray way off in a plain of olive scrub. In one canto, *The Event,* the same endless horizon suddenly takes on a narrative interest, for it tells of the arrival of the space shuttle at Edwards Air Force Base and of the people, colored silhouettes on a blinding flat, who are awaiting it. The future—a dot in the sky—is about to descend into this immemorial place. Or is it the Second Coming these cowhands, army personnel, and sightseers are about to witness? Biblical parallels are certainly a part of Misrach's overview of his desert campaign. His notion of *The Flood* is filled out by the Salton Sea, an utterly still body of water that has inundated telephone poles and swamped a gas station and a kiddy slide (fig. 12). Such limpid scenes have an eerie, unforced beauty that whispers to us of retribution. And he concludes with *The Fires,* vegetation burnoffs, often uncontrolled in their sweep, which he photographed at such close range as to almost make us feel their scorch (fig. 13).

For all their ominousness, however, these crackling vistas are not yet infernal, as are a later group Misrach calls *The Pit,* and his latest book, the even quieter *Bravo 20: The Bombing of the American West.*[7] The Pit acts as a dirge to thousands of livestock that died of unexplained or unexamined causes and were thrown into remote Nevada dumps (fig. 14). Their hooves and hides protrude from the silt like so much refuse. The burnoffs provided a startling new subject for Misrach's photography; his dead animal pictures amount to a scathing political exposure.

13 Richard Misrach, *Desert Fire #249*, 1985, from *The Fires* canto in *Desert Cantos*

14 Richard Misrach, *Dead Animals
#327*, 1987, from *The Pit* canto in
Desert Cantos

15 Richard Misrach, *Bomb Crater
    and Destroyed Convoy*, 1986, from
    *Bravo 20: The Bombing of the
    American West*

16 Roger Fenton, *The Valley of the
    Shadow of Death*, 1855. Salt print.
    The Royal Photographic Society,
    Bath, England

Yet both subjects are treated with a caressive regard that is eloquently incongruous. A tension is set up between the magnitude of the description, the physical presence of large prints, and the dread of their subjects—disgorged, as it seems, into our own space, from which we are not meant to escape. Hitherto, his attitude toward the desert was one of almost anthropological curiosity, and we were cast as wayfarers there with our guide, who saw with real opulence. Presently, he maintains his vision and takes us into a holocaust.

Misrach was not the first to discover the devastation wrought at Bravo 20, the United States Navy's bombing range in Nevada, nor the first to learn that it had all been illegal for more than twenty years. The worst kinds of violence had been committed there, to the deafening accompaniment of supersonic jets. He happened upon the place in his travels, joined the activists who had come in to resist the military, and made his reflective pictures of the scenery. They show a cratered landscape, barren of all but the most stubborn plantlife, yet littered with thousands of bombs and shells (fig. 15). These photographs inadvertently recall Roger Fenton's pictures over a 140 years ago of the Crimean battlefields, strewn with cannonballs that resemble the feces of some obscene metal bird (fig. 16). But Bravo 20's ready-made quality as a moralized landscape lies in the fact that it is not a battlefield but a practice zone. Misrach has no trouble in revealing how a macho culture has literally vomited all over the very same environment that in yesteryear it had held up as the territory of its heroic aggressions. Because they show the results of the United States military purposefully at work rather than just one of its accidental by-products, Bravo 20's wastes are even more demonstrative than those pitiable animals brought down by chemical or radioactive taint.

The economy of the tacky develop ments out in the western drylands—the dreck—is deeply entwined with our militarism. The people of Fallon, Nevada, though terrorized by the noise, were loath to protest the armed forces' usurpation of their nearby ground because it brought revenue into their town. It seems as if we have extreme difficulty either in adapting ourselves to nature or protecting it from us. In speculating along these lines, Misrach has never argued for anything so radical as removing people from the land. But he has proposed that Bravo 20 be turned into a national park as the country's first environmental memorial. Sightseeing routes within it would be called "Devastation Drive" and "Boardwalk of the Bombs"—apt names for a horizon that deserves to be considered prodigiously wrong.

Notes

1   Théophile Gautier, *Guide to the Louvre*, quoted in Frank Jewett Mather, Jr., *Western European Painting of the Renaissance* (New York: Tudor, 1948), p. 746.

2   Georg Gerster, *Grand Design* (London: Paddington Press, 1976), pp. 17–18.

3   *Los Angeles Spring: Photographs by Robert Adams* (New York: Aperture Foundation, 1986).

4   *The American Space: Meaning in Nineteenth-Century Landscape Photography*, with introduction by Robert Adams (Middletown, Conn.: Wesleyan University, 1983), p. 3.

5   Richard Misrach, *Desert Cantos* (Albuquerque: University of New Mexico, 1987).

6   Ibid., p. 96.

7   Richard Misrach, *Bravo 20: The Bombing of the American West* (Baltimore: Johns Hopkins University Press, 1990).

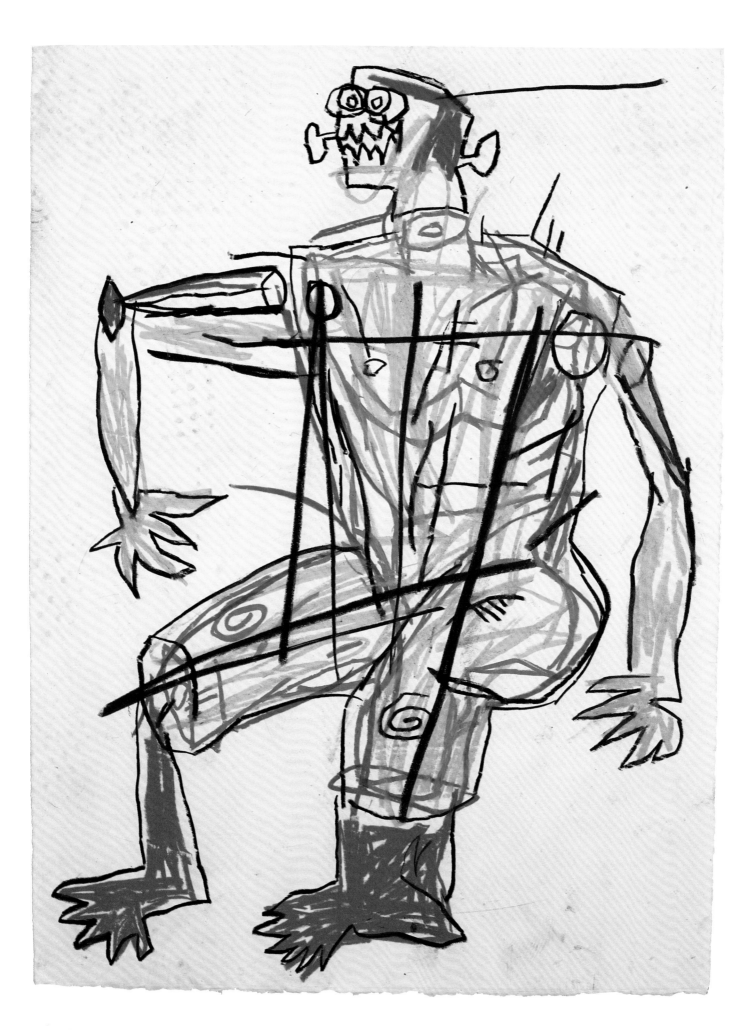

The Appropriation of Marginal Art in the 1980s

Donald Kuspit

In the 1980s a certain climate of opinion facilitated the commercial appropriation and intellectual administration of marginal art. Such art was looked upon with favor by the powers-that-be because of the "horizon of expectations," in the phrase of reception-theorist Hans Robert Jauss, that was used to justify mainstream eighties art. Before examining this conceptual horizon, however, it seems important to make a few general points, both to establish our parameters of meaning and to gain some historical perspective.

First, the concept of "marginal art" is virtually indefinable, having been given a variety of incommensurable meanings. The dialectic between marginal and mainstream art is, using an expression of the philosopher Ludwig Wittgenstein, "a language game." If, in a true Wittgensteinian sense, every language game is a reimagining of life, then the marginal/mainstream language game is a reimagining of the life of art.

Second, at least since Gauguin, avant-garde artists have used marginal ("primitive") art as a seemingly inexhaustible, magical means of artistic rejuvenation. Indeed, insistence on marginality is the cornerstone of their vanguardism, for the marginal is the last-ditch defense against decadence. The current appropriation of folk and graffiti art is simply another instance of this process of revitalization through incorporation of the marginal, the crucial difference being that it is as commercial as it is stylistic or iconographic. One socio-artistic group renews itself by consuming another in a conspicuously economic as well as an aesthetic way; in fact, today aesthetic interests follow the path cut by economic initiative. This fin de siècle pattern of appropriation is the reverse of the pattern dominant at the beginning of the twentieth century, when Cubism and Expressionism employed marginal artifacts before these artifacts had become economically important art. Also, the line between marginal artifact and mainstream art has become so thin today—both are readily reducible to symptoms of material culture—that the transition from one to the other occurs with less intellectual handwringing and fanfare than it once did.

Third, the distinction between mainstream and marginal is a social construction that says more about the mainstream's creative desperation and pursuit of novelty than it does about the sociohistorical—or, for that matter, stylistic—reality of what it labels marginal. It places necessity within the mainstream rather than within the marginal culture. Also, like the sophisticated-naive, cosmopolitan-provincial, and insider-outsider polarities implicit in it, the relationship between the opposing terms is in historical flux and, more crucially, has no single logic. It is oppositional thinking structuring a relationship hierarchically for a variety of often-conflicting motivations. So unstable is the hierarchy that it tends to be perverse. The moment "mainstream" seems more intrinsic to the meaning of art than

Keith Haring, *Purple Heart*, 1989.
Acrylic on canvas, 60 x 60 in. Estate of
Keith Haring

Edgar Tolson, *Paradise*, 1968.
Carved and painted white elm with
pencil, 12 7/8 x 17 x 10 in. National
Museum of American Art,
Smithsonian Institution, Gift of
Herbert Waide Hemphill, Jr., and
museum purchase made possible by
Ralph Cross Johnson

"marginal" or vice versa, the other term asserts itself, shouting "unfair" and "fraud."

Fourth, the appropriation of the marginal by the mainstream is dialectical, in that the marginal is legitimated by the mainstream and the mainstream acquires the aura of authenticity and integrity supposedly innate to the marginal. Once appropriated by the avant-garde, the artifacts that embody marginality slowly but surely become mainstream, eventually acquiring the status of high art even though they were initially valued because they had nothing to do with its conventions. In its turn, the avant-garde acquires the exotic look of being at the limit of civilization—of being a primordial response to life—that marginal art affords. Of course, avant-garde art domesticates this look as much as it idolizes it and begins to manipulate and even manufacture it.

For all these paradoxes, mainstream avant-garde and marginal art benefit from their association, but not mutually. It is the mainstream that initiates the process of appropriation, that seeks out and needs the marginal, not vice versa. It is the mainstream that scavenges the margins of civilization for raw artistic material. But who said the marginal is marginal? It never thinks of itself that way: It is just itself. Only to the mainstream is it the alluring "alternative," the exciting "other," a welcome breath of fresh air in the stale room of tradition. Unlike the mainstream, the marginal is not an institutional system that must perpetually challenge itself by importing the heterogenous and discordant. The mainstream is neither a serious part of the consciousness of the marginal nor a clue to its raison d'être. Thus, at issue are the self-esteem and self-characterization of the mainstream, not of the marginal. The mainstream needs to appropriate the marginal to develop in order to convince itself of its own validity and legitimacy.

Appropriation is paradoxical in yet another way: it signals not only the self-doubt but also the imperialism of the avant-garde mainstream. They converge in its paranoid determination to colonize and control whatever outlandish art exists beyond its pale. This is not just blind power-hunger, a compulsive extension of the mainstream's rule, but a necessary narcissism. Unless it is actively integrating—*dominating*—some kind of marginal art, the mainstream risks the ultimate entropy: loss of belief in itself. It needs to aggrandize a "lowerclass" art in order to feel "upperclass." Moreover, it garners sociopolitical credit for its "discovery" of and "responsibility" to the "lesser" art, almost as though bringing alien art into the fold were a civic service. But behind the noblesse oblige of appropriation lurks a latent authoritarianism.

Once taken into the mainstream, marginal artists may become hungry for the rewards—money and reputation—it can offer and may even fantasize that they are mainstream, or "professional," marginalists. This is likely to lead to the loss of the innocence, directness, and immediacy of expression that led the mainstream to adopt them. They win a predictably ironical place in the mainstream but lose the significance of being "basic" that gave them mainstream value in the first place. They become minor artists rather than standing apart from the major-minor distinction in a place of emblematic uniqueness. When the artistic "fundamentalism" of marginal art is truly unforced, it seems more inherently singular than any other art.

In the 1980s the two major artistic positions were Neo-Expressionism and Neo-Conceptualism. Marginal artists are usually regarded as quasi-Expressionists. It is significant that they are never thought of as quasi-Conceptualists.

Neo-Conceptualism keeps alive the idea that art is a concept up for grabs. Art is assumed to have a speculative existence

Robert Longo, *Dickhead*, 1988.
Cast bronze, granite, 19 x 12 x 11 in.
Private collection

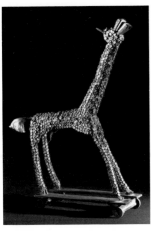

Unidentified artist, *Bottlecap
Giraffe*, ca. 1966. Carved and
painted wood, bottlecaps, rubber,
glass, animal tail and fur, and sheet
metal, 72 1/2 x 54 x 17 1/2 in.
National Museum of American Art,
Smithsonian Institution, Gift of
Herbert Waide Hemphill, Jr., and
museum purchase made possible by
Ralph Cross Johnson

to the extent that it tends to evaporate the moment it is concretized. Thus, art is supposedly always the triumph of mind over matter, but it is not always clear what is in mind when art is spoken of. ("Mind over Matter" is the name of a recent Whitney Museum exhibition of six young Conceptualist "sculptors," a term I put in quotation marks to suggest the nominal character of all conventional categorizations of art by the Conceptualists.) It seems that marginal art can be regarded as at least naively conceptual, for it brings the idea of art into question, however unwittingly. It would require elaborate theory to explain what one means by calling it "art," whether with a large or small *a*. But of course marginal art is neither philosophical in intention nor even generally intellectual, as Conceptual art imagines itself to be. Much of it is illustrative and seems to have an obviously practical intent, or else it seems naive about what it expresses and how it does so. Marginal art appears so conspicuously "real world" in purpose that it cannot help but be suspect as art.

None of this is sufficient to make marginal art quasi-Expressionist art. What does seem to justify the expressionistic label is the recognition that marginal art, like Expressionism, is urgently physical (as opposed to Conceptualism, which no doubt marginalizes and despises both) and, like Neo-Expressionism, overtly subjective. Neo-Expressionism makes the subject an issue of art, particularly the subject damaged by history as well as conflicted in itself. Its sense of subjectivity is in dialectical relation with the objectively inhumane world. Georg Baselitz and Anselm Kiefer are exemplary in this respect; they confirm Theodor W. Adorno's conception of art as the only space in the modern world where the inward injury of a subject violated by history can be articulated without being falsified. Where eighties Neo-Expressionism restores explicit interest in subjectivity

to modern art—a subjectivity to which the Pop, Minimal, and Conceptual art of the 1960s was indifferent—expression of the subject is a constant in marginal art.[1]

In Neo-Conceptualist art, the status of the object, including the art object, is at issue. With irony that is not always clear, "commodity" conceptual art of the 1980s presents commodities as art objects. In so-called reproduction art, often famous art objects are re-presented in what Marchel Duchamp called "assisted form." This is done to bring out their commodity identity, to undermine their aura, and to suggest that they are social constructions rather than personal creations. There is a strong element of reprise in both Neo-Expressionism and Neo-Conceptualism; in the latter it is often parodic. Both are self-consciously postmodernist, looking back to and integrating modernist styles, sometimes pulverizing them to stylish pulp in the process.

Marginal art does not truly belong to either camp. Yet it can be interpreted as having ideological elements of both: as a means of expressing a sense of injured subject and as "injured" art. That is, it conveys the problematic condition of the modern subject, always on the verge of disintegration, and the equally problematic, relativistic character of art in the modern world, a condition that precludes its conclusive conceptualization. However, insofar as the international art scene is concerned, marginal art exists in an underground limbo, for it has no stylistic credibility. Although it is obliquely Neo-Expressionist and Neo-Conceptualist in orientation, it bears little stylistic resemblance to them. It may use impulsive, distorted representation and language but not the same way they do. Marginal art in general is not deliberately concerned with style, that is, formal innovation. Nevertheless, marginal art has come to be regarded as significant during postmodernism, a time of stylistic incoherence. Indeed, postmodernist artists can be

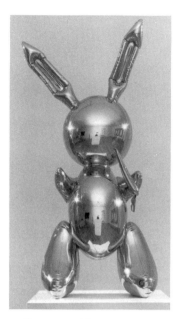

Jeff Koons, *Rabbit*, 1986. Stainless steel, 41 x 19 x 12 in. Private collection

Unidentified artist, *Optician's Sign*, twentieth-century braized and painted sheet brass, porcelain and metal electrical sockets, electrical wiring, and replacement incandescent bulbs, 12 x 24 3/8 x 2 in. National Museum of American Art, Smithsonian Institution, Gift of Herbert Waide Hemphill, Jr., and museum purchase made possible by Ralph Cross Johnson

said to have fetishized incoherence, as though that were innovative in itself and enough to generate aesthetic momentum. Even more than modernism, postmodernism is a scavenger of raw artistic material. More threatened by decadence, it is more willing to risk its all on novelty and to use whatever stylistic and ideological means it can to make itself seem alive. Marginal art fits very well into its "program."

The infusion of the marginal into mainstream modernism had a strong utopian flavor. Whether advocating the subjective utopia of instinctive expression or the objective utopia of harmonious society, modern art pursued stylistic novelty to foster an artistic anticipation of a brave new world and to enliven the appearance of the cowardly old one. Artistic innovation represented the will to achieve revolutionary change, both individually and socially. Postmodernism is a fall from this innocence: It disbelieves in artistic, personal, and social utopias—in revolutionary possibilities—because it has seen them fail. Therefore it looks to the past rather than future, for it admits no forward psychosocial position to advance to, or even imagine. Unable to represent such a position, art becomes more dependent on the past as a source of novelty than on modernism. Post-modernism is inherently more conservative.

But this is a peculiar conservatism: Postmodernism regards the styles of the past as so many casts, like the figures of Pompeii. They are hollow novelties, of interest only for their uncanny appearance, not for what they meant when they were alive. Novelty for its own sake—the appearance rather than the substance of novelty—is important to postmodernism. While it accords the art it appropriates an abstract historical significance, this turns it into a kind of pillar of salt. Appropriated by postmodernism, marginal art becomes merely another shallow novelty,

losing its import as a symbol of the subject. Marginal art serves this historical craving for dead novelties—that is, the ideologizing and objectification of novelty.[2]

It is no historical accident that marginal art has been assimilated as the ultimate novelty during postmodernism. In postmodernism, novelty is a sign of the implicitly futile sociohistorical dead end we find ourselves in. For postmodernism, the art historical "difference" of a particular style becomes a reified novelty. Its psychosocial significance forgotten—lost to history, as it were—it exists as an aesthetic shadow of itself. Novelty thus becomes regressive rather than progressive. Today it is a trophy of true belief reified as a decorative end in itself. The postmodernist art world's aggrandizement of marginal art is thus an instance of its fetishization of novelty as the most essential commodity.

Unexpectedly, the appropriation of marginal art also implies nostalgia for "true" novelty—neither that of the commodity nor of modernist utopianism. Marginal art comes to stand for the novelty of "Being," completely beyond appropriation—Being that can never be "had" simply for the asking. There is wonder at objects of marginal art today, a special respect for them, for they alone among works of art seem to embody the Being that is fundamentally incommensurate with "Having." The distinction between these radically different orientations is a new way of making the distinction between mainstream and marginal art meaningful. The former is presumably the product of Having, the latter of Being. Marginal art restores faith in art as such, implying that it need not be a symptom of the decadence that comes from Having alone.[3]

Thus, the attitude about marginal art is paradoxical. In the eighties it became clear that art was less and less in an authentically marginal position—that, in Luis

Anselm Kiefer, *Bruch der Gefässe (Breaking of the Vessels)*, 1990. Lead books in iron bookshelf, iron, lead, copper wire, glass, charcoal, aquatec, 150 1/2 x 135 7/8 x 59 in. The Saint Louis Art Museum, St. Louis, Missouri

Howard Finster, *The Model of Super Power Plaint (Folk Art Made from Old T.V. Parts)*, 1979. Painted plastic and metal electronic television parts, glitter, mirror, wood, and metal, 20 x 6 5/8 x 7 5/8 in. National Museum of American Art, Smithsonian Institution, Gift of Herbert Waide Hemphill, Jr., and museum purchase made possible by Ralph Cross Johnson

Buñuel's words, of the permanent outsider. At the same time, there was great eagerness for marginality—indeed, an anxious clinging to it as an indication of authentic artistic being and Being as such. Tied up with the idea of marginality as a demonstration of authenticity is the idea of greater-than-ordinary openness to and depth of experience and, correlatively, extraordinary power of Being. Presumably the lives of those on the social margin are more to the existential-artistic point than those in mainstream America or those who accept establishment values, including stylistic values. Even as the marginality of contemporary art dwindled by reason of its economic and academic assimilation and consumption—its eager

socialization into the mainstream, making it the darling of the art establishment—and the very idea of marginality came to be doubted (except as a way of distinguishing the have-nots from the haves), artistic marginality came to be apotheosized as an aesthetic in its own right and as the touchstone of authenticity in art. In other words, the less artistic marginality became a reality, the more the fantasy of it had to be maintained. Indeed, the less clear its meaning, the more crucial it seemed, to the extent that artistic marginality has become the new sign of quality, as has recently been implied by *New York Times* art critic Michael Brenson.[4]

Essentially, what is involved in the

Haim Steinbach, *Untitled (Igorot backpack, rice container)*, 1989. Plastic laminated wood shelf with objects, 49 1/2 x 48 x 23 in. Private collection, New York

Unidentified artist, *Standing Articulated Figure*, ca. 1920. Carved and painted sequoia and black ash, painted metal, wire, and metal hardware, 32 3/4 x 13 3/8 x 9 in. National Museum of American Art, Smithsonian Institution, Gift of Herbert Waide Hemphill, Jr., and museum purchase made possible by Ralph Cross Johnson

postmodernist celebration of the authenticity of marginality (often conflating social with artistic marginality)—exemplified by such self-taught artists as Jean-Michel Basquiat, Thornton Dial, Sr., and Howard Finster—is the idea that art must be perverse and that marginal art is particularly perverse. (Being self-taught is an important sign of authenticity, for it suggests that the artist is not repressed by the art establishment and society in general, and so is freely expressive.) Self-taught marginal art is highly esteemed because it seems inherently perverse, especially in its physicality, and its much-noted awkwardness is the sign of this perversity. The perverse is what looks obscene in the etymological sense of the term: what is experienced as the obverse of the scene. The obscene turns out to be something quite specific: in Erling Eng's words, "a modified reproduction of the past of [the] particular scene, whether the past be a verifiable memory or a mythic form."[5]

This partly explains the obsessive historicism of eighties art. The past is inherently obscene, for it is perversely behind the scene of the present and it perversely undermines the possibilities of the future scene. The eternal return of the past intimates the spuriousness of present and future novelty—that present and future novelty cannot help but be a disguised repetition of the already secretly familiar. Thus, the obscenity of novelty is that it makes no difference, changes nothing. Nonetheless, the perversity of the marginal use of material is that it is made to suggest an obscene, forgotten sense of Being. Our sensitive respect for the awkwardness or stylelessness of marginal art suggests that we unconsciously regard it as Being made manifest. It is an emblem whose awkwardness indicates that it has become what it signifies. Unfortunately, the awkwardness of marginal art is later institutionalized as the ultimate novelty.

Another understanding of the perverse is perhaps more directly to the point regarding the taste for self-taught marginal art: the perverse embodies the specifically infantile—the past all adults share. The taste for self-taught marginal art has to do with the implicit belief that it returns us to the level of inchoate, inarticulate, emotionally archaic experience. Adorno thinks that one of art's tasks is to signal such experience without rationalizing and socializing it.[6]

From this point of view, the Neo-Expressionism of the eighties reemphasizes what is most fundamental to and inescapable in experience. The difference between Neo-Expressionism and self-taught marginal art (which is often regarded as a provincial variant of it) is that the former does this in and through a sophisticated articulation of a complex awareness of objective history, often national history, as in the case of German Neo-Expressionism. Folk art, which is perhaps the quintessence of self-taught marginal art, lacks such a sophisticated awareness, even if it sometimes alludes to historical events. Instead, it returns us to a kind of prehistorical awareness, reinstating with special purity what has been called the child's vision of the world—a vision regarded as fundamental to much modern art. Neo-Expressionism and self-taught marginal art share an assertiveness, a physicality, and an awkwardness that accord well with this calculated "infantilism," except in the latter it is not so calculated. The conspicuous physicality of self-taught marginal art conveys a sense of inchoate, inarticulate experience in a much less pretentious way than in postmodernist Neo-Expressionism.

Janine Chasseguet-Smirgel defines the perverse as a "reconstitution of Chaos, out of which there arises a new kind of reality, that of the anal universe." This involves turning the "psycho-sexual genital dimension . . . upside down," sometimes by parodying it.[7] The marginality

Elaine Reichek, *Yellow Man*, from the *Tierra del Fuego* series, 1986. Oil and photo on wool, 71 x 115 in. Collection of the artist

Bill Traylor, *Dancing Man, Woman, and Dog*, ca. 1939–42. Crayon and pencil on paperboard, 22 x 14 in. National Museum of American Art, Smithsonian Institution, Gift of Herbert Waide Hemphill, Jr., and museum purchase made possible by Ralph Cross Johnson

achieved by such parody—involving, as Chasseguet-Smirgel argues, the fantasy of eliminating the difference between the generations (so that eternal infancy seems to reign) and the sexes (the homogenization of sexuality)—keeps art eternally on the margin—indeed, makes it that of Buñuel's permanent outsider. It can never be completely assimilated by mainstream, establishment culture—what we might call genital culture—which believes that there is a right side up and that differences must be maintained. Establishment culture prefers differentiated order to undifferentiated chaos, and its interest in chaotic self-taught marginal art is an effort to place it in the order. So, it declares such art emblematic of another "order" of things, thereby legitimizing— and neutralizing—expressive chaos.

The inherent marginality of the artistically perverse is sometimes described by critics as radically subjective and "personal," sometimes as intransigent or irreducibly "idiosyncratic." That is, the artistically perverse is what does not and never can fit in properly, for it lacks propriety; it is intrinsically indecorous, which is why it terrorizes. Indeed, much eighties art aims to terrorize, as Lucy Lippard suggested in her long review of the 1980 Times Square show, with its

"shock and schlock." Shock and schlock are, to use another slogan, a kind of "generosity of expression."[8] And a pointless generosity it is, this expressivity that exists as an end in itself, ostensibly with no rhetorical purpose, although no doubt subliminally oratorical.

Now such generosity of expression, inwardly and often openly occupied with sex and death (to allude again to the title of Lippard's article), involves an attempt to be private. "It is private," as Edit de Ak eloquently put it in her article on Francesco Clemente, because "it can be measured by its idiosyncracies." The artist regresses to the idiosyncratic private—that is, the perverse personal—and expresses himself with no audience necessarily in mind because he feels he "has no chance" in life and art and wants to use his sense of futility in art—an allusion to Wolfgang Max Faust's conception of the psychosocial basis of German Neo-Expressionism.[9]

This notion is the last piece to be put in place to arrive at the conception of the marginality of eighties Neo-Expressionism—a conception much more directly to the point of self-taught marginal art, which is much less "learned" than Neo-Expressionism. This suggests that self-taught marginal art came to be acclaimed in the eighties because it was recognized as an even more important justification for art—proof of its human necessity— than Neo-Expressionism. Indeed, it seems to be a more authentic realization of the generically expressionistic ideal of perverse and perversely private art. It is more inherently marginal, as it were.

The interesting question, of course, is what social success will do to self-taught marginal art. Has the success of making record album covers killed the Reverend Finster's art, as some think? Certainly his recent production does not have the same unaffected look as his early work. Did success kill John-Michel Basquiat, or was it in the cards of his personality that he

Justin McCarthy, *Washington Crossing the Delaware, Variation on a Theme #3*, ca. 1963. Oil on fiberboard, 27 1/2 x 48 1/4 in. National Museum of American Art, Smithsonian Institution, Gift of Herbert Waide Hemphill, Jr.

Sherrie Levine, *Untitled (The Bachelors: "Gendarme")*, 1989. Cast glass, 10 x 4 x 3 3/4 in. Private collection

would overdose on drugs? The answers are unclear, but the questions are real and suggest the destructive intention—envy?—lurking in the postmodernist welcome given self-taught marginal art. It is a perverse welcome, indicative of postmodernism's decadent belief that only a perverse attitude can save art from its own success and that in general such an attitude is the last stand possible against society. But what happens when a perverse aesthetic becomes the only way to success, the only way to become an establishment artist? However, self-taught marginal art has not been quite as successful as postmodernist Neo-Expressionist art, with its stylized marginality, partly because self-taught marginal art exists not only on the margin of art but also on the margin of life. In contrast, postmodernist art exists on the margin of past modern art—its prey. For self-taught marginal art, the margin is not an official position that is a matter of aesthetic choice, but a state

of emotional life.

For all its ambiguities, the establishment success of self-taught marginal art hints that the official art world is uncertain about its own values. Endorsement of self-taught marginal art is not simply another phase in what has been called the democratization of culture, but an indication of official culture's unconscious uncertainty that its values are lasting or even truly significant. That self-taught marginal art is perverse in yet another way supports this idea. If, as Arnold Hauser has written, the "genuinely artistic presents the picture of an existence which makes sense and which has reached its goal and its end, an existence which has been mastered and controlled," while at the same time not "remain[ing] close to life," then the awkwardness of self-taught marginal art, the sense of something out of control in it, is not genuinely artistic.[10] For it suggests an existence—not only art—that is unmastered rather than mastered, that makes no sense rather than makes sense, as well as an art that is all too close to life rather than at a discrete aesthetic distance from it—an art under the illusion of being in control of life.

Self-taught marginal art is thus inherently beyond the control of socio-artistic authority. In endorsing and embracing it, such authority, however unwittingly, implies its own groundlessness, inner awkwardness, and lack of mastery—its unconscious recognition that its authority is dubious, even as it uses that authority to legitimate and give authority to self-taught marginal art. But then, in paradoxically moving it from the margin toward the center, thus suggesting that self-taught marginal art articulates the perversity that is implicitly regarded as central in art today better than the postmodernist art that is officially regarded as central, socio-artistic authority shows its own perversity.

Notes

1   Theodor W. Adorno, "Commitment," in *The Essential Frankfurt School Reader*, ed. Andrew Arato and Eike Gebhardt (New York: Continuum, 1985), p. 312. With characteristic irony, Adorno has remarked that to make an aesthetically pleasurable image of the subject's hurt is already to falsify it.

2   So-called folk art ("so-called" because the Nazi conception of "folk" has made clear how much of a sociopolitical construction it is), in particular, satisfies postmodernism's fascination with dead novelties.

3   I am alluding to Erich Fromm's distinction between the Having and Being modes of existence, fundamentally different ways of defining it. In *To Have or to Be?* (New York: Harper & Row, 1976), pp. 76–77, Fromm writes that in the former mode "all that matters is my acquisition of property and my unlimited right to keep what I have acquired." Collecting, for example, is motivated by the desire to own and have total power and superiority over something. In contrast, in the latter mode, to exist means "to love, to transcend the prison of one's isolated ego, to be interested, to 'incline,' to give" (p. 88), ultimately involving being actively present in a shared relationship (p. 81).

4   Michael Brenson, "Where Has the Quality Gone?" *New York Times*, 22 July 1990.

5   Erling Eng, "Psyche in Longing, Mourning, and Anger," in *Facets of Eros, Phenomenological Essays*, ed. F. J. Smith and Erling Eng (The Hague: Martinus Nijhoff, 1972), p. 79.

6   Theodor W. Adorno, *Aesthetic Theory* (London: Routledge & Kegan Paul, 1984), p. 82.

7   Janine Chasseguet-Smirgel, *Creativity and Perversion* (London: Free Association, 1985), p. 17. Parody in part explains such appropriationists as Mike Bidlo, et al., making these Neo-Conceptualists unconscious marginalists. Indeed, they reduce what they quote to cheap anal material. This contrasts with the Neo-Expressionists, who can be regarded as self-conscious marginalists, for they assume that chaos is an "elevating" state.

8   Lucy Lippard, "Sex and Death and Shock and Schlock: A Long Review of The Times Square Show," *Artforum* 19 (October 1980): 50–55. On "generosity of expression" see Rene Ricard, "Not About Julian Schnabel," *Artforum* 19 (Summer 1981): 79.

9   Edit de Ak, *Artforum* 19 (February 1981): 37; Max Wolfgang Faust, " 'Du hast keine Chance. Nutze si!' With It and Against It: Tendencies in Recent German Art," *Artforum* 20 (September 1981): 33–39.

10 Arnold Hauser, *The Sociology of Art* (Chicago: University of Chicago Press, 1982), p. 37.

Patriarchy Fixed in Stone

Gutzon Borglum's Mount Rushmore

Albert Boime

Gutzon Borglum often sought the perspective provided by the tramway cage, suspended from a cable that stretched thirteen hundred feet between Mount Doane, the project's operating base south of the monument, and an A-frame atop Roosevelt's head. From its base, the tramway cage ascended four hundred feet to reach the monument. Borglum's fear of vandalism made him take great comfort in the monument's inaccessibility.

The gargantuan heads of Mount Rushmore's four Great White Fathers—all intellect and logic, disembodied and soulless—stare down from the lands of their victims, the vanquished Native Americans. The faces are ostensibly benign, but the story behind their creation reveals the darker side of this American monument and the sculptor who chiseled it into being.

Indefinitely postponed by the sculptor's death and the outbreak of World War II in 1941, Mount Rushmore National Memorial's dedication has finally been set for 4 July 1991, the monument's fiftieth anniversary. The quintessential flag-waver, George Bush, is scheduled to attend the extravagant, star-studded ceremonies—on the order of the hoopla staged for the Statue of Liberty's centennial—to formally dedicate the sculpture and kick off a nationally televised tribute.

Considered America's "shrine" of democracy and as popular a national icon as the Statue of Liberty, Gutzon Borglum's Mount Rushmore has served satirists and cartoonists as a source of inspiration since its inception. The memorial's colossal faces carved in granite have come to symbolize, in the words of the sculptor's son, "an accomplishment born, planned, and created in the minds and by the hands of Americans for Americans. . . . There on the mountain the sculptor has spoken eloquently with his art, an eloquence that says simply, 'This is what it means to be an American!' "[1]

Gutzon Borglum (1867–1941), the sculptor of Mount Rushmore, was a singularly energetic and versatile artist who had to overcome any number of human and material impediments to realize his ambitious scheme. Not the least of these were the problems of working at great heights while suspended in space. Equally challenging were the difficulties in developing a system of transferring the models' measurements to the mountain surface so that untrained miners and laborers working with jackhammers and dynamite could perform the work of assistant sculptors. He himself had no reservations about his qualifications for making "a nation's memorial" to Washington, Jefferson, Lincoln, and Teddy Roosevelt that would project "a serenity, a nobility, a power that reflects the gods who inspired them and suggests the gods they have become."[2]

Borglum always claimed that the idea of the mountain memorial, which he wanted to dedicate to democracy, was to represent American ideals. The strain of "democracy" that he and his peers advocated, however, contained an essential ambivalence—an ambivalence that shaped Mount Rushmore's Rock of Ages less into a hymn to democracy than into another Art Deco expression of the 1930s in which authoritarian impulses and imperialist politics were masqueraded.[3]

The son of Danish immigrants who settled in the West, Borglum internalized the fierce chauvinism of his parents. His heritage made him a belated and anachronism heir of "magisterial aeshetics," my

William Tylee Ranney, *The Scouting Party*, 1851. Oil on canvas, 22 x 16 in. Thyssen-Bornemisza Foundation, Lugano, Switzerland

term for the imperial point of view that is often expressed in American landscape painting of the nineteenth century and that remains deeply embedded in the national consciousness. The elevated vantage point—and the sense of mastery and control that vantage point inspires—is the metaphorical embodiment of the aspirations of Manifest Destiny. Borglum the explorer-artist-spectator stood at an observation point that submitted the vast reaches of the wilderness to a gaze symbolizing the exercise of unlimited physical and intellectual power. This controlling line of sight, or "magisterial gaze," is a pervasive motif in American literature and landscape painting, in which the experience of power and domination often takes place on a lofty vantage point, as in William Ranney's *The Scouting Party*. With its monstrous, omniscient heads looming over the western landscape, Mount Rushmore literally crystallizes this experience into rock hardness. Borglum's staring effigies are in fact surrogates for the sculptor-spectator himself, surveying the endless tracts of land and consuming them with his gaze, internalizing the government's actual expansionist ideology—allegorized by the cyclopean busts—and converting it into an aesthetic response to the landscape. In this sense,

Mount Rushmore prefigures the Orwellian gaze with a quartet of Big Brothers.

Borglum recorded his feelings when he stood for the first time on the crest of Mount Rushmore, towering 6,200 feet above sea level: "I was conscious we were in another world . . . and there a new thought seized me—a thought that was to redirect me and dominate all my carving—the scale of that mountain peak." He continued:

We looked out over a horizon level and beaten like the rim of a great cartwheel 2,000 feet below. We had reached upward toward the heavenly bodies . . . and it came over me in an almost terrifying manner that I had never sensed what I was planning. Plans must change. The vastness here demanded it.

In justification of his visionary monument, he wrote, "Everything in modern civilization has so expanded that the very scale, the breadth of one's thought, is no longer limited by town, city, county or state, but daily reaches to the boundaries of the world." And he immediately drew the conclusion that it was wholly "natural and consistent with the great modern awakening that I should have turned to the huge cliffs of our land, the lofty granite ledges, and in them carve monuments and there leave records of the founding of our great nation and the development of our civilization."[4]

Borglum's visionary transformation of a mountain into gigantic father figures sharing an omniscient gaze may be traced in part, I believe, to the unusual circumstances surrounding his birth and early childhood. He was the child of a plural Mormon marriage between his father Jens Borglum and the sisters Ida and Christina Mikkelsen. All three were Mormon converts who had left the hostile religious climate of Denmark for a better life in the United States. Jens and Ida were initially

P. Steiner, "Your Face in Stone,"
New Yorker (12 November 1990)

This insightful satire democratizes
the "Great Man" complex
associated with Borglum's
monument and, indeed, all
colossal memorials dedicated to
the celebration of famous white
patriarchs.

married en route to Salt Lake City, where
their first son, Miller, was born in 1865.
The following year Christina arrived from
Denmark, and all three were subsequently
united in marriage. They then traveled by
wagon train to the Idaho Territory, where
Christina gave birth to Gutzon on 25
March 1867. (The next year Christina
bore another son, Solon, whose later
success as a sculptor piqued Gutzon's
competitive streak.) Restless and ambitious, the Borglums kept moving—from

Idaho to Utah to Nebraska to Missouri to
California. This movement from one
frontier line to another recapitulated the
striving of their pioneer predecessors.
Quarrels between Ida and Christina and
pressure on the plural marriage from the
outside, however, led to the family
breakup. In Omaha it was decided that
Christina, Gutzon's mother, should
withdraw from the marriage, after which
Ida, Jens, and the three sons proceeded to
St. Louis. Ida, now the nominal mother

Borglum, suspended in a bosun's chair, supervises work on the Lincoln head. The "skin" of Lincoln's face is pockmarked by a uniform pattern of drill holes, the result of a process called honey-combing, which allows rock to be broken away in relatively thin layers.

Borglum was scrupulous about work conditions on the mountain. Not a single worker was ever seriously injured during the entire project, although there were several close calls.

of the three boys, and the elder Borglum swore the children to secrecy about their Mormon past. Recalling his mother's tearful departure, Borglum reflected: "I never forgot it, but I wondered why. I thought she was going to stay with us. She and father had always been with us. I could not understand." Borglum, then four or five years old, clearly felt deserted by his biological mother, but he was never allowed to mourn his loss and had to carry a "guilty secret" with him into adulthood. As he confessed: "By the time I was seven, I knew what it meant not to have a mother of my own. I thought I didn't want to stay around things that reminded me of her any more. So I ran away." Later autobiographical statements reveal Borglum's denial and even outright prevarication concerning the circum-

stances of his birth and the identification of his mother—he veered from Ida to Christina and often cast blame on a cruel stepmother for a brooding, unstable childhood.[5]

The rage and paranoia that lay just beneath Borglum's expansive personality—ready to flare up instantly with little provocation and inevitably creating conflict in his business and social relationships—most likely developed from this childhood trauma of abandonment, which probably was at the root of his chronic fighting with his father and his frequent attempts to run away during adolescence. His first attempt to stabilize his life took the form of an early marriage to his matronly and highly devoted art teacher, Elizabeth ("Lisa") Jaynes Putnam. Eighteen years his senior, Lisa was then

This photograph of Lincoln's head, probably taken from atop Washington's head, provides a good view of the complex scaffolding designed by Borglum as a working platform.

Lincoln figured prominently in Borglum's project. Borglum even named his son after the president who preserved the union.

nearly the same age as his mother. Borglum kept news of their relationship secret from his father and other members of the family until after the marriage. Later, he abandoned this wife for another woman and then proceeded to efface Lisa from his history. A creator of monuments to public history, he was a destroyer of his own personal history.

The circumstances surrounding his childhood may also help explain the contradiction inherent in Borglum's aggressive pursuit of the friendship of the rich and powerful, while simultaneously regarding himself as an outsider. I believe that it is not possible to isolate his sculptural aspirations from the impact of his early experience. The representation in perpetual, enduring granite of four powerful males whose steady countenances suggest the security of omniscient and omnipotent fathers may be traced to

Tseng Kwong Chi, *Mt. Rushmore, South Dakota*, 1990. Gelatin silver print.

Tseng Kwong Chi, who photographed himself at key American tourist sites to explore their spatial and symbolic impact, here appears dwarfed by the magisterial gaze of the four Great White Fathers.

Greta Pratt, *Mt. Rushmore*, 1990. Gelatin silver print.

Pratt's photograph presents Mount Rushmore as the ultimate tourist fantasy and the culmination of state historian Doane Robinson's dream for South Dakota.

Borglum's childhood trauma. Such protective males would never leave a child in the clutches of an uncaring or unsteady woman and would themselves remain a stable force to dissipate the child's inner rage. In building monuments to withstand time and nature (he had a horror of vandalism and delighted in the memorial's inaccessibility), Borglum was creating a heavy armor to guarantee the continuity and coherence he lacked in his childhood. The hardheartedness of his actual parents was transmuted into rock-hard metaphors of perpetual loving care.

His anxiety about "fathering" can be seen in his own relationship to his son Lincoln, whom he kept close to his side at all times even into adulthood, much to his mother's distress. Lincoln in fact gave up the idea of his own career to devote his life to the Mount Rushmore project, which he helped realize after his father's death in 1941.

All four figures represented on Mount Rushmore constitute a monument to Borglum's patriarchal preoccupations with the common man. Although he internalized the aristocratic view of the

artist-genius who deserves unqualified support from society, he held populist convictions about the small farmer and urban laborer. Washington, Jefferson, Lincoln, and especially Theodore Roosevelt embodied for the sculptor the strong and wise ruler's compassion for the underdog. As an answer to his personal sense of parental loss, the psychological role of these colossal father figures in Borglum's life helps explain his own paternalistic attitude toward his employees. He fulminated continuously against corruption in high places—one of his most audacious adventures being his investigation and condemnation of the aircraft industry during World War I—because it threatened his sense of the good father.[6] But unlike the authentic muckraker and Populist, he almost always took his case directly to the presidents or institutional heads to warn them against corruption from below, invariably sparing them any blame, which he placed on bureaucratic middle managers.

Borglum's maturation coincided with the consummation of the new industrial order in America at the end of the

Alfred Hitchcock's spy thriller
North by Northwest (Metro-
Goldwyn-Mayer, 1959) exploits
the Shrine of Democracy as the
symbolic backdrop for the
undoing of foreign thugs and
their local collaborators and the
salvation of the enlightened
American heroes.

century, when the imaginative ideal of the
pioneer who could chart new worlds in
the wilderness was giving way to the
postbellum myth of enterprising captains
of industry who could restructure the
world through their inventive genius and
daring. Borglum's contribution to
American culture may be seen as an
expression of his need to fuse both ideals
in his life and work. He lived out the
western fantasy of rugged individualism
and dominion over larger and larger units
of land, but he accomplished his goals
with modern technology and an army of
subordinates. He carved a granitic
mountain as a piece of sculpture with
pneumatic jackhammers and plugs of
dynamite.

It is no coincidence that Mount
Rushmore was conceived from the first as
a tourist site not in its original state like
Niagara Falls or Yellowstone National
Park, but in an altered state wrought by
human artifice. The initial idea for a
monument carved into the Black Hills
sprang in 1923 from Doane Robinson,
state historian for South Dakota, who felt
that natural scenery was not enough to

lure tourists—that "something of special
interest to make it impressive" was
required.[7] Robinson received fundamental
help from South Dakota's senator Peter
Norbeck, an influence peddler in Washington involved in the development of the
state's recreational and scenic areas.
Mount Rushmore was to represent not
only the wild grandeur of its local geography but also the triumph of modern
civilization over that geography through
its anthropomorphic representation. God-
created man could now recreate nature in
his own image, realizing through modern
technology the old myth of the artist as
usurper of the Creator's prerogative. Like
Disneyland, Mount Rushmore transformed history into theater, something
only a megalomaniacal actor with bound-
less energy and confidence could have
pulled off. This desire to transform the
environment seemed part of Borglum's
character: when he purchased several
properties in North Stamford, Connecticut, in 1910, he promptly created a vast
estate and named it "Borgland."

Borglum was remarkable for his
abundant creative and entrepreneurial
capacities. His ambition embraced not
only the symbolic shaping of material
through an art of the imagination but the
physical subjugation of the material world
as well. He was able to map out his
schemes, however, only through a vulgar
kind of representation that resembled
popular illustration. Because he confused
bigness with greatness, he thought of
himself as an artist producing monuments
that rivaled the achievements of the
ancients. But Mount Rushmore, like the
Statue of Liberty, succeeds primarily
through the impact of scale rather than
through its aesthetic quality. Actually,
because Borglum transferred the conventional formula of the bust to a wholly
unprecedented context, Mount Rushmore
can be regarded as a kind of inverse
version of those plastic reductions of the
Statue of Liberty and the Eiffel Tower

that serve as decorative paperweights. While the paperweights miniaturize the original work and shift its context from the outdoors to the indoors, Mount Rushmore magnifies what is typically ornamental and shifts it from the indoors to the outdoors. This notion of the bust transplanted to a "natural," public setting becomes somewhat analogous to the idea behind topiary design. In this sense, Rushmore seems to be more kitsch than art.

The Fathers of the Country, like ordinary fathers, required a place of residence. Borglum's theme for Mount Rushmore was "the founding, preservation, growth, and development of the nation."[8] The sculptor elaborated on his concept:

The Memorial at Mount Rushmore is the first monument erected on the Western Hemisphere dedicated to a conception and the organization of this great Western Republic. It will include its struggles to maintain its unity as well as record its territorial completion and development.[9]

Seeking information on Thomas Jefferson from George Gordon Battle at the outset of his Mount Rushmore commission, Borglum stated:

Jefferson's place in this memorial is more important even than Washington's. By that I do not mean to eclipse Washington one iota, but Jefferson purchased the Louisiana Territory, in the center of which, on a spur of the Rocky Mountains, this memorial is located. I am literally converting a spur of the Rockies into a memorial and a monument to the great Western Republic.

Borglum understood Jefferson's acquisition to be the key to the unfolding of the saga of Manifest Destiny:

It was the acquisition of the Louisiana Territory that led to the colonization of Texas by Americans and that eventually to the Mexican trouble. It was the struggle over the precise relationship of Texas to the United States that led to the acquisition of California. It was the opening of the Northwest by Lewis and Clark, the direct agents of Jefferson, that developed the Oregon Trail and that, in turn, determined the boundary with Canada. In other words, it was Jefferson's political strategy in securing the Mississippi that incidentally gave us the Continent westward to the Pacific.[10]

Mount Rushmore allegorizes the idea of Manifest Destiny and inadvertently invokes all the tragedy this "doctrine" implied for native peoples. Borglum's professed intent demonstrates that his imagination had been nurtured in part by William Gilpin, the nineteenth-century lyricist of the Rockies and of Manifest Destiny: "I want, somewhere in America on or near the Rockies, the backbone of the Continent, so far removed from succeeding, selfish, coveting civilizations, a few feet of stone that bears witness, carries the likenesses, the dates, a word or two of the great things we accomplished as a Nation, placed so high it won't pay to pull down for lesser purposes." Although it did not illustrate an obvious narrative, Borglum's program for the memorial clearly suggested a summary of American conquest. His wife Mary, who served as his amanuensis, wrote that the memorial constituted her husband's "sincere patriotic effort to preserve and perpetuate the ideals of liberty and freedom on which our government was established and to record the territorial expansion of the Republic."[11]

Borglum's choice of four presidents for the Mount Rushmore memorial testifies to his position as a latecomer to the stage of magisterial aesthetics: each of the four had a role in founding and consummating the myth of America's Manifest Destiny. Their roles are clear: George Washington, who dominates the ensemble by project-

Roosevelt's head was dedicated in 1939. Roosevelt was the only "modern" president represented on Mount Rushmore. The choice aroused controversy, but Borglum felt that Roosevelt, a close personal friend, completed the work of Manifest Destiny with the Panama Canal and made America a world power.

ing out the farthest, extensively surveyed what was then the western wilderness; Thomas Jefferson, deliberately positioned to face west, was responsible for the Louisiana Purchase, which doubled the nation's land mass, and for the Lewis and Clark expedition, the first to explore a land route to the Pacific and eventually open the West to settlement; Abraham Lincoln, for whom Borglum named his

son, preserved the Union; and Theodore Roosevelt, Borglum's favorite, engaged in political machinations that led to the building of the Panama Canal (thereby fulfilling Columbus's dream of finding a water route to the Far East) and that consummated the American empire by facilitating access to the West and quickening the industrial development of the nation. Borglum's original plan was also designed to include a huge panel in the shape of the Louisiana Purchase. Inscribed in eight-foot-high, five-inch-deep gilded letters was to be his selection of the nine great events in American history. Significantly, seven of these—after the signing of the Declaration of Independence and the framing of the Constitution—had to do with the acquisition of territory: the Louisiana Purchase, the admission of Texas to the Union, and the acquisition of Florida, California, Oregon, Alaska, and the Panama Canal Zone.

Borglum's nationalist project could not have been better timed. The post–World War I era was marked by a social narrowness and growing intolerance of foreigners, with white, Protestant Americans of older stock displaying overt hostility against Asians, African Americans, Catholics, and Jews. In 1924 Congress passed the National Origins Act, which limited immigration, especially from southern and eastern Europe, and included a provision that forbade the immigration of Asians. It was during this same period that the spectacular rise of the Ku Klux Klan reached its zenith. The prim Vermonter Calvin Coolidge, who presided over the dedication pageant at Mount Rushmore in 1927, was the president who signed the National Origins Act into law.

Coolidge's trip to South Dakota in 1927 was also motivated by his desire to placate the impoverished farmers of the western and midwestern states. Farm politics particularly irritated Washington, D.C., during Coolidge's second term, when farmers stepped up their demands for a government marketing plan. Coolidge consistently vetoed agrarian legislation designed to alleviate the plight of American farmers. Perhaps Coolidge saw in the Rushmore project a cheap means of mollifying regional anxieties and rural resentment against his farm policy by tapping into the farmers' ethnic prejudices as well as their identification

with the continent's first European settlers. In any case, Coolidge signed the bill that established the Mount Rushmore National Memorial Commission and allocated $250,000 toward its completion.

The signing of the bill took place in February 1929, when only six days remained in Coolidge's presidency, leaving Herbert Hoover to do the practical work of organizing the commission. Congressional support for the Rushmore bill manifested the heady optimism of the 1920s, when general prosperity seemed to bear out the national promise of unlimited expansion. Only in this climate could Borglum and his confederates persuade the government of his project's symbolic significance. With the stock market crash in 1929 and the Great Depression of the 1930s, however, what had been a luxury item for Coolidge and Hoover became a necessity for Franklin Roosevelt. Roosevelt actively supported Mount Rushmore, exploiting its popular appeal to promote his New Deal policies. Roosevelt's philosophy of spending the country out of the Depression played a role in Borglum's success: Mount Rushmore could be classified as a large-scale public project designed for hiring the unemployed, another instance in which federal money could be used to create jobs.[12]

Roosevelt traveled to South Dakota in 1936 to be present for the unveiling of Borglum's Thomas Jefferson. The president's trip coincided with an extensive tour of the West, ostensibly to evaluate the effects of the long drought but actually to campaign in traditional Republican strongholds during an election year. During Roosevelt's previous campaign, South Dakota had slipped into the Democratic camp for the first time in its history, and Roosevelt wanted to make sure it stayed there this time around. Significantly, the president's Mount Rushmore speech emphasized his attempt to preserve the democratic principles embodied in the monument's effigies.[13]

Gutzon Borglum, *Staging in California*, 1889. Oil on canvas, 60 x 108 in. Joslyn Museum, Omaha, Nebraska, Gift of J. L. Brandeis and Sons

He took advantage of the occasion to include Mount Rushmore as part of his national crusade to restore confidence in the government and regenerate the nation's morale; at the same time, he fended off conservative critics who accused him of behaving like a dictator with his sweeping New Deal measures.

Borglum's penchant for "can-do" leaders and obsession with territorial aggrandizement predisposed him to feel most at home with robber barons like railroad tycoon Collis P. Huntington and newspaper czar William Randolph Hearst. Despite his respect for the two Roosevelts, Borglum considered a railroad magnate like Huntington to be greater than either. His belief in the need for a dominant authority to maintain social order is evident in his 1931 letter to his dear friend Lester B. Barlow, the eccentric founder of the Nonpartisan League of America, who considered Hoover a "robot." Borglum complained that America lacked someone with "guts" who could "take over the Presidency and put the company in order." He found his model in Europe: "There is only one man in all Europe with vision and courage and fortunately has the power to carry it out, that's Mussolini."[14] Borglum clearly

admired those with the power to move mountains, irrespective of their politics or ethics.

He profoundly admired western explorers and entrepreneurs like Thomas Hart Benton (the granduncle of the painter) and Benton's son-in-law John Charles Frémont. Like them, he imagined himself a "lone crusader" in the quest to make an enduring monument for the American republic. It was Benton who, in an address proposing a transcontinental road in 1849, declared that it would be crowned with a colossal statue of Columbus, "hewn from a granite mass or a peak on the Rocky Mountains . . . pointing with outstretched arm to the western horizon, and saying to the flying passengers—'There is the East; there is India.' " Borglum shared Benton's reverence for Columbus, who, in his mind, "did more for mankind than any other since Christ" and "who started into this great unknown, untraveled, and discovered this country."[15] For Borglum, Columbus's genius represented the legacy of the Renaissance within America.

Young Borglum's orientation was decisively affected by the achievements of Benton and Frémont. The reviews of his painting *Staging in California* brought

For the unveiling of the Jefferson head on 30 August 1936, Borglum draped a huge flag over the boom of the pointing machine used to transfer measurements from model to mountain. At a prearranged signal, Lincoln Borglum detonated charges of dynamite to slowly shift the boom and pull the flag away from Jefferson's face. Further demonstrating his flair for dramatic dedications, Borglum proclaimed in a stentorian voice, "I want you, Mr. President, to dedicate this memorial as a shrine to democracy; to call upon the people of this earth for one hundred years to come, to read the thought and see what manner of men struggled here to establish self-determining government in the western world."[17]

Hat in hand, Borglum shares his vision for the developing memorial with President Roosevelt.

or in the face of the ocean. We do not value enough the effect of space for the eye; it reacts upon the mind, which unconsciously expands to larger limits and freer range of thoughts.[16]

When he first dedicated Mount Rushmore in 1925 by climbing its vertical walls and planting a flag on its peak, Borglum was emulating Frémont's dramatic unfurling of the flag on the summit of the Rockies. Although Borglum's dedication occurred much later, it is certain that he and the Frémonts hit it off nicely. Jessie Benton Frémont recommended Borglum to members of her social and political circle in Los Angeles, leading to the admiration and purchase of his work. When Borglum and his wife headed for Europe by way of New York in 1890, they carried letters of introduction from Jessie Frémont to her friends across the United States, together with more than fifty paintings they hoped to sell along the way. Eventually Jessie Frémont introduced Borglum to Theodore Roosevelt, then New York's police commissioner, with whom Borglum became a close friend and political ally.

Borglum's preoccupation with national conquest is reflected in the themes of his earliest works. He sculpted *Death of the Chief* (1891) while in Paris, and in 1893 he began, but never completed, a monumental canvas called *Noche Triste* (or *The Conquest of Mexico*) for the World's Columbian Exposition. The latter depicts Cortez's battle for survival against his formidable Aztec foes. Borglum's fascination with the conquest theme was also apparent in his symbolic dedication ceremony for Mount Rushmore on 1 October 1925. On top of the mountain, huge flags representing the former European owners of the land that encompassed Mount Rushmore were dramatically raised and lowered by assistants in French, Spanish, and English costumes. The Indians—always hired by Borglum to

When Roosevelt addressed the crowd at the unveiling of the Jefferson head, he seized the opportunity to make political hay in a campaign year. His attendance was due in no small measure to Borglum, who had written to the Democratic party chairman to warn him of the Republican nominee's imminent victory unless the president appeared at the unveiling.

him to the attention of Jessie Benton Frémont, Benton's daughter and Frémont's wife, who became Borglum's most enthusiastic champion. When she persuaded her husband to sit for Borglum, she brought together men who typified two generations of the American male, each desiring to transfix the world with his magisterial gaze. As Frémont, the intrepid mountain climber, wrote in his *Memoirs*:

Shut in to narrow limits, the mind is driven in upon itself and loses its elasticity; but the breast expands when upon some hill-top, the eye ranges over a broad expanse of country,

perform at dedication and unveiling ceremonies—were represented by one Sioux brave in full native regalia.

Borglum's experience was grounded in the annexation of territories grabbed from Spain, Mexico, and native peoples in the nineteenth century. Consistent with the pattern of destruction characteristic of national exploration and empire building, the creation and the dedication of the Mount Rushmore monument was one more symbol of the white man's racist and intolerant Indian policy. While nascent environmentalists and other groups are recorded as having opposed the defacing of the mountain, there is scant reference to Sioux Indian protest or to the violation of their rights. Ironically, Mount Rushmore stands between what are now the boundaries of Harney National Forest and Custer State Park, named for two of the most hated names in the Sioux lexicon. Both Harney and Custer engaged in Sioux massacres that included the murder of women and children and led illegal expeditions into the Black Hills to provoke Native Americans to hostile confrontation.

The Black Hills, of which Mount Rushmore is part, were then known as the sacred site of Paha Sapa, holy mountains where ceremonies were held for the spirits of dead warriors and where the young came alone to meditate and pray for guidance from the Great Spirit. No Sioux lived in the Black Hills, the revered center of Sioux spiritual life. But the harmonious relations between Native Americans and the land were disrupted by the Yankee expansionists. As more and more wagon trains and empire builders invaded Sioux hunting grounds, Indians retaliated by raiding the trains. Civil War generals still thirsting for blood, like Sherman and Sheridan, treated Indians as an enemy foreign nation. Sheridan—the subject of a flattering equestrian statue by Borglum in Sheridan Circle, Washington, D.C.— uttered the famous comment, "The only

good Indians I ever saw were dead" (which became, in the popular version, "The only good Indian is a dead Indian"). Following the bloody Sioux war from 1865 to 1867, the United States negotiated the Fort Laramie Treaty of 1868, which established, for the exclusive use of the Dakota Indians, the forty-one-thousand-square-mile Great Sioux Reservation that encompassed the Black Hills. The treaty was ratified by the Senate on 16 February 1869 and signed by President Andrew Johnson a week later.[18]

Again, however, whites violated their contract when surveyors for the Northern Pacific Railroad extended their survey through the Sioux reservation and the government provided troops to protect them. In 1874 General Custer led an army of one thousand men into the Black Hills under the pretext of surveying for a possible fort site. Deliberately constructing a glowing official report on the fertility of the region and the possibilities for cattle grazing, Custer shrewdly tacked on near the end of his report the news of the discovery of a gold vein.[19] As might be expected, the news leaked, spurring tens of thousands of gold prospectors to swarm into the Black Hills. The government, making only half-hearted attempts to honor the treaty, thus relinquished its commitment to the Sioux during a period of economic depression and high agrarian unemployment. The government then offered to buy the land, but the outraged Sioux refused and reacted violently. Eventually President Grant resorted to all-out war, during which Sitting Bull and Crazy Horse annihilated Custer and his elite Seventh Cavalry at Little Big Horn. But the full weight of the U.S. Army began to take its toll. The Indians, suing for peace, were compelled to assemble in barren preserves in Indian territory, where they were ravaged by hunger and disease. The military, once again in violation of the Fort Laramie Treaty, then forced

Gutzon Borglum, *Sheridan Monument*, ca. 1908. Bronze, 132 in. high. Sheridan Circle, Washington, D.C.

Tatanka Yotanka, or Sitting Buffalo Bull, best known as Sitting Bull. Photograph by David F. Barry, 1885. National Anthropological Archives, National Museum of Natural History, Smithsonian Institution

selected chiefs to enter into an agreement to turn over to the United States government the land—more than seven million acres—that comprised the Black Hills.[20] The last incident of the Sioux wars was the sickening Wounded Knee massacre in 1890, in which U.S. troops slaughtered two hundred largely unarmed Lakota men, women, and children.

Although the wars were over, the Sioux were now forced to undergo a different kind of attack on their society, customs, religion, and tribal unity, as the government tried to integrate them into white society as permanent second-class citizens. The Sioux fought back in the white man's court, trying to obtain satisfaction for the theft of their land and the violations of the treaties. With Sioux litigation still in progress at the time he planted the American flag on the summit of Mount Rushmore to dedicate the site for the memorial, Borglum would soon be swept up in the network of Native American claims. As if to stake out the territory, the sculptor then proceeded, like a typical colonial, to desacralize the holy place by defacing it permanently with the effigies of four Great White Fathers hewn directly into the granite. Thus, the harmony that the Native Americans had established with their environment was disrupted in a double sense by Borglum's monument—first, a religious and cultural site had been violated; second, an integral feature of the indigenous landscape had been permanently altered. Borglum's memorial, which constituted the crowning touch to western expansion, literally etched the magisterial gaze into the conquered landscape.

It is no wonder that the Sioux came to despise the pale face's monumental impress on their sacred hills, a humiliating symbol of their oppression. As Lame Deer, a Sioux medicine man, interpreted it:

What does this Mount Rushmore mean to us Indians? It means that these big white faces are telling us, "First we gave you Indians a treaty that you could keep these Black Hills forever, as long as the sun would shine, in exchange for all the Dakotas, Wyoming and Montana. Then we found the gold and took this last piece of land, because we were stronger, and there were more of us than there were of you, and because we had cannons and Gatling guns, while you hadn't even progressed far enough to make a steel knife. And when you didn't want to leave, we wiped you out, and those of you who survived we put on reservations. And then we took the gold out, a billion bucks, and we aren't through yet. And because we like the tourist dollars, too, we have made your sacred Black Hills into one vast Disneyland. And after we did all this we carved up this mountain, the dwelling place of your spirits, and put our four gleaming white faces here. We are the conquerors."

Lame Deer noted the psychological impact of the great white heads on the tourists who look up to them "and feel good, real good, because they make them feel big and powerful." They strut and think, "We are white, and we made this, and what we want we get, and nothing can stop us." Lame Deer concluded: "And this is what conquering means. They could just as well have carved this mountain into a huge cavalry boot standing on a dead Indian." As one type of symbolic protest against this desecration, Native American males would often form a death-defying human chain just to urinate down on the noses of the faces. Mounted police had to stand guard out of fear that Native American protestors would dump red paint on the faces. Led by leaders of the United Native Americans and the American Indian movement, Sioux women and men—some of whose ancestors had been killed at Wounded Knee—occupied the site behind Mount Rushmore in the summers of 1970, 1972, and 1973, occasionally demonstrating on top of the heads for the return of their

The signing of the Fort Laramie Treaty in 1868 foreshadowed one of the grossest violations by the U.S. government of its contractual bonds with Native Americans and left a lasting feeling of bitterness among the Dakota Sioux. It was signed into law by President Andrew Johnson, shown here with a delegation of Dakota and other Indians at the White House. Photograph by Alexander Gardner, 1867. National Anthropological Archives, National Museum of American History, Smithsonian Institution

rightful land and an end to institutionalized racism in South Dakota.[21]

Although Borglum was often sensitive to the plight of the Indians, his interest was primarily paternal and self-serving.[22] His attitude resembled that of President Coolidge, who, in preparation for the dedication ceremonies at Rushmore in 1927, greeted a delegation of Sioux and donned a chief's feathered bonnet. In his address, however, the president stressed that the monument, in its location and design, was "distinctly American in conception, in its magnitude, in its meaning," ultimately representing "a picture of hope fulfilled. Its location will be significant," Coolidge unequivocally proclaimed, going on to describe the site "here in the heart of the continent, on the side of a mountain which probably no white man had ever beheld in the days of Washington, in territory acquired by the action of Jefferson." Coolidge made it known that the monument cemented

forever the white man's grasp on the sacred land.[23]

Unlike Coolidge, however, Borglum often translated his paternalism into direct action on behalf of Native Americans. When he learned that the Oglala Sioux were starving in the drought and depression of the 1930s at their Pine Ridge, South Dakota, reservation, Borglum—impatient with the responses to his many requests to politicians for help—rounded up cattle and clothing for the stricken tribe. An example of the official government attitude was the response to his call for help from Ray Lyman Wilbur, secretary of the Interior under Herbert Hoover. Wilbur argued that empty Indian dwellings do not necessarily imply hunger, since Indians indulge excessively in "feasts" one day and are destitute the next. "The real Indian," he asserted,

continues to be essentially a primitive man and as such is quite naturally satisfied with

The last incident of the Sioux wars was the Wounded Knee Massacre of 1890, during which U.S. troops slaughtered about two hundred largely unarmed Lakota men, women, and children. National Anthropological Archives, National Museum of Natural History, Smithsonian Institution

primitive conditions. Regardless of what we may do to hasten the progress of their evolution toward a higher civilization the fact remains that the major part of such progress can only be worked out by the Indian himself after there has been aroused in him the will to better his mode of life.[24]

Borglum shared this attitude, although he evidently felt more keenly the historical injustice perpetrated against Native Americans. Although he was sympathetic to the plight of the indigenous peoples and to the abuses against them, Borglum nevertheless did not accept the Indian as a potentially full and equal partner in his vision of America. He used the Sioux in dedication ceremonies as colorful accessories but still considered them wards to be taken under protective custody.

Borglum's earliest childhood memory was of a "Sioux Indian's face pressed closely against the window of our main room." He was so frightened that he hid in the folds of the clothing of his grandmother, who had been telling him Norse stories. Borglum suffered nightmares of Indian raids, with the fierce Vikings of Denmark and the Sioux Indians fused forever in his imagination. Indeed, Borglum's childhood dread of Native Americans on the frontier became public knowledge, subject even to satire by one West Coast cartoonist. In another anecdote, Borglum recalled that during an expedition to Oregon his father was selected to converse with a delegation of Indians encountered on the trail. One of them asked permission to examine Borglum's revolver and accidentally shot himself with it. The chief blamed Borglum for this mishap and demanded that he be turned over to the chief's people for punishment. This request was denied, and the Indians departed shouting threats.[25]

These childhood memories and imaginative reconstructions of frontier life—his earliest paintings, drawings, and

Following his inaugural drilling at Mount Rushmore's dedication ceremony on 10 August 1927, Coolidge accepted the chief's bonnet from the Oglala Sioux as well as the honorary title "Wanbli Tokaha," Chief Leading Eagle. Coolidge's visit to South Dakota was a turning point in the monument's history. In addition to his direct support, the project benefitted from the publicity generated by the visit.

sculpture represented western landscapes, horses, Indians, and cowboys—help explain his ambivalence toward Native Americans. Borglum's mixed feelings are reflected in a 1934 letter in which he claimed to have known American Indians since "babyhood." He acknowledged that Americans had stripped the Indian of everything "we wanted and punished him or imprisoned him if he complained." At the same time, he revealed his belief that Native Americans had had time to reflect on right and wrong and should now accept "as justified our [i.e., the descendants of the pioneers] 'right to be free and pursue happiness.' "[26]

Borglum's involvement with the Sioux during the early years of the monument's development may also be attributed to a shrewd political sense. Among Borglum's personal papers is a report on a 1931 class

action suit on behalf of the Sioux against the United States.[27] It should be noted that during 1930–31, the Sioux Nation's action against the United States, known as the Black Hills Claim, was reaching a final judgment. This suit demanded various benefits as well as reparations for past injustices. The pressures of this major suit and the hardships of the period may have prompted Borglum to intercede on behalf of the Indians. His letter of 2 October 1932 to the Interior Department's Joseph M. Dixon demonstrates that he was in direct communication with the Sioux delegates, even mediating their quarrels with the government. The month before, he had written to Secretary Wilbur from his home in Stamford, Connecticut, to say that he would "be very earnestly questioned" when he returned to the Dakotas and that he was "very anxious to bring back to these people something besides regrets and delays." Borglum's paternalistic attitude is then spelled out:

I had thought of asking the Department to give me some authority with the Sioux tribes in South Dakota so that I could, without interfering with their agents, develop a simple plan of life for them and restore a little of their confidence in the white man's administration.

He concluded his letter with a blistering attack on the Indian Bureau, saying it "is so incompetent that only the dumb patience of the Indian himself has protected this government from the severest censure."[28] Borglum's protectiveness, however, was probably fostered less by his concern for the Indians' welfare than by his own anxiety about his tenuous connection with the sacred hills he was then subjecting to jackhammer and dynamite.

Borglum was useful to enterprising Native Americans who played up to his desire for "local color" in connection with his ceremonies. Chief Henry Standing Bear asked Borglum to use his influence with the organizer of the upcoming Pageant of America, at which the chief hoped to "head and handle the Indians should they want to use them and to put on for them Indian act or play." Despite his obvious affection for the Sioux chief, Borglum's exaggerated and hyperbolic responses to Chief Standing Bear's periodic requests suggest his political manipulation of the Pine Ridge community:

I wish you would write to me rather fully about what is on your mind. I want you to know that I am the friend of your people and when I say that I mean that I place friendship and good honest service to the Indian as one of the first obligations of the American people and the Government of the United States toward the original inhabit-

ants and owners of this country—and that I will always do everything I can—perhaps more than I can afford—to do what is right and proper for the American Indian.[29]

Borglum's aid to the Sioux during the Depression and his periodic gifts to them for performing at his dedication sideshows endeared him to a certain number of the chiefs, who made him an honorary member of the Sioux with the name "Inyan Wanblee"—Chief Stone Eagle. Yet in 1938, at the height of the Sioux protest against Washington, when Chief James Red Cloud requested that he grant Native Americans equal time on Mount Rushmore by carving the head of his father or one of the great Sioux chiefs, the man who could reshape mountains claimed to be "helpless."[30]

Seven years earlier the Oglala Sioux had first requested a monument to their people on the order of Mount Rushmore. Chief Standing Bear wrote Borglum in December 1931:

When I visited the reservation last summer I heard that you were sculptoring the face of George Washington in the Black Hills which is fine. But would it not be most appropriate to have the face of the great Crazy Horse placed there too. I spoke of this to the people at Kyle last summer and they agreed with me. Crazy Horse was the guardian of the Black Hills—the great patriot—and is still so revered by all the Sioux today even those who catered to the white man. Crazy Horse stands out as not [sic] other Sioux in history and when he met death no one took his place. With him the nation fell and the Sioux went into bondage. He is deserving of honor. I do not, of course, know how you feel about the matter but it does appear as a most fitting tribute to pay to a great American.[31]

Chief Henry Standing Bear's apparent acceptance of Borglum's defacement of the sacred place can be understood as a strategem to encourage the sculptor to embrace the interests of the dispossessed owners of the land. But Crazy Horse had no place in a memorial dedicated to the Great White Fathers; it was, in fact, his very absence that signified their triumph. Despite Borglum's aid to the Sioux and his awareness of the injustices meted out to them, he needed the Black Hills—sacred Indian land—for the embodiment of his vision of empire. The Native American claim to the land made it all the more appropriate for his shrine of democracy: the spread of the republic was, after all, the story of the conquering white men and their accomplishments, and the carving of Mount Rushmore attested to this spirit of conquest.

Native Americans did not want Borglum's charity; rather, they wanted him to convey to the Great White Father in the White House their request to fulfill the treaty of 1868. Borglum, however, advised them against going to Washington to demand restitution for their stolen land. He suggested that they instead barter their votes for political favors and even plea for charitable donations:

There is only one way to get land for your children and your wives for the very hot months to give a little green and a little shade, that would be for a few fine men to contribute it to you and to give you a deed for it so that the Government or no one else could ever take it from you.

In addressing the idea for an Indian counterpart to Mount Rushmore, however, Borglum's disregard for the Native Americans he claimed to support is apparent: "I have never received a nickel for the work of the last year—for the carving of the head of Lincoln. How could I ever carve a head of your Father?"[32]

Borglum resisted blaming these problems on the Great White Father in the White House or his chiefs, but focused instead on "the little men"—the same "little men who kill your buffalo and take them away—meat and hides. The Chiefs in Washington know nothing about these things, and you must be patient." He viewed himself as a "progressive," which to him meant possessing "an independence of thought and a desire on the part of the individual to place policy and action above party habits and convention."[33] Unfortunately, this often meant working out a plan of action to suit his own interests.

Borglum's true position on the Native American question may have been best stated in his letter to P. E. Byrne, author of *Soldiers of the Plains*, who wrote to Borglum in 1927 to propose "a fitting memorial to *THE INDIAN*." Byrne's letter ended with something of an appeal for a "national monument worthy of the Indian warrior at his best, and of America's contribution to the story and the glory of the vanquished." Borglum replied that he was sympathetic to the project but was unclear as to what shape it should take and preferred that such a memorial be embedded into a more general monument of frontier life. As he explained, it was

a matter of fact [the Indian] has done nothing himself, and he became great only when he was fighting to resist civilization; that is he showed phenomenal mental ability, great fighting qualities, but he has contributed nothing to literature; nothing to science. In his great human qualities he is certainly our equal. So, when I seem to criticize him don't think it is because of any lack of love for him.[34]

Borglum's apologetic note at the end of the passage clearly resulted from his sense of having gone too far in disparaging Native Americans to an author bitterly critical of their treatment.

Borglum's divided sentiments toward Native Americans came to the fore again

in 1932, when Chief James Red Cloud wrote to thank him for the gifts of blankets and clothing that he had requested from the Great White Father. Red Cloud had heard that Borglum was preparing for a journey to Washington, D.C., and he wanted him to marshal a delegation of Pine Ridge Sioux to the president to discuss the violations of the old treaties and the miserable conditions of Native Americans. He explained:

We are a vanishing race and our bows and arrows are no longer useful. Our eyesight is dim, our muscles are stiff and we are like women. We are told that we must farm and work like our pale face brothers. We do not like to be forced to live like white people. We are happier when we are in Council or dancing. We are not lazy like the pale face says we are, but our civilization is different. The Black Hills still belong to us, and if the treaty of '68 is carried out, we will be happy and will not ask help from the Red Cross.[35]

Red Cloud concluded his appeal with a request to Borglum, should permission for the Pine Ridge group to meet with the

Makpiya-luta, or Red Cloud.
Photograph by David F. Barry, n.d.
National Anthropological Archives,
National Museum of Natural History,
Smithsonian Institution

president be denied, to "plead with the Great White Father to fulfill the 'Treaty of '68.'" Since the chief's plea would have meant giving back Mount Rushmore, Borglum could only have received it with his customary ambivalence.

The District Council of Pine Ridge, however, resolved that all plans for a Washington visit should be arranged by the members themselves. If Borglum were to act on their behalf, it should be only as a messenger of statements made and prepared by them. They rejected any advocacy role by whites. Borglum, in turn, rejected the Pine Ridge Council's resolution and seemed deeply offended by its implications. In a petulant tone, he declared to the council's president:

This means that I must hold my tongue and do nothing for you, that I must not go to the great white father with your story and your needs. I shall respect your wish. It is bad; some evil spirit has done this, driven from you a good friend. I shall not go to Pine Ridge, shall not go to the great white father, shall not go to the Indian Office and shall make no suggestion for you have told them to give "no consideration to any request I make."

He concluded that he would never "come to you again."[36]

Yet Borglum himself seemed to understand the Indians' mistrust of whites. In January 1932, he wrote to James H. McGregor, superintendent of the Indian Bureau in Pine Ridge, and admitted his astonishment at the readiness of Native Americans to trust whites and his regard for their "sincerity and earnestness." As he rather cynically put it:

This amazes me the more when I see so much myself to distrust, in those in charge. Their gratitude to me is pathetic, it does not please nor deceive me, it is pathetic, it shows me how eager they are to grab at a new straw, a new hope to lean upon and to this I now see clearly, from my records, they would have had practically nothing, had not someone "outside" insisted on meat rations, clothes, blankets, presented those needs to Washington and followed each item to its successful conclusion.[37]

Closely related to Borglum's paternalistic attitude was his idealization of the Native American as a "noble savage." This paternalism shows through in his letter of December 1931 to General Douglas MacArthur, then chief of staff of the United States Army:

[The Indian of South Dakota is] a capable, high spirited, intelligent human being, left over from the Stone Age. Without our metal they would still be using flint pointed arrows or volcanic glass for their tools. They are the nation's wards. From our standpoint of civilization, under the restrictions we have prescribed by law and which are in force, they are helpless, practically homeless. They don't know how to live as we do and will not for some hundreds of years even arrive at the pueblo stage.[38]

Borglum then recounted his achievements on behalf of Native Americans and stressed the incompetence of the Indian Bureau. It seems fair to conclude that if Borglum could not perform at the center of events as the "father who knows best," he wanted no part of collective action.

Borglum's racist, paternalistic attitudes toward Native Americans were emblematic of his overall political and cultural sensibilities. For Borglum, in spite of his own Danish-Mormon heritage, Anglo-Saxon origins most truly marked the ideal individual. His racist beliefs characterized many of his dealings—he hired, for example, no African Americans or Asian Americans to work on Mount Rushmore. His fierce anti-Semitism, however, best illustrates the extent of his prejudices.

On the eve of America's involvement in World War II, Borglum wrote, "We

The Stone Mountain sculpture was conceived in 1915 but ended in a fiasco in 1925 due to squabbles over financing and control of production. The profile head of Lee alone was completed but was later effaced by the sculptor who was subsequently hired to complete the job. But it was never carried out.

will not get into the war [because we are] utterly sick of it and no combination of Jews, Communists, and [John L.] Lewis et al, can force us into it."[39] His attitudes here echoed those of Gerald L. K. Smith, Father Charles Coughlin, and other leading anti-Semites, who believed there was an international conspiracy of mostly Jewish bankers to subvert traditional Christian values. Although he spoke out against the Nazis, Borglum and others like him helped establish the "intellectual" foundations of fascism and institutionalized racism.

Borglum's involvement with the darker side of right-wing politics also included an ill-fated association with the Ku Klux Klan, which lent its support to a plan for Borglum to create a monument to the Confederacy at Stone Mountain, near Atlanta, Georgia. Although the plan was never carried out, Borglum found the KKK's views congenial. He not only added a Klan altar to his design for the memorial but also became a Klansman himself. He was attracted to the Klan's outsider, populist status and hoped to see it become a major political force that would put a member in the White House and influence national policy.[40]

Borglum identified with those in high public office and symbolically expressed power himself through his love of the colossal. His attraction to adventure and danger was part of his desire to emulate the western "macho" ethos, at odds with an effeminate character he perceived Jews to possess. He dissociated himself from the stereotype of the sensitive "artiste" and made much of his boxing and wrestling skills. He had a contradictory personality, perhaps also marked by an element of self-hate: while identifying, for example, with Populists and farmers (whom he wanted to see wrest power from the bankers and brokers), he pursued his fame within the wealthy strata

he professed to despise.

As an artist, Borglum was equally conservative, opposing the Works Projects Administration's support for artists during the Depression and rejecting the tenets of modernism. "Cubism," he once wrote, "is the extreme of our inability." His ambition was for popular success— not even his most monumental projects transcend the look of popular illustration. "Art is not self-sustaining," he wrote when he turned thirty, "until it becomes commercially valuable, and a man is not to be counted until he is in popular demand."[41] His technique was to aggrandize style with scale.

Borglum's sculpture on Mount Rushmore was an artist's fantasy of immortality come true. His obsession with fame, the force behind his best known work, could not have found a more appropriate site: his Mount Rushmore is packaged in a form geared to popular consumption. Almost overnight, Borglum turned Mount Rushmore, originally the outcome of a geologic process spanning some sixteen million years, into a colossal piece of kitsch, which his Native American critics have compared to a gigantic paperweight, among other things.[42]

Borglum, by contrast, compared Mount Rushmore very favorably with the Egyptian and Greek monuments of antiquity, even declaring it "infinitely greater than anything those ancient civilizations had accomplished.[43] In effect, he attempted to re-create nature in his own image. Mount Rushmore was to be a monument that would resist change and outlast corruption in society. In trying to tame a hostile environment as the pioneers had tamed the frontier, Borglum deeply carved into the Indians' holy mountain an eternally tangible yet spiritually shallow magisterial gaze.

Notes

I want to express my gratitude to Clare Spark for her insightful comments. I also want to thank James A. Chambers and Jim Popovich of the National Park Service, Mount Rushmore National Memorial; Frank Wheeler of the Atlanta Historical Society; and Delia Gilliland of the DeKalb Historical Society, Decatur, Georgia, for providing me with valuable research materials. Above all, I am grateful to Eric Boime for his diligent research, wise selection of archival materials, and critical comments that provided the basis for this paper.

1   Lincoln Borglum, *Mount Rushmore, The Story Behind the Scenery* (Las Vegas: KC Publications, 1977), p. 4. I found the following works on the subject indispensable to my study: Gerald W. Johnson, *The Undefeated* (New York: Minton, Balch and Company, 1927); Robert J. Casey and Mary Borglum, *Give the Man Room* (Indianapolis: The Bobbs-Merrill Company, 1952); Gilbert C. Fite, *Mount Rushmore* (Norman: University of Oklahoma Press, 1964); Karal Ann Marling, *The Colossus of Roads: Myth and Symbol Along the American Highway* (Minneapolis: University of Minnesota Press, 1984), pp. 83–89; Howard Shaff and Audrey Karl Shaff, *Six Wars at a Time* (Sioux Falls: The Center for Western Studies, 1985); Rex Alan Smith, *The Carving of Mount Rushmore* (New York: Abbeville Press, 1985).

2   L. Borglum, p. 8. See also Gutzon Borglum, "Engineering Problems to be Met in Mountain Sculpture," *The Black Hills Engineer* 18 (November 1930): 308–34.

3   It may be noted that one of the worst tyrants of the post–World War II era—Ferdinand Marcos of the Philippines—took Mount Rushmore as a source of inspiration in helping him to polish his image and shore up his program of "constitutional authoritarianism." Troops were ordered to dispossess recalcitrant Ibaloi Indians of their land in Tuba, Benguet Province, which was then converted into Marcos Park—a vast recreation site crowned with a gigantic concrete bust (estimated between eighty and a hundred feet high) of Marcos. See

A. Le Mont Wilson, "Monument for Marcos" (paper from Public Sculpture seminar, University of California at Los Angeles, 1987).

4   Borglum, quoted in Smith, p. 96; Gutzon Borglum, "Mountain Sculpture," *Scientific American* 148 (January 1933): 7–8.

5   Borglum, quoted in Casey and Borglum, pp. 28–29. For details on his parents' marriage see Borglum, "Mountain Sculpture," pp. 46–48; Shaff and Shaff, pp. 9–20.

6   Although Borglum once backed prolabor policies, his earlier reformist position was predicated on his paternalistic and benevolent disposition. He had no use for militant labor unions, especially as he became an entrepreneur himself. He paid his own nonunionized workers for their high-risk tasks a pitiful fifty cents to a dollar an hour, depending on the skills involved; see L. Borglum, p. 42.

7   Doane Robinson, *A Brief History of South Dakota* (New York: American Book Company, 1931), p. 227. See also Smith, p. 24.

8   L. Borglum, p. 13.

9   Gutzon Borglum, "The Political Importance and the Art Character of the National Memorial at Mount Rushmore," *Black Hills Engineer* 18 (November 1930): 285.

10 Borglum to George Gordon Battle, 27 September 1932, Gutzon Borglum Papers, Manuscript Division, Library of Congress (hereafter cited as Borglum Papers; unless otherwise noted, all citations of letters to and from Gutzon Borglum are from this source).

11 Borglum, quoted in L. Borglum, p. 48. Mary Borglum to "The Answer Man" radio program, 25 July 1949, Borglum Papers. Gilpin's geopolitical theory paid special attention to the Black Hills, whose fertility and "ever-varying scenery" would eventually attract "the densest population." He also noted that over the Black Hills rises the Cordillera of the

Sierra Madre, "the backbone of the world"; see William Gilpin, *Mission of the North American People, Geographical, Social, and Political* (Philadelphia: J. B. Lippincott & Co., 1873), p. 16.

12 In typical fashion, Borglum attributed his success in gaining Roosevelt's support to his own personal charm: "I just came from the White House—after a 3 quarters hour with the President, selling him Mount Rushmore—and I was a hundred per cent successful"; Borglum to his friend J. S. Lankford, April 1934, Gutzon Borglum Collection, Archives of American Art, Smithsonian Institution, roll 3056.

13 See Smith, pp. 311–12, 314.

14 Borglum to Lester Barlow, 29 August 1931. For Barlow's reference to Hoover, see "Barlow Looks to Young Business Men for Help," undated *New York Times* clipping, Borglum Papers.

15 Benton, quoted in Fite, *Mount Rushmore*, pp. 34–35; Borglum, draft for an address delivered in Kansas City, Mo., dated 15 April 1920, Borglum Papers.

16 John Charles Frémont, *Memoirs*, excerpted in *The Expeditions of John Charles Frémont*, ed. Donald Jackson and Mary Lee Spence (Urbana: University of Illinois Press, 1970–1984), 1:5. On Jessie Benton Frémont, see Shaff and Shaff, pp. 33–35, and Smith, pp. 50, 54.

17 Smith, p. 314.

18 See Robinson, *A Brief History of South Dakota*, p. 140.

19 Doane Robinson, *A History of the Dakota or Sioux Indians* (1904; reprint, Minneapolis: Ross and Haines, 1956), pp. 408–13.

20 For this sordid history, see George E. Hyde, *Red Cloud's Folk: A History of the Oglala Sioux Indians* (Norman: University of Oklahoma Press, 1937), pp. 217–19, 230–49, 277–85.

21 John Fire/Lame Deer and R. Erdoes,

Lame Deer: Seeker of Visions (New York: Simon and Schuster, 1972), p. 91–93, and chap. 5. See also Ernest M. Halliday, "Carving the American Colossus," *American Heritage* 28 (June 1977): 19–20. Ironically, the issue of *Scientific American* featuring Borglum's article "Mountain Sculpture" also contained a piece entitled "The Disappearance of the Red Man's Culture" (see n. 4).

For conservative responses to the demonstrations at Mount Rushmore in the early 1970s, see W. Morrell, "Kooks' Plea to Sioux Fails: Weather Helps Cool Threat to Mount Rushmore," *Los Angeles Herald-Examiner*, 25 November 1970; "Rushmore Encampment Must Stop," *Sioux Falls Argus-Leader*, 16 December 1970; "21 Indians Arrested Atop Mt. Rushmore," *Sioux Falls Argus-Leader*, 7 June 1971.

Not all Sioux, however, opposed the monument. The medicine man Black Elk went to pray on Mount Rushmore two days before Franklin Roosevelt attended the unveiling of the Jefferson head. He prayed for "unity of my people and the whites in the name of brotherhood" and for protection of Borglum and his men at work; quoted in Raymond J. DeMallie, ed., *The Sixth Grandfather* (Lincoln: University of Nebraska Press, 1984), pp. 65–66.

22 Borglum wrote to his friend, Dr. J. S. Lankford: "I have a new toy. I've been feeding eight-thousand Indians this winter. . . . I have provided them with clothing and blankets and now I'm developing a scheme to reorganize their life so they will be happy and I'll make the government do it. That's play . . . and a rest!"; Gutzon Borglum Collection, roll 3056.

23 Coolidge, quoted in Smith, pp. 152–53.

24 Ray Lyman Wilbur to Borglum, 22 October 1931. On Borglum's help, see Borglum to Congressman Edgar Howard of Nebraska, 12 January 1932. Noting that he had been sending the stricken community "about a thousand pounds of beef a week" for three months, Borglum stated emphatically, "Though knowing Indians, modeling, sketching, painting them, I was *shocked, ashamed, embarrassed* as an American, to see and realize . . . that we had shown so little sense, so little humanity, so little common justice as to allow the, not long ago, owners of all this territory, to be *robbed, bullied* and *starved* as we have *robbed, bullied* and *starved* these human beings."

25 Borglum, quoted in Shaff and Shaff, pp. 20–21. On his father's encounter with Indians, see Casey and Borglum, p. 27.

26 Borglum's draft of a letter to unknown addressee, 3 March 1934.

27 See the report "Sioux Nation Against the United States," 31 October 1931, Borglum Papers.

28 Borglum to Joseph M. Dixon, 2 October 1932; Borglum to Ray Lyman, 22 September 1932.

29 Chief Henry Standing Bear to Borglum, 4 December 1934; Borglum to Chief Henry Standing Bear, 16 January 1933.

30 Borglum to Chief James Red Cloud, 30 January 1938.

31 Chief Henry Standing Bear to Borglum, 4 December 1931. Borglum's disciple Korczak Ziolkowski launched a Crazy Horse monument a few miles from Mount Rushmore in 1947. Since his death, his family has continued to work toward the project's completion.

32 Borglum to Chief James Red Cloud, 30 January 1938.

33 Borglum to Joseph M. Dixon, 2 October 1932.

34 P. E. Byrne to Borglum, 10 August 1927; Borglum to Byrne, 30 November 1927.

35 Chief James Red Cloud to Borglum, 21 January 1932.

36 Borglum to "The President of the District Council and the District Council," 10 March 1932.

37 Borglum to James H. McGregor, 21 January 1932.

38 Borglum to General Douglas MacArthur, 24 December 1931.

39 Borglum to Amy Bassett, 6 September 1939. In an unpublished manuscript entitled "The Jewish Question," Borglum wrote that "Jews refuse to enter the mainstream of civilization, to become producing members of the world community. They do not share or create, but choose instead to clannishly hold onto their ways and with mere money buy and sell the efforts of others"; excerpted in Shaff and Shaff, pp. 103–9.

40 For Borglum's association with the KKK, see Shaff and Shaff, pp. 5–6, 145–51, 187–89, 195–203.

41 Borglum, draft of a letter to the *New York Times*, 18 July 1922, and quoted in Casey and Borglum, p. 57.

42 See John Fire/Lame Deer and R. Erdoes, p. 91.

43 See Borglum to Senator William Borah of Idaho, 12 March 1936.

Disneyland, 1955

Just Take the Santa Ana Freeway to the American Dream

Karal Ann Marling

The opening—or openings—of the new amusement park in Southern California did not go well. On 13 July, a Wednesday, the day of a private thirtieth anniversary party for Walt and Lil, Mrs. Disney herself was discovered sweeping the deck of the steamboat *Mark Twain* as the first guests arrived for a twilight shakedown cruise. On Thursday and Friday, during gala preopening tributes to Disney film music at the Hollywood Bowl, workmen back in Anaheim, some twenty-three miles away, struggled to finish paving the streets that would soon lead to Fantasyland, Adventureland, Frontierland, and Tomorrowland. Last-minute strikes had compelled the builders to haul in asphalt all the way from San Diego.

The invitation-only press preview and dedication, broadcast over a coast-to-coast TV hookup on 17 July, was a disaster from start to finish. At dawn, with carpenters and plumbers still working against the clock, traffic on the freeway was backed up for seven miles, and gridlock prevailed on the secondary roads surrounding the former orange grove along Harbor Boulevard. Studio publicists had issued twenty thousand tickets to reporters, local dignitaries, Disney employees, corporate investors, and Hollywood stars—including Eddie Fisher, Debbie Reynolds, Lana Turner, Danny Thomas, and Frank Sinatra. By midmorning, however, more than thirty thousand people were already packed inside the earthen berm that was supposed to seal off Disney's domain from the cares of the outside world. Some of the extra "invitees" flashed counterfeit passes. Others had simply climbed the fence, slipping into the park in behind-the-scene spots where dense vegetation formed the background for a boat ride through a make-believe Amazon jungle.

Afterwards, they called it "Black Sunday." Anything that could go wrong did. The food ran out. There weren't enough drinking fountains. A gas leak temporarily shut down Fantasyland, site of many of the twenty-two new Disney-designed rides the crowd had come to inspect. It was terribly hot, too. Main Street USA melted, and visitors' high heels stuck fast in the fresh asphalt. The nervous proprietor (who had spent the night in the park) accidentally locked himself in his apartment above the turn-of-the-century firehouse near the front gate. As the moment approached for the boss to welcome a vast, stay-at-home audience to his California kingdom through the magic of television, Walt Disney (1901–1966) was nowhere to be found. And somehow, ABC's twenty-four live cameras managed to cover all the glitches: the ladies walking out of their shoes; "Davy Crockett," star of Disney's new weekly series, drenched by a hyperactive sprinkler system as he thrashed about on horseback in Frontierland's western scenery; the regal Irene Dunne showering announcer Art Linkletter with glass and soda water while attempting to christen the *Mark Twain* on televised cue.

The Carolwood-Pacific line, the railroad train in the garden of Disney's new Holmby Hills house, was the real inspiration for Disneyland.

A souvenir map of Disneyland in the 1950s shows the various "lands," the peripheral railroad, and the controlled access to the park through the stage-set re-creation of Main Street USA.

Bob Cummings and Ronald Reagan shared the network hosting duties—and a whole range of maddening "technical difficulties"—with Linkletter. Sometimes the screen simply went blank. Audio and video transmissions winked on and off at will. When the voice-over described Cinderella's coach at the head of a passing parade, the picture showed Roy Rogers and Dale Evans. Linkletter strolled blithely through the portcullis of Sleeping Beauty's Castle and emerged from the other side, seconds later, without his microphone. Walt Disney accidentally appeared on camera ahead of schedule, chatting with the crew and wondering aloud how the show was going. "'Dateline Disneyland,'" concluded the *New York Times*, had "captured some fun and fantasy, the elements . . . that are supposed to make the place tick." But despite such flashes of honest spontaneity, the tightly scripted ninety-minute program—like the whole Disneyland enterprise—had serious flaws. It was entirely too "Hollywood," according to the *Times*: slick, commercial, star-studded, glitzy.

And too reverential, too much like "the dedication of a national shrine." Cummings, for instance, repeatedly assured viewers that cultural history was being made in Orange County before their very eyes: "I think that everyone here will one day be as proud to have been at *this* opening as the people who were there at the dedication of the Eiffel Tower." And the commemorative plaque, which Disney read aloud during his segment of the broadcast, was both portentous and vaguely imperialistic in tone:

To all who come to this happy place . . . Welcome. Disneyland is your land. Here, age relives fond memories of the past, and here youth may savor the challenge and promise of the future. Disneyland is dedicated to the ideals, the dreams, and hard facts that have created America . . . with the hope that it will be a source of joy and inspiration to all the world.[1]

Park officials, of course, had no time to brood over iffy reviews: the *real* opening, for the general public, was less than twelve

Hosts of the televised opening, 17 July 1955: Ronald Reagan, Bob Cummings, and Art Linkletter. The presence of these small-screen stars of the period signaled the importance of television to the genesis, iconography, and formal design of Disneyland.

hours off, and, if Sunday's mobs were any portent of things to come, Monday was going to be wild. Dave McPherson, a senior at Long Beach State College, stationed himself at the ticket window at 2:00 A.M., just about the time the state police began to report abnormal traffic volumes building along the periphery of Anaheim. By 8:00 A.M., two hours before the posted start of business, eight thousand merrymakers had already queued up behind McPherson, and the hundred-acre parking lot was almost full. At 10:00 A.M., Walt Disney appeared and personally greeted the first two kids in line: little Christine Vess, age five, from North

Hollywood, and her seven-year-old cousin, Michael Schwartner, of Bakersfield. Although the children got all the media attention, the clear majority of those who followed Disney inside were grown-ups, determined to experience for themselves what only the elite had been privileged to enjoy the day before. They swarmed over the park, eating everything in sight, dropping garbage everywhere, tossing their kids from hand to hand to get them a seat on the King Arthur Carousel, nearly swamping the *Mark Twain* in their eagerness to clamber aboard. But they came, they had a wonderful time, and, in defiance of

The steamboat *Mark Twain* plies the Rivers of America at Disneyland, carrying visitors back into a special, 1950s version of American history.

strong negative criticism from travel writers, influential columnists, glossy news magazines, and itinerant intellectuals, they kept on coming in enormous numbers, more than a million of them in the first seven weeks alone, exceeding all estimates and giving backers reason to believe their risky, $17 million investment might someday pay off.

Indeed, even before the previews began, speculation about costs and profits all but overshadowed discussion of the park's entertainment value. And while the press did not fail to wax eloquent about the chronic traffic tie-ups around Disneyland, most of the first-year complaints came down to dollars and cents. "Walt's dream is a nightmare," wrote one particularly disillusioned member of the fourth estate.

To me [the park] felt like a giant cash register, clicking and clanging, as creatures of Disney magic came tumbling down from their lofty places in my daydreams to peddle their charms with the aggressiveness of so many curbside barkers. With this harsh stroke, he transforms a beautiful dream into a blatant nightmare.[2]

Other critics agreed. To them, Disneyland was just another tourist trap—a bigger, pricier version of the Santa Claus villages and the seedy Storylands cast up by the postwar baby boom and the blandishments of the automobile industry. It was "commercial," a roadside money machine, cynically exploiting the innocent dreams of childhood. On his second visit to the complex, a wire service writer cornered Disney and asked him about his profit margin. Walt, whose stake in the success of the venture was as much emotional as it was financial, was furious:

We have to charge what we do because this Park cost a lot to build and maintain. I have no government subsidy. The public is my subsidy. I mortgaged everything I own and put it in jeopardy for this Park. Commercial? . . . They're crazy! We have lots of free things [here]. No other place has as high a quality. I stand here in the Park and talk to people. It's a most gratifying thing. All I've got from the public is thank-yous.[3]

Middlebrows continued to carp about the potential profitability of Disneyland, as if capitalism were an unfamiliar concept or Disney's park, by virtue of its use of characters that all Americans knew and loved from his cartoon features, ought to have been in the public domain—free, or almost free, like a national park or national shrine. With few exceptions, highbrow critics of the 1950s despised Disneyland for similar reasons. Writing for the *Nation*, the novelist Julian Halevy took exception to an enterprise that charged admission to visit ersatz environments tricked out as Never-Never Land, the Wild West, or the Amazon basin. At Disneyland, he argued, "the whole world . . . has been reduced to a sickening blend of cheap formulas packaged to sell." The sin of commercialism, in other words, was compounded by the fact that Disney's Amazon was not the real thing:

[The] overwhelming feeling that one carries away is sadness for the empty lives which accept such tawdry substitutes. On the river boat, I heard a woman exclaim glowingly to her husband, "What imagination they have!" He nodded, and the pathetic gladness that illuminated his face as a papier-mâché crocodile sank beneath the muddy surface of the ditch was a grim indictment of the way of life for which this feeble sham represented escape and adventure.

Like Las Vegas, Halevy concluded, Disneyland was vulgar—American culture at its most corrupt, contemptible, dollar driven, and bogus.[4]

One rabid critic faulted Adventureland's Jungle Cruise for its fake, "papier-maché" crocodiles.

Disneyland had its champions, too. The science fiction writer Ray Bradbury went to Disneyland in the company of the actor Charles Laughton and loved the place, as much for the fact that the robot crocodiles were made out of plastic as for any other reason. Unlike the genuine article—dangerous and often invisible to passing boatloads of tourists—the toothy Disney version was perfect: tireless, predictable, and benign, the very ideal of "croc-ness" on a sparkling clean Amazon in Anaheim, California. Disney's land as a whole was a lot like that plastic crocodile. It was utopian, perfected—or perfectible.

What is most important about Laughton and Bradbury's excursion to Disneyland is the ripping good time the pair had "laugh[ing] at the wild palaver of our riverboat steerman's jokes, duck[ing] when pistols were fired dead-on at charging hippopotamuses, and bask[ing] face up in the rain, eyes shut, as we sailed under Schweitzer Falls."[5] The Jungle Cruise was a visceral, sensual experience, like stepping, somehow, into the Technicolor confines of *The African Queen* and becoming a member of the cast, bound for some exotic coast in the company of Bogart and Hepburn.

In fact, the ride had been loosely based on the adventure described in that popular 1951 film and on its picturesque river craft. But, in the end, the matinee voyage and the Disneyland cruise were very different propositions. The movie, like all movies, was perfect: the actors, the director, and the editors reshot and tinkered until they got everything right. When *The African Queen* played in the neighborhood theater, filmgoers saw a finished work of art up there on the screen, a moving picture, complete, remote, unreal—and detached from themselves, despite the implicit intimacy of the darkened room. What Disney's "imagineers" added to the movie by transferring it in three dimensions to Anaheim was the missing quotient of "reality": running water, gunshots, grinning crocodiles that swam and snapped their jaws to expose pointy, plastic teeth. If there were no mosquitoes, no "Montezuma's Revenge," no accidental distractions from the narrative unfolding along the river, there was an abundance of convincing atmosphere to smell and to feel dripping down one's neck. The once-passive viewer now became an actor, a real-life participant, "face up in the rain" as a rackety little boat plowed under Schweitzer Falls. During the 1950s, Walt Disney often said that movies were beginning to bore him, because when they were done, they were done. But because it was *real*, Disneyland could never be completed. It was always perfectible—and that was the challenge. That was the real fun.

The intellectuals who hated Disneyland did not reckon with all that fun. Nor, it would seem, did they share in the genuine pleasure of being only slightly terrified by a plastic (*not* papier-maché) crocodile on a nice, clean (never, *never* muddy) Amazon less than three feet deep. Whatever else it aspired to be, Disneyland was an amusement park, a place for good times, for the willing suspension of disbelief. It was not a zoo or a scientific expedition gone awry: it was a place where plastic crocodiles were better than live ones, since half the fun came from noticing that the beasts were *almost* real. The tension between perfection and reality, between the real and the more-or-less real, was a primary source of the visitor's delight. The critics, undelighted, saw only plastic and profits in a society hopelessly corrupted by TV, suburbia, tail fins, and too few distinctions of caste and class. "Ours is not so much an age of vulgarity as of vulgarization," wrote a bilious Louis Kronenberger on the declension of American culture in the 1950s: "Everything [is] tampered with or touched up, or adulterated or watered down, in an effort to make it palatable, in an effort to make it pay."[6]

Disney among the Highbrows

Highbrow hysteria over Disneyland and the potential profits to be made there was symptomatic of a deeper problem that had plagued the Disney studio since the early 1940s and the release of *Fantasia*. An effort to bridge the gap between elite culture and mass entertainment, *Fantasia* combined cartoon imagery with classical music conducted by Leopold Stokowski of the Philadelphia Orchestra. Although, for a variety of reasons (including glitches in a new movie sound system), the film was a commercial failure, it typified an optimistic strain in prewar aesthetic thinking that admitted no hard-and-fast barriers between high and low art. Throughout the late 1940s, despite the scorn of the critics, Disney still clung gamely to his vision of creating a middle-brow, middle-class art. Salvador Dali took up residence at the studio to work on a domesticated version of *Fantasia* based on the music of the Americas. But on the weekends the Surrealist was sometimes found tootling around the Disney family's backyard in suburban Los Angeles on

Walt's new steam locomotive in the company of movie stars and rail buffs. The train was a symbol of transformation, of movement, a sign that Disney was about to leave high art and its troublesome practitioners behind. When the *New York Times* critic Bosley Crowther came to visit in the early 1950s, he found his old friend uninterested in making movies, with or without Salvador Dali. Instead, noted the puzzled Crowther, Walt was "almost weirdly concerned with the building of a miniature railroad engine and a string of cars."[7]

This new Walt accepted and even accentuated the distinction between art and the typical Disney product. In his authorized autobiography, outlined by the studio but presented in the guise of a series of 1956–57 *Saturday Evening Post* articles by his elder daughter, Diane Disney Miller wrote:

The sophisticates and the eggheads . . . write off Dad's work as "Disney's picture post-card art," but Dad is unconcerned. He says, "If picture post-card art moves millions of people, then I like it. If I'm corny, then millions of people in this country must be corny too.

We're not trying to entertain the critics. . . . I'll take my chances with the public."[8]

Togetherness and Automobility

The public liked Disneyland. On New Year's Eve, 1957, attendance reached the ten million mark. Statistics further indicated that a hefty 40 percent of the guests had come from outside California, often driving long distances to reach their destination. If the highway and the habit of "automobility" were major factors in Disneyland's success, the outing in the family car was also a key element in the standardized creation story Disney used to explain how he had come to build America's first theme park. In the Diane

Disneyland's horse-drawn trolley represents one of many possible means of moving around the grounds. Like the suburban culture to which it appealed so strongly, the park is about mobility.

Disney series, it all begins with "Daddy's Days," those spare afternoons when a busy father finds time to take his two little girls to the zoo or the merry-go-round in Griffith Park. Other anecdotes find the trio bound for an unspecified kiddieland or a ma-and-pa amusement park on La Cienega Boulevard. Despite all the variations in detail, the meaning of the narrative never varies. There are always two crucial lessons to be learned from the "Daddy's Days" tale: the importance of family entertainment and the baleful condition of the old Coney Island–style amusement park. "I would take them to the merry-go-round" or the Ferris wheel, Walt Disney remembered,

and sit on a bench eating peanuts while they rode. And sitting there, alone, I felt that there should be something built, some kind of a family park where parents and children could have fun together.

The so-called parks the Disneys haunted on Saturdays and Sundays were "dirty, phony places, run by tough-looking people." There was a crying "need for something new," he thought, "but I didn't know what it was."[9]

The unspoken urge to build "some kind of a family park" brought the two divergent sides of Disney's personality together for the first time. The Walt Disney of the big, looping signature was a busy studio head, but he was family man too: a typical Los Angeles commuter, a suburbanite with a comfy, unpretentious house in Holmby Hills. The difference was in the backyard. In the Disney garden, everybody could play in a cunning replica of the dwarfs' cottage from *Snow White*, complete with picket fence and gingerbread gables, built by the studio shop as a present for Diane and her sister Sharon. Here, in his own backyard, in the expanding leisure hours that had suddenly become a factor in the life of the nuclear family, the interests of the businessman and the father began to converge. Compared with the average, seedy kiddieland, the Snow White cottage suggested that the Walt Disney Company could probably do a vastly superior job of promoting weekend togetherness.

While Disney's interest in family activities anticipated the concept by a decade or more, the actual smarmy word *togetherness* was coined by *McCall's* in the 1954 Easter issue and became the rallying cry of a moral crusade endorsed by anxious editors, clergymen, and advertisers. Togetherness legitimized the new, postwar suburban family—affluent, isolated, reared on a bland diet of TV and TV dinners—by stressing the compensatory benefits of a greater paternal role in the household. Togetherness made fathers into full domestic partners with their wives and provided healthy male influences in the formation of young psyches. Togetherness meant, in effect, that Daddy occasionally changed diapers, helped with the shopping and the vacuuming, and took charge of the kids on Saturday or Sunday afternoons. And whatever its erotic burden of ornamental chrome, the bloated American automobile of the 1950s was as large as it was because it was a *family* car, perfect for jaunts and outings with Daddy at the wheel, Mommy right beside him, and Sis and Junior squealing with anticipation in the spacious backseat.

According to the ads, the car promised freedom—"freedom to come and go as we please in this big country of ours," Ford rhapsodized.[10] It also liberated the family from the conformity of the suburb, from rows of identical houses, rigid social rituals, unspoken codes of conduct, and written rules governing the proper trimming of lawns. The car allowed the family to escape the pressures of modern times: out there, on the freeway, it was still possible to play the part of the pioneer, headed bravely off into that unknown America of the presuburban past, in search of adventure and self-exploration. The automobile let the family outrun its fears of recession, of a sudden end to the prosperity of big cars and weekend fun— or its countervailing fears of prosperity and the soulless materialism of which Americans were so often accused.

Early visitors to Disneyland seem not to have noticed any correlation between driving to the park and what they did when they got there. Mainly they went for another long ride: on the old-fashioned steam train, circling the grounds; on the Model-T—era fire trucks and the horse-drawn trolleys along Main Street; on the *Mark Twain*, coursing through Frontierland; on the Jungle Cruise through Adventureland; on Tomorrowland's rocket to the moon; on Mr. Toad's wild putt-putt through Fantasyland. Eschewing conventional shows and walk-through attractions, Disneyland was premised largely on vehicles, many of them designed to conjure up a faraway, long-ago world of adventure and restless freedom. In 1971 the late Reyner Banham became the first to posit that what happened inside Disneyland bore a direct relationship to what was going on outside the gates:

Set in the middle of a city obsessed with mobility, a city whose most characteristic festival is the Rose Parade in Pasadena, fantastically sculptured Pop inventions entirely surfaced with live flowers rolling slowly down Colorado Boulevard every New Year's Day—in this city Disneyland offers illicit pleasures of mobility. Ensconced in a sea of giant parking-lots in a city devoted to the automobile, it provides transportation that does not exist outside—steam trains, monorails, people-movers . . . not to mention pure transport fantasies such as simulated space-trips and submarine rides.[11]

For Walt Disney and his fellow commuters, Disneyland's rides made a daily chore into a treat by isolating and emphasizing the pleasurable aspects of driving. What was a metaphoric escape on the freeway, for instance, became a real or an almost real escape aboard the *E. P. Ripley*, the first steam locomotive put into service on the Santa Fe and Disneyland Railroad that circled the park. In a society

Walt Disney's obsession with trains began at the Santa Fe depot in Marceline, Missouri. The structure shown here replaced the original station, but this train would inspire Disneyland's earliest Tomorrowland "future-liners."

in which the ticket to adulthood was the driver's license, the Disneyland transportation system permitted regression to childhood through the simple expedient of inviting grown-ups to become passengers. And the destinations were no longer the office, the shopping center, or some sleazy, little amusement park. Disney's boats and trains went instead to the places of the heart, to a happy past, to memories or dreams of a perfect childhood.

The Carolwood-Pacific Railroad

Mrs. Disney believed that Disneyland sprang directly from her husband's lifelong obsession with the Atchison, Topeka and Santa Fe Railroad. The main line ran through his boyhood hometown, Marceline, Missouri, on its way to Kansas City and distant California. During his teenage years Disney had worked (like Thomas Edison before him) as a weekend news- and candy-butcher on the run from Kansas City to Chicago, and he spent an exciting summer in 1917 plying his trade on the West Coast route. In 1923 Walt had taken that same train to Hollywood to seek his fortune in the cartoon business: corporate lore had it that Mickey Mouse was later invented in a westbound Pullman car out of Chicago, somewhere between Toluca, Illinois, and La Junta,

Colorado, as a disappointed Disney returned from New York after learning that his first animated hero had been stolen by an unscrupulous distributor. Thereafter, in times of distress, a train trip became his antidote of choice. Plagued by financial worries, Disney had a full-blown nervous breakdown in 1931. "I simply went to pieces," he told his daughter, and, on the advice of his doctors, he boarded the Santa Fe for a therapeutic trip.[12] In the late 1940s, the doctors suggested more time away from the office, in pursuit of a hobby, perhaps. And Walt Disney turned to trains again. He built a railroad on the canyon side of his own Holmby Hills backyard at 355 Carolwood Avenue, high above the UCLA campus, between Bel Air and Beverly Hills.

Direct inspiration for the one-eighth-scale home railroad came from the studio. One of the most engaging inventions in *Dumbo*, released in 1941, was *Casey, Jr.*, the determined little engine. While *Dumbo* was still on the drawing boards, animator Ward Kimball bought a real, full-size 1881 mining engine and a passenger car and took the boss for a ride on his five-hundred-foot track. Soon Kimball had added a second working locomotive and an abandoned western station to his garden in the San Gabriel Valley. Fellow animator Ollie Johnston remembered what happened next:

Walt Disney's railroading hobby gave him the illusion of control over an increasingly chaotic and ungovernable world.

Ward Kimball had his steam engine back in '40 or '41. He got this big steam engine from the Nevada Central . . . I think. Walt was always interested and then, along in 1946, I started building a miniature engine . . . and I think it was the next Christmas, Kimball came into the room and said, "Hey, let's go up to Walt's office. He's got a Lionel train up there that he set up for his nephew." So we went up to his office and while we were looking at the model, Walt turned to me and said, "I didn't know you were interested in trains." I told him I was building a steam engine. He said, "You are? I always wanted a backyard railroad myself." So he came out to where we were

building mine, in Santa Monica. He came out two or three times and he started to get ideas on how he was going to build his. They started building it here in the shop, several months later.[13]

Disney recouped part of the cost of the work done on his first engine by selling duplicate sets of the scale drawings to an eager public. Both Kimball and Johnston collected railroad memorabilia in addition to building models and restoring old trains. This widespread craze for railroading in the 1940s and 1950s was an aspect of the broader popular interest in "Americana." Antiques gave mobile Americans a

The Disney farm outside Marceline, ca. 1925. Disney remembered every detail of the place. In the 1940s, he built with his own hands a small replica of the family barn, alongside his backyard train layout.

Walt and his sister Ruth, ages seven and five, respectively

sense of rootedness; hobbies and crafts attached leisure activity firmly to the den or basement workshop of the family home. With his daughters approaching the stage of roving adolescence, Disney frequently tried to justify his own train on the grounds that it would keep the girls and their friends close to home. Mainly, however, the distaff side of the family proved indifferent to his hobby, and the Carolwood-Pacific served instead to keep Walt Disney at home, where his social life revolved almost completely around his pastime. Ward Kimball attended gatherings at Disney's new Holmby Hills residence:

It was here that he started throwing his own railroad-type parties, inviting a few close friends to ride on his miniature train. Sometimes he would ask me to come out and take care of running the train while he was busy making ice-cream sodas in his own full-sized soda fountain by the pool. I remember one party in particular because it had a rather bizarre guest list headed by actress Una Merkel, the agent Jules Stine (whom Walt kept calling "The Octopus") and Salvador Dali, the surrealist.[14]

But the train was clearly much more than a conversation piece for movie-colony parties; it answered a deeply felt need on Disney's part, becoming an extension of his personality and a reflection of his autobiography. Only the most intimate of friends received cards making them honorary vice presidents of the line. And before the new house was built, its president and chief engineer had rejected several spectacular sites because they were too small for a workable layout. Never noted for his personal extravagance, Disney had nonetheless spent a small fortune to relocate power lines so they could not be seen by the passengers; he spent another huge sum on a concrete tunnel running under the garden so as not to disturb Mrs. Disney's flower beds. He also presented Lillian with a bona fide legal document giving him control of the right-of-way in exchange for such aesthetic considerations. With his own hands he built the little freight cars (one passenger to a car) and a caboose (fitted out with miniature bunks and newspapers printed to scale) in a trackside workshop that was a precise replica of the barn on his forty-eight-acre boyhood farm back in Linn County, Missouri.

Disney's ties with Marceline remained strong throughout his life. Walt, at right, and his brother, Roy, at far left, returned to the Linn County farmstead in 1956.

at last firmly in control. Perched atop the cab of a one-eighth-scale steam engine, modeled after the Southern Pacific's old number 173, Walt Disney was master of all that he surveyed, the engineer of his own destiny, in charge of his future and of his own miniaturized and idealized past.

The Chicago Railroad Fair

Ollie Johnston saw a direct connection between the Carolwood-Pacific and the genesis of the park in Anaheim. "The next thing you knew, Walt was thinking about putting a railroad around here, at the Studio," he insisted.

There was a guy in Los Gatos who had some engines that were used in the 1915 [Panama-Pacific] Fair in San Francisco, and Walt was thinking of buying those. Then he got to thinking there wasn't enough room here and before long there was a Disneyland.

But the Chicago Railroad Fair of 1948 was the crucial event that linked the model train to a new kind of themed amusement park in Walt Disney's own mind. The trip to Chicago was part of Disney's regimen of relaxation. Told to get away from the studio completely, he seized upon, as the ideal cure for the blues, a display of railroad rolling stock and memorabilia being mounted in Burnham Park. Ward Kimball was easily persuaded to come along. And when the two train fans boarded a passenger coach to start their adventure, they discovered that E. P. Ripley, president of the Santa Fe, had left an open invitation for them to join the engineer in the cab. "I had never, ever seen [Walt] look so happy," Kimball said.[15]

Sponsored by thirty-eight major American carriers, including the Santa Fe, the railroad fair ostensibly honored the centenary of the first steam locomotive to enter Chicago, the nation's greatest rail

The geographer Yi-Fu Tuan maintains that the planned and planted garden—or backyard—is, by its very essence, a statement about the dominance of the human personality over nature. The garden imposes order over chaotic natural growth: in that one place, the householder tames and subdues the primal forces of growth, death, and regeneration—the forces of time itself. Via twenty-six hundred feet of railroad track circling his backyard, Walt Disney was likewise able to control his environment, to travel back into a rural childhood perfected by memory. He could make his cartoons come to hissing, chugging, three-dimensional life. Bedeviled by the vagaries of finance and artistic taste in his business life, here in his own backyard Disney was

center. A replica of the city's first station was built on the fairgrounds. A working model of the newspaper printing press Edison used aboard the Grand Trunk Western in 1862 was also prominently displayed. Mrs. Casey Jones, the eighty-four-year-old widow of the legendary engineer, rode at the head of the opening day parade. But the Railroad Fair was not an idle exercise in retrospection. Despite the plethora of railroad relics, the fair was being held to drum up business and investment capital for modern-day lines, hard hit by the competition from cars and planes and burdened with an inventory of equipment all but worn out by hard use during World War II. "Few railroads could sell stock today," a trade journal confessed as the $2 million extravaganza geared up for the summer on the site of the old Century of Progress Exposition.[16]

The Railroad Fair took on something of the futuristic flavor of its predecessor, with displays of the rolling stock of the 1950s and 1960s, including various sleek, domed passenger cars and the Chesapeake and Ohio's mysterious "X" train, designed for speeds approaching 150 miles per hour. The crisp, uniformed attendants, the banners and flags, the orderliness, and the festive atmosphere also rekindled the utopian optimism that visitors to the 1933 Chicago Exposition and the 1939 New York World's Fair remembered so well. But for every train of tomorrow showcased in Chicago in 1948, there were dozens from yesterday. A retrospective mood prevailed by careful design. Experts had calculated the number of active railroad model makers at 100,000; most of them were steeped in the arcanum of railroad lore, as were the many thousands more who collected "railroadiana," took pictures of rare and unusual sights at trackside, and went on trips under steam power. The total annual investment of these hobbyists was more than $10 million, and organizers of the Chicago Fair of 1948 were eager to tap their

interest, enthusiasm, and goodwill. Besides, as one rail executive put it, there were really 144 million train buffs in the United States: everybody who had ever dreamed of adventure when a whistle pierced the silence of the night, who had ever imagined standing in the crowd at Promentory Point when the golden spike joined the rails, who had ever thought of heading out to L.A. for a fresh start aboard the Santa Fe's California Limited.[17] So, with a perfunctory nod to tomorrow, the Railroad Fair set about indulging the American appetite for pistons, steam, smokestacks, cowcatchers, and the fabled historical romance of the rails.

The fairgrounds gave pride of place to the old steam engines. Strung out along the shore of Lake Michigan, the fair was separated from the city and the rest of Burnham Park by a narrow-gauge railroad called the Deadwood Central. A ticket to ride cost ten cents. Serving two stations (copies of historic depots in the Wild West), one at either end of the tract, the six-car train was the first thing a visitor encountered and the actual means of transit from one attraction to another. Between the right-of-way and the water, the exhibits were deployed along the tracks in no particular order: a carousel, equipped with coach seats instead of wooden horses, cheek by jowl with the "Florida in Chicago" venue, which contained a full-size southern mansion, a sandy Gulf Coast beach with an orange juice bar, and a motorized diorama showing scenes evoked by Stephen Foster tunes. Most of the exhibits, in fact, recreated in convincing atmospheric detail some exotic vacation spot best reached by train.

The Great Northern, the Northern Pacific, and the Burlington, for instance, collaborated on a massive display that aimed to replicate famous points of interest in the Rocky Mountain and Pacific Coast regions. These included a real working dude ranch, transported to

The *Great Locomotive Chase* (1956), a Disney movie utilizing steam engines destined one day to circle Disneyland, premiered in Marceline at the Uptown Theater.

Chicago piece by piece; a colossal mechanical statue of Paul Bunyan that wagged its head and talked; a rodeo; dioramas and panoramas of all kinds; and a much-improved version of Old Faithful "operated by trained engineers, resorting to some very tricky work with steam pipes and water pumps." Whereas the original in Yellowstone Park erupted once an hour, Chicago's Old Faithful was scheduled to go off every fifteen minutes for the convenience of busy tourists with other

things to see. Many were bound for the Santa Fe exhibit, which consisted of a southwestern Indian village, with a trading post, a curio shop, a crafts building, an Apache *wikiup*, a Navajo medicine lodge, a full-scale pueblo, and more than 150 natives in residence, performing their dances and selling their wares to fair goers. "You'll think you really are on an Indian reservation . . . when you visit the Santa Fe Village," read the ads in the nation's newspapers. Nearby, the scene changed abruptly to the French Quarter in New Orleans, courtesy of the Illinois Central. Here, by some miracle of showmanship, were the iron balconies, "the quaint narrow streets, the tiny shops, and the hidden courtyards that have [always] captivated travelers."[18]

"Villages" were not new to big expositions, of course. Since the nineteenth century, communities of Philippine tribesmen, Native Americans, and other picturesque peoples had been a regular feature of world's fairs, along with reproductions of historic buildings, dioramas, models, and the like. Walt Disney had seen such sights at New York's 1939 "World of Tomorrow," and Chicagoans were quick to compare the environmental displays of 1948 with the popular Belgian Village built for the Century of Progress Exposition fifteen years earlier. Indeed, the Railroad Fair occupied the portion of the old exposition grounds once devoted to the Alpine Village, the Hawaiian Village, the Spanish Village, a Mayan temple, and a replica of Fort Dearborn. What was different about the Railroad Fair was the coherence and concentration of the experience—the sensation of having dropped in on most of the nation's beauty spots in a single day via a magical train.

Reality rarely intruded. Even dining was apt to be a part of the illusion of being in Yellowstone or the Southwest. Thus it was possible to have lunch served by a cowhand from the business end of a

chuck wagon and dinner in the dining car
of a Rock Island streamliner fitted out as a
Mexican hacienda staffed by grandees in
appropriate costume. "By dramatizing . . . ,
by making every exhibit a novelty in
entertainment as well as education," the
New York Times remarked, "the railroads
have graphically driven home a realization
of how much they mean in our national
economy."[19] Although their success in
conveying economic realities remains
arguable, the railroads succeeded in
vivifying the sense of being there by
making the American scene come alive to
the senses. All that was missing was a
narrative, a story that tied together,
somehow, all the stops on the itinerary of
the Deadwood Central: the Old West and
the Wild West, the Vieux Carre, a
tropical beach, and the transportation
technology of the future.

The story line was supplied by a four-
times-a-day play—"Wheels A-Rolling"—
enacted by moving locomotives. The
lakefront "stage" was a pair of tracks,
framed by huge concrete wings. Specta-
tors sat in a grandstand facing the water
and watched as each engine puffed into

view. A narrator described its significance
over a loudspeaker, and in the open space
between the two sets of tracks, actors
mimed famous scenes from railroad
history. During the course of the hour's
presentation, 220 actors, by virtue of swift
costume changes, played 800 roles in a
saga that stretched from 1673, when the
canoe was the most up-to-date means of
transportation, to the present day,
represented by the last word in passenger
coaches and diesel locomotives.

Of the pageant's twelve acts, those that
got the biggest hand depicted the passage
of Lincoln's funeral train, the driving of
the Golden Spike, the famous race
between the B & O's *Tom Thumb* and a
horse, and "a Harvey House scene."[20]
Fred Harvey's turn-of-the-century hotels
on the Santa Fe route were also an
important precedent for the Railroad Fair
itself. Designed to encourage tourism by
providing intriguing destinations for
passengers, Harvey Houses used pseudo-
southwestern architecture, menus, and
gift shops to create an all-encompassing
atmosphere of authenticity, like that of
the 1948 Indian village. In both cases,

"Villages" at the Chicago Railroad Fair, like this pueblo re-creation, inspired Disney's later simulated environments, replete with period restaurants, souvenir shops, and employees in old-fashioned costume.

unlike the genuine article, the replica offered predictable quality, safety, and every civilized amenity. The experience became an unscripted play, with the touring tenderfoot in a starring role.

Walt Disney, as the fair organizers were well aware, knew all about the Harvey Houses. Because of his interest in railroading, he was no doubt familiar, too, with Edward Hungerford's other railroad pageants, the best known of which, "Railroads on Parade," had been mounted at the New York World's Fair in 1939. But Disney's fame alone was probably sufficient reason for his temporary inclusion in the cast of "Wheels A-Rolling" as an engi-

neer and dramatic performer. According to Ward Kimball, during their stay in Chicago,

sometimes Walt would be invited to don period costume and take part in some of the historical episodes. I remember one in particular where he was part of the Santa Fe's Harvey House bit. Walt would watch the other actors and play it accordingly, all in pantomime. In the meantime, I was busy filming the whole show and Walt's cameo appearance from the orchestra pit. We were both acting like a couple of kids.

All the way home, Disney talked to Kimball about building an amusement

A typical Harvey House in Santa Fe, New Mexico, ca. 1930, hints at Walt Disney's Frontierland.

park. "Disneyland was already forming in his mind. Of course, he thought [it] should have an almost full-sized steam train . . . that he could have fun operating himself on days when the park was closed."[21]

Los Angeles vs. Disneyland

As it was finally built, some six years later, Disneyland owed a great deal to the 1948 Chicago Railroad Fair. First and foremost, of course, was the Santa Fe and Disneyland line that defined the boundaries of the park, served as the chief artery of internal transportation, and even determined the scale of the buildings adjacent to the tracks. The park's separate "lands," each with a historic or geographic theme reiterated by every aspect of the environment, down to the very shops and restaurants and the costumed employees in charge of them, recalled the "village" layout in Chicago with its period eateries and trading posts. Even the kinds of places and concepts singled out for special treatment by the fair's planners—the Old West, the technological future of railroading, tropical Florida, the age of steam— bore more than a passing resemblance to Disneyland's ultimate constituent parts, from Main Street USA to Tomorrowland. Only Fantasyland was not taken from the prototype because, in Disney's scheme of things, a good measure of the fantasy would be supplied by the visitor who became a cowboy or an astronaut for an afternoon, much as Disney had once lost himself in the role of a Santa Fe engineer making a whistle stop at a Harvey House.

Finally, although Disney included a Tomorrowland corresponding to the Chicago railroad pageant's conclusion, when the trains of the future were introduced, the real emphasis in both cases fell on the past—on the culture of railroading that the automobile had all but eradicated. Disneyland presented wilderness

(albeit artificial) too remote for the ruinous embrace of the highway. Preserved there, somehow, were places out of time, bypassed by the interstates. Disneyland had bustling towns, each one with a depot, but no suburbs, no carports. And there were only two ways to reach these little Disneyland cities: on foot, or the more dramatic way preferred by the founder—aboard an obsolete, steam-belching, doomed-to-destruction railroad train. In that sense, Disneyland was a tacit protest against modern America, on the wrong side of the tracks, to which Walt Disney consigned the cars and the parking lots. Disneyland was old-fashioned and urban. It was everything that L.A. was not.

In Disney's considered opinion, Los Angeles was a very dull place. "You know," he told Kimball in the late 1940s,

it's a shame people come to Hollywood and find there's nothing to see. They expect to see glamour and movie stars and they go away disappointed. Even the people who come to this studio. What can they see? A bunch of guys bending over drawings. Wouldn't it be nice if people could come to Hollywood and see something?[22]

Clearly, however, Disney exaggerated the nullity of Southern California to prove a need for the kind of park he was determined to build. It seems obvious, in retrospect, that such tourist attractions as Los Angeles did possess before the advent of Disneyland exerted an important influence on it.

One seminal tourist mecca was Olvera Street, a permanent sort of world's fair "village" constructed in the old, historic heart of downtown Los Angeles in 1929 as a Mission-period pedestrian mall lined with more than seventy shops, cantinas, and stalls full of souvenirs. From the 1920s through the Depression era, the Spanish colonial style adorned buildings that dramatized tourist fantasies associ-

The Chicago Railroad Fair's "Gold Gulch" would one day become Anaheim's Frontierland.

ated with the good life in California. Union Station, where nubile starlets posed atop their steamer trunks; the amusement piers near Naples and Santa Monica, where the silent movies had come for background settings; and movie palaces like the famous Carthay Circle, where *Snow White* premiered—all were lushly Spanish in flavor. They denied humdrum reality by recontextualizing life as it was lived in California in fabulous, make-believe settings. The pleasures of consumption, shopping, and dining were particularly susceptible to enhancement by architectural means. The Farmers'

Market of 1934, one of Disney's favorite haunts, was a "let's-pretend" midwestern farmscape identified by a trademark windmill. Sunset Boulevard's Crossroads of the World, completed in 1936, invited shoppers to browse through boutiques matrixed in a half-timbered European village, a lighthouse, and a ship, in addition to the usual early California presidio. Restaurant Row, on La Cienega, ran the gamut from a hot-dog stand operating out of a giant plaster-over-chicken-wire frankfurter to sit-down establishments that looked like grass shacks, Spanish castles, and colonial inns.

Olvera Street, another Disney favorite, combined history, exoticism, and shopping—the key ingredients of Disneyland's Main Street USA.

In its upscale manifestations, the architecture of illusion generally parted car and driver. The buildings of the past stood for preautomotive behavior, associated with the luxury, ease, and sensuality of premodern times. To shop at Crossroads of the World was to purchase the joy of free, unhurried time, the bliss of walking through unfamiliar townscapes, pausing to savor the sensual delights of touch, sight, and smell—or precisely what Disney would offer to the masses in 1955 in Anaheim. But the downscale version of such fantasy architecture—drive-in restaurants shaped like giant, fairy-tale shoes or derby hats, gas stations in the form of mosques (complete with lady pump-jockeys in Moorish veils), Hansel and Gretel cottages housing real estate offices or eccentric studio executives—could be seen on virtually any street corner during the years when Disney was beginning to dream of an alternative to amusement park and city alike. "If, when you went shopping, you found you could buy cakes in a windmill, ices in a giant cream-can, [and] flowers in a huge flower-pot," wrote a bemused British tourist in 1938, "you might begin to wonder whether you had not stepped through a looking glass or taken a toss down a rabbit burrow and could expect the Mad Hatter . . . to appear round the next corner." In 1939 Aldous Huxley, who would soon write the first draft of the script for Disney's *Alice in Wonderland*, described a typical Los Angeles suburb as a succession of implausible villas in which "Gloucester followed Andalusia and gave place to Touraine and Oaxaca, Dusseldorf and Massachusetts."[23]

History had no dominion over such a world. Instead, time was contingent and malleable. Without a past firmly situated in relationship to the future, there were no beginnings or endings, no death. Storybook architecture rewrote the story of the human condition in California, the Golden State of perpetual youth. Although some critics have attributed the imaginative vernacular of Los Angeles to sheer hedonism or to a liberating awareness of the distance between the West Coast and the old eastern rules of decorum, most commentators have posited a tenuous linkage between make-believe buildings and the movie industry. "Motion pictures have undoubtedly confused

Los Angeles's Union Station, where starlets (and Walt Disney) boarded the Santa Fe. The Mission style, popular from the 1920s, made the whole of Southern California into a kind of historical theme park.

Once introduced by an old-fashioned windmill, the Farmers' Market was one of Walt Disney's favorite haunts and an inspiration for his own theme park's make-believe architecture.

architectural tastes," the California architect Richard Neutra concluded in 1941:

They may be blamed for many phenomena in this landscape such as: Half-timber English peasant cottages, French provincial and "mission-bell" type adobes, Arabian minarets, Georgian mansions on 50 x 120 foot lots with "Mexican Ranchos" adjoining them on sites of the same size. A Cape Cod fisherman's hut (far from the beach and fish) appears side by side with a realtor's office seemingly built by Hopi Indians.[24]

Neutra's target was the suburbs of Los Angeles, but he could just as well have been describing Walt Disney's plans for a little park adjacent to his own backlot property.

Disney's Park and the Backlot Tour

Public interest in the backlots of the major studios was intense throughout the 1930s and early 1940s. Where did the magic come from? Was this the place? The Disney studio, which moved into new quarters in Burbank in 1940 during the last stages of the work on *Fantasia*, had been besieged for years with requests for tours and had answered these, in part, with a sequence in *The Reluctant Dragon* of 1941 dramatizing how animators took a cartoon from idea to finished product. But Disney thought that actually watching the process in the flesh would bore most tourists silly. They wanted movie magic, not the tedious reality of work. They wanted a taste of Hollywood's razzle-dazzle, whereby faraway times and places came to life on the silver screen. They wanted to be there as part of the illusion. "Walt's original idea, back in the '40s," says Disney Company president Michael Eisner, "was that Disneyland should be a tour of our studio."[25] The ultimate backlot, a film set on a titanic scale, Disneyland was the by-product of Walt Disney's unrealized plans for the greatest studio tour of all.

People who knew Walt Disney claim to have heard him talking about his future amusement park as early as 1920. Corporate records from the early 1930s document discussion of a two-acre park (never built) at the old studio; the files also contain actual sketches for rides prepared at the end of the decade. But the move to Burbank accelerated things. The Buena Vista Street facility was a personal triumph for Disney, a mark of his status in

A view of the first "magical little park" Disney planned to build on a lot adjacent to his Burbank studio: Disneyland would be a glorified, self-guided studio tour.

the industry and an expression of his ideals as a artist/Hollywood mogul/ businessman. Thus the architect Kem Weber gave Disney a sleek, Moderne design, in keeping with the latter's utopian vision of a workplace in which employees called the boss "Walt," attended free classes at a company art school, formed corporate orchestras, and jitterbugged happily during their lunch hour. With their banded chrome decorations and campuslike setting, the studio buildings were a model factory of tomorrow, suggestive of a benevolent and enlightened management. The appended park was a further sign of executive goodwill. The first detailed plans for Disneyland coincide, in fact, with the move to Burbank and mandate that a "magical little park" of eight acres be set aside for tourists and, on the weekends, for studio employees and their families.

The proposed contents of Mickey Mouse Park were sparse and simple, a nicer version of what a parent might take his child to see in nearby Griffith Park: a "singing" waterfall, statues of the Disney characters to pose with for snapshots, pony rides, and a working steam locomotive. The war, financial pressures, and a bitter strike in 1941 all dampened

enthusiasm for the project. But with his postwar shift from filmmaking to railroading, it became clear that Disney had designs on sixteen undeveloped acres on Riverside Drive, along the banks of the Los Angeles River. The land was across the street from his plant, from which his hypothetical train could run straight into Griffith Park. Renderings of this enlarged plan introduce the concept of theming for the first time. Gone are the waterfalls and statues. In their place was to be Old Town, a false-front western set organized around the depot and a right-of-way that skirted an Indian encampment and a midwestern farmstead. A stern-wheeler was to circumnavigate the tract inside the railroad tracks on a man-made waterway, and a Pony Express stage was to link the wilderness with the Old Town station.

An in-house memo of 31 August 1948 also lists a general store, pack mules—all appurtenances of the future Frontierland —a carnival section with the "typical Midway stuff" (lampooned in the 1940 Disney feature *Pinocchio*), and an old-fashioned townscape that sounds a lot like Anaheim's Main Street USA:

The Main Village, which includes the Railroad Station, is built around a village

*green or informal park. In the park will be
benches, a bandstand . . . trees and shrubs.
It will be a place for people to sit and rest;
mothers and grandmothers can watch over
small children at play . . . .*

*Around the park will be built the town.
At one end will be the Railroad Station; at
the other the Town Hall. The Hall will be
built to represent a Town Hall, but actually
we will use it as our administration building. It will be the headquarters of the entire
project.*

*Adjoining the Town Hall will be the Fire
and Police Stations. . . . In [the police
station] we could have a little jail where the
kids could look in.*

And there was more: a quaint commercial
district with an ice cream parlor, a
bookshop, a hobby shop, an art gallery, a
post office, a doll hospital, stores for
candy and toys and play clothes, and "a
restaurant for birthday parties."[26] Linked
to the more active attractions of the
western and the carnival sections by a
variety of buckboards, surreys, and horse-
drawn trolleys, Main Village was meant
for leisurely strolling and sitting in the
shade. It was Olvera Street with an
Americana veneer, the pedestrian shopping mall with a touch of fantasy, a whole
streetful of backlot–cum–Los Angeles
eccentricities of architecture, a model
railroad layout enlarged to usable scale.

None of it, however, impressed the
Burbank City Council. Ignoring Walt's
emphasis on the family, council members
persisted in thinking of any amusement
park as a potential liability. "We don't
want the carny atmosphere in Burbank,"
cried one lawmaker. "We don't want
people falling in the river, or merry-go-
rounds squawking all day long." The
acreage was swallowed up by the Ventura
Freeway, and Disney went back to
tinkering with trains and models. His
brother Roy wondered if the dreaming
and experimenting did not fascinate him
more than the doing anyway. "Walt does

a lot of talking about an amusement park
but . . . I don't know how deep his
interest really is," Roy Disney wrote to an
associate in 1951. "I think he's more
interested in ideas that would be good in
an amusement park than in actually
running one himself."[27]

Yet it was becoming increasingly
difficult to separate Walt Disney's
interests, ideas, and pastimes from the
park scheme. One of the most compelling
ingredients in the evolving Disneyland of
the late 1940s and early 1950s, for
example, was also one of the most personal: a walk-through museum of automata—moving, miniature scenes from
his own films and from American history—made by Walt Disney himself. On
his 1931 sabbatical, Disney had purchased a mechanical bird from a New
Orleans antique shop. Fascinated by the
technology that made the creature move
its tail and chirp, he brought the 100-
year-old automaton back to the studio
and had it taken apart. To Disney, the
bird was a three-dimensional cartoon, one
of his own animal characters come to life,
and so he collected for further study other
toys operated by springs and gears. When
he began to build miniature furniture and
appointments for the cars in his railroad
train, the connections between the singing
bird and the train chugging through his
garden suddenly jelled.

Disneylandia

In 1951, in a model train shop in London, Disney ran into Harper Goff, an
illustrator whose renderings of American
historical scenes for *Esquire* and other
magazines were well known. Goff had
also worked in Hollywood, most recently
doing storyboards for live-action films at
Warner Brothers. "I've got a little thing
up my sleeve that I really want to do,"
Disney told the illustrator by way of
inducement to join the enterprise. "It's

The automata and working miniatures that made up "Disneylandia" translated model railroading into a new, robotic dimension essential to the eventual success of Disneyland. This technology made Granny Kincaid's cabin, a scene from a Disney movie, into a three-dimensional reality.

sort of a 'Kiddieland,' and I want it to be called 'Walt Disney's America.' I don't want to just entertain kids with pony rides and slides and swings. I want them to learn something about their heritage." It soon became known that, with the help of studio artist Ken Anderson, Disney was engaged in a secret project, code named "Disneylandia." A touring attraction that could reach children in their own home-towns, Disneylandia was to consist of twenty-four peep-show views of salient moments in the American past, enlivened by little figures that could actually talk and gesticulate. Plans called for Anderson

and Goff to paint the scenes in great detail, à la Norman Rockwell. Then Disney would go home and build them to scale in his workshop, with some help from company mechanics. "I'm tired of having everyone else around here do the drawing and painting," Disney admitted to Anderson.

I'm going to do something creative myself. . . . I want you to draw . . . scenes of life in an old Western town. . . . I'll carve the figures and make the scenes in miniature. When we get enough of them made, we'll send them out as a traveling exhibit.[28]

By the time the model making began, the iconography of Disneylandia had expanded from the Old West to include a broader swath of history and, under the rubric of Americana, the history of Walt Disney's own career as a filmmaker. If movies and cartoons gave ideas a visible form, Disneylandia would make those flat, cinematic images real and palpable. The first tableau actually completed, for instance, was based on a set from the 1948 live-action–cartoon feature *So Dear to My Heart*, a Disney period piece dealing with small-town life in 1903, complete with county fair, locomotive, and genial Main Street merchants. The scene chosen for miniaturization was the interior of Granny Kincaid's cabin, crammed with lilliputian models of a spinning wheel, a family Bible, and a flintlock rifle mounted on the wall. Thanks to a system of cams and cables, Granny herself rocked by the fireside and spoke with the recorded voice of actress Beulah Bondi. And tantalizing slices of an old-fashioned kitchen and a bedroom with a four-poster were visible behind her. These half-seen fragments—a view out a window in one scene would hint at the milieu of the next—were to interconnect a coherent reconstruction of small-town America.

The second tableau was a music hall, with a dancing man doing his routine. Buddy Ebsen was hired to perform an old-time dance on camera, the film was rotoscoped to break fluid action down into its constituent parts, and a nine-inch entertainer (operated by a console larger than the scene itself) strutted his stuff before a velvet curtain. The third and final scene combined the elaborate movements of the dancer with the vocal capacity of Granny Kincaid in a barber-shop quartet that sang "Sweet Adeline" for almost ninety seconds, with dramatic arm waving and head tilting.

From the first, Disneylandia was plagued with problems. The model making went slowly. Although the miniatures worked, the operating equipment was cumbersome: studio technicians admitted they had duplicated the eighteenth-century technology of mechanical toys without improving it much and argued unsuccessfully for full-size figures that could be crammed full of more sensitive hydraulic and pneumatic controls. To Disney, the magic of the scenes derived from their tiny size, but miniaturization, according to the accountants, also meant that few viewers could see a given segment of the show at once, and those who deposited their quarters in the slot to start the machinery were liable to spend a lot of time ooohing and aaahing over each little room. At twenty-five cents a head, the chances of breaking even, given the enormous costs of the project, were slim indeed. So Disneylandia was folded into the master plan for an amusement park. Along with life-size versions of the Old West and Granny's Cabin, the layout sketches for the Anaheim site captured the essence of the small town, of American history and heritage, basic to the unfinished miniature exhibit.

Main Street USA

Disneylandia ultimately spawned the slithering plastic crocodiles of Adventureland and the flying witches and fairies of Fantasyland. But its most important legacy was Main Street USA, the grand, ceremonial entrance to Disneyland. Like the train track and the depot defining the margins of the park, Main Street was another Disney hobby given larger, national significance in the fluid landscape of Anaheim in 1955.

In *The Lonely Crowd*, a study of the changing American character published in 1950, David Riesman took up the subject of hobbies. The intensity with which the average, middle-class American pursued after-hours woodcarving or outdoor cooking or model making initially puzzled

Main Street architecture: a shopping mall in movie-set disguise.

the sociologist because such private interests seemed at odds with the "outer-directed" personality typical of the period. The "outer-directed" corporate man took his social cues from those around him and, Riesman concluded, "remains a lonely member of the crowd because he never comes really close to . . . himself." But the use of leisure for craftsmanlike activities by these same nine-to-five conformists struck him as anomalous, an expression of autonomy and individual competence that ran counter to the workday norm. In such moments of basement tinkering, Riesman posited, the hobbyist "can often rediscover both his childhood and his inner-directed residues by serious craftsmanship."[29] To make a model—to recreate, in Disneyland's case, the Marceline, Missouri, of a turn-of-the-century boyhood—was to return to those happy, bygone times as a competent adult. To make a model was to construct, or reconstruct, one's own biography. To make a model of an ideal past was to reject an imperfect present.

In Disneyland, the present—suburban reality, 1955-style—was abandoned in the parking lot, along with the family car. Although ticket buyers would ultimately face a choice between Fantasy-land, Frontierland, Adventureland, and Tomorrowland, they were first forced to negotiate a common entranceway defined by the architectural and techno-logical symbolism of an American past that coincided with Walt Disney's own. Here, too, his hobbies displaced the realities of the workplace on a scale that demanded the same "inner-directed" ethos of others. Everybody walked under the railroad tracks and past the station where the old steam locomotive chuffed to a halt. Everybody walked down Main Street USA, under its gingerbread cor-nices, past windows bearing the names of Disney's father and his friends in-scribed in gilded letters. That kind of experience, writes the landscape historian John Stilgoe, is a primal one, a rebirth, a common affirmation of American identity:

Main Street USA

[The] small-town depot appears again and again in American literature as a liminal zone through which young people pass into adulthood, into adventure, and into real or seeming wisdom, and through which they sometimes return to find the towns of their youth, rarely beautiful but more often tawdry, "run-down" in the American expression that connotes a town hit by a train.[30]

In Disneyland, the Main Street complex leads to adventure and sometimes to

wisdom, thanks to imbedded lessons about the space program and the conquest of the frontier taught in the adjacent "lands." But its liminal markers set off a world in which everybody—and the nation itself—is young again and therefore perfect: spanking clean, freshly painted, orderly, peaceful, happy, and never "run-down."

Main Street is Kansas Street in Marceline, Missouri, as Walt Disney remembered it from a distance of half a century. Diane Disney called it "his dreamlike re-creation of Marceline's main stem," and her father confirmed her insight when he explained the meaning of Main Street USA in terms of the collective memory of his generation. "Many of us fondly remember our small hometown and its friendly way of life at the turn of the century," Disney remarked. "To me, this era represents an important part of our nation's heritage." The Missouri town first encountered by the four-year-old Walt Disney was far from perfect, however. Richard Francaviglia's historical reconstruction of Marceline circa 1905 reveals a raw, treeless, unlovely place, a visually incoherent mosaic of signboards, telegraph poles, and bulky, vaguely classicized buildings all competing for attention along the rutted, unpaved length of Kansas Street. The Disneyland version of hometown America, as one of the staff members described it, "is what Main Street *should* have been like."[31]

Main Street, Disneyland, has none of the vile features observed by Sinclair Lewis's heroine when she made her famous thirty-two-minute tour of Gopher Prairie's Main Street back in "19-aught-something": no saloons, no malodorous pool halls, no sidewalk loafers casting bold glances at the passersby. Instead of jostling one another for the shopper's favor, the buildings are all of a piece, roughly equal in height, complementary in color, and ebulliently overdecorated with Andy Hardy Victorianisms. There

Main Street USA

are too many awnings, too much fretwork and gilt, creating an intensity, a concentration of sensation that is almost urban, despite itself. But the wealth of decoration, in the end, reads as wealth or material well-being, and the overall effect, thanks to clever manipulations of scale, is intimate, even comforting.

Disney's one-eighth scale locomotive ultimately determined the dimensions of his park. When measured drawings for the train were enlarged to adapt it to Disneyland, it was determined that a six-foot doorway was adequate for a passenger car. Everything else was proportioned to that module, by eighths, like the little freight stations and villages on a railroad layout beneath a Christmas tree. "It's not apparent to a casual glance that this street is only a scale model," Disney stated, pointing at the Italianate storefronts that stretched away toward Sleeping Beauty's Castle. "We had every brick and shingle and gas lamp made 7/8 of true size."[32] Actually, it was more complicated than that. Like Baroque masters of illusionism, or the clever set decorators they were, Disney's "imagineers" built Main Street in forced perspective, with the upper stories much smaller than the lower ones, giving the impression of diminution by distance while keeping the overall height of the cornice lines suburban, unthreatening, and low. The ground floor, in each case, is seven-eighths the size of a "real" turn-of-the-century commercial structure; the second story is in five-eighths scale (also used for the *Mark Twain* and the Santa Fe and Disneyland line); but the top story is only one-half as large as its generic prototypes.

Along with Levittown and places like it, Main Street USA's size answered Lewis Mumford's call for a postwar "return to the human scale" that made neighborliness and intimacy possible.[33] Its size domesticated, its atmosphere comfy and benign, Main Street evokes the mood of Disney's own small-town movies and the

front-porch television tradition that began with *Father Knows Best* in 1954. On Main Street, the grown-up suddenly becomes a kid again—a Bud or a Betty from television's fictional Springfield, USA. Main Street's scale captures the sense most adults experience when they return to their hometowns and notice how small, how toylike their cherished places of childhood have become. Built from the blueprint of memory, Main Street was capable of shrinking the past and stripping away the nasty facts of yesterday, exalting instead the positive values that recollection has burnished to a golden luster. Main Street is thus a plaything, a dream at nap time, a TV sitcom, better than reality has ever been.

The sense of well-being Main Street imparts is also related to scale, for, paradoxically, if reduced size summons up childhood memories and emotions, it also makes the adult feel ten feet tall, larger than life, and therefore immune from harm. With its dollhouse ice cream parlors and toy-town candy shops, Main Street is just unreal enough to be unthreatening. In 1928 the novelist Glenway Wescott, taking the reader back to the luminous nighttimes of his own Wisconsin youth, remembered such a Main Street scene:

As the sun hurried west . . . everywhere men and women and children were made eager by the thoughts of the night . . . for the night was Saturday night and they were going to town. . . . And in Middle America, in the numberless small towns that serve the people of the farms, there is no more magical time. It is the sweet reward of the long week's labor; it is their opera, drama, their trip to Zanzibar.[34]

The Main Street of old was Zanzibar, Rome, and Paris, the Fourth of July and Christmas, rolled into one. So is Main Street USA, a memory first softened by the blur of nostalgia and then coaxed into

The Santa Fe and Disneyland depot at the head of Main Street USA—the liminal border between fantasy and reality, the suburban present and small-town past

a three-dimensional existence, just that way—pristine and eternally lovely—in the architecture of Disneyland.

Disney's make-believe Main Street shares much common ground with 1950s suburbia: the sense of uniformity, order, community, and safety, a sort of smiling "I Like Ike" friendliness conveyed by each perky awning. But as a model community, Main Street also stands in obvious contrast to the American city from which the suburbanite had fled. People-sized, organized around the meanderings of pedestrians, its deepest meaning is revealed by its opposition to Los Angeles and to the creeping steel-and-concrete urbanism outside the park. Perhaps, then, Main Street is the real national Fantasyland, since Los Angeles and its environs in 1955 constituted the future that had already come to pass for small-town America. Or perhaps, secure from bulldozers and the ravages of urbanization, it is a compensatory monument to Anaheim and all the other vanished Main Streets of the postwar era. Southern Californians, according to one trenchant social commentator struggling to make

sense of Disneyland's popularity, habitually "imagine ivy-covered, leaf-strewn squares, and villages clustered around white frame New England churches, and, lacking them in reality, create them in plastic towns to which they go to find themselves." The architect Charles Moore calls Main Street the town square of Los Angeles, a public environment otherwise missing from a city of freeways and housing tracts:

In an unchartable sea of suburbia, Disney has created a place, indeed, a whole public world, full of sequential occurrences, of big and little drama, of hierarchies of importance and excitement. . . . No raw edges spoil the picture . . . everything is as immaculate as in the musical-comedy villages that Hollywood has provided for our viewing pleasure for the last three generations.[35]

Within his own mythological system, the small town Disney fetishized was a part of a larger Hollywood drama. Called upon to explain the village huddled at the foot of Bald Mountain in the spectacular

Inscriptions on the windows refer to the founder's own relatives and associates. Elias Disney, for example, was Walt's father. The signs are a clear admission of Disney's personal stake in his latest, greatest project.

(overleaf) Kansas Street, Marceline, Missouri—the prototype for Main Street USA

finale of *Fantasia,* he said that "it sort of symbolizes something. The forces of good." At Disneyland, the same archetypal set introduces the whole show. As the visitor strolls past the storefronts, the townscape itself unwinds a narrative describing in a welter of props what it was like to be in America in the early 1900s, when the movies shown in the Main Street Cinema were new, when the horseless carriage was still an oddity, when life was very, very good. "Here is a period in America . . . when progress was a good word and . . . there was an intense optimism about what we were doing with our lives," says a park official, "reading" the cinematic story being told in the passage from turnstile to castle.[36] Disney placed great stock in what he called the "weinie" theory of crowd movement whereby an eye-catching object—a "weinie," like the castle at the end of Main Street—pulls the guest in that direction, past the prompts and cues that make up the visual script along the way. Each Disneyland visitor thus becomes an actor in a drama arranged, like a movie, in an edited sequence of sights and sounds.

Likewise, the person who takes a seat on any one of the park's many rides immediately becomes a cast member in the Disney feature to which the attraction alludes. "Snow White's Adventure," one of the original Fantasyland rides, is a case in point. Tucked behind the safety bar of a moving, "dwarf-carved" vehicle of simulated wood, the visitor experiences exactly what Snow White did in the 1937 movie. The Wicked Witch offers a poisoned apple. The dwarfs mine their diamonds and tramp homeward. To maintain the illusion, Snow White herself is nowhere to be seen in representational form: the passenger–turned–movie-star fills in for her, living out her adventures for as long as it takes the simulated-wooden car to negotiate the darkened tunnel. And so it is the visitor who is menaced, attacked, and scared half to

death by things that go bump in the night, in a clash of good and evil that ends only when the car shoots back into the blessed sunlight.

The flat, unnuanced contrasts between good and evil, light and dark, so evident in the cold war politics of the 1950s, underlie the filmic narratives of Fantasyland. Along Main Street, however, evil exists only in terms of its absence, as the banished antonym of civic virtues like cleanliness or picturesque charm, and the storytelling proceeds by subtler means. Since the visitor revises the script by making choices—to enter one store and not another, to dawdle, to rush through—mood becomes almost as important to the perception of meaning as any particular storyline that is spelled out in gilded signage and period costume. As act 1, scene 1 for Disneyland, Main Street is appropriately pleasant, reassuring, and undemanding. At world's fairs and other public amusements studied by the Disney team, each structure competed with all the rest for the audience's attention. But Main Street architecture, from its shared roofline to its limited decorative vocabulary, functions in noncompetitive aesthetic harmony "because there's an attempt to relate one idea to the next," declared a studio animator who helped Disney build his park.

This comes from the motion picture background. . . . Colors are harmonized very carefully. It may not have an impact at a logical level, but I'm sure people respond to it, whether they're trained in this or not.[37]

Because Main Street USA was built by filmmakers, not by architects, its appearance was calibrated to achieving a desired emotional effect. Form follows function—or script—unashamedly, as it does more often than not in commercial, roadside architecture. "What is Main Street?" asked the Manhattan developer Mel Kaufman after a pilgrimage to Disneyland.

ZURCHER

Disney visits the Zurcher Building in Marceline, 1960. It is said to have been the inspiration for one of the storefronts on Main Street USA.

It is an ordinary shopping center where they sell souvenirs, film . . . ice cream, have a movie house—all functioning as would any ordinary shopping center. Except for one thing. It's a stage set of Main Street circa 1900.[38]

It is no ordinary shopping center, of course, this evocative blend of history, autobiography, mythmaking, and Holly-wood set. But Main Street USA *is* a functioning commercial district, which, at its inception, looked backward to Los Angeles's Olvera Street and forward to Victor Gruen's Southdale, the first fully enclosed suburban mall, which opened in Minneapolis in 1956. Indeed, Main Street is a mall in its own right, since the disposition of interior space permits free movement from one shop to another along the entire length of the block. And by virtue of Main Street's controlling position in the layout of the park, shopping becomes a key motif in the iconographic structure of Disneyland. On the one hand, the psychology of the place makes for low sales resistance. "Unlike in society's modern cities," a Disney planner boasted, "they drop their defenses [here]. . . . Actually, what we're selling is reassurance."[39] On the other hand, while the ambience makes for enormous profits, it also exalts the central act of street corner capitalism—the buying and selling of merchandise, which goes on at a frantic pace behind the pretty, filigreed facades of what amount to antique shops in reverse: old-fashioned stores stocked with the latest in Mickey Mouse memorabilia. Period decor legitimates consumption by equating the business of Main Street USA with the very historical fiber of the nation. At the gateway to the cold war moralism of Walt Disney's reconstructed America, Main Street USA celebrates the real-life pleasures of exuberant postwar consumerism.

A Williamsburg or a Greenfield Village adapted to the social climate of the 1950s, Main Street USA affirms that the good life—utopia—is American, middle-class, and midwestern. The rest of Disneyland, to which the thoroughfare leads, represents a world view grounded in Main Street's values. Frontierland sets forth the story of how the West was made safe for homesteaders—and suburbanites. Adventureland appropriates the Third World and untamed nature to serve as the frontiers (and boutiques) of today, while a corporate Tomorrowland, intent on the conquest of space, is the profitable frontier of the future. As for Fantasyland, its flirtations with the dark and irrational only serve to affirm the ideological clarity with which the progress of the American adventure, from cowboy to astronaut, is described in nuances of architecture, cuisine, and gift shop souvenirs. But Main Street USA remains the allegorical touchstone for this "Disneyized" history of the nation: "It is what America was," writes a cultural geographer, "and provides the bedrock security for what it is to be." And so a powerful dramatization of history and destiny arises directly from Walt Disney's own childhood memories. In an act of almost stupifying self-assurance, he made himself—his life, his imagination, his movies—the objective correlative for American culture, past, present, and future. In the words of a promotional brochure for the park, "Disneyland reflects Walt's personal experiences, his dreams, his ambitions and special interest which are universal interests."[40]

The Aesthetic of Television

If not universal, these interests were well known to most Americans through the medium of film. Main Street USA pushed to the foreground scenic backgrounds of *So Dear to My Heart* and *Lady and the Tramp* (released when Disneyland opened in July 1955). Fantasyland brought back Tinker Bell, Snow White, Pinocchio, and Alice, stars of the animated fairy-tale features. Adventureland alluded to Disney's True-Life Adventure series of nature documentaries. Tomorrowland, the least developed of the quadrants in 1955, was based on 1954's *20,000 Leagues under the Sea*, a live-action, sci-fi thriller, loaded with special effects. Hence the characters and themes of Disneyland

were familiar to adults who had grown up with Disney cartoons and who were now, as parents, taking their own children to see the latest from the same studio. Everybody knew Walt Disney, if not from his movies, then from the products related to them: the books, watches, lamps, toys, clothing, and novelty items—even a line of canned foods marketed under the Donald Duck label. In a pluralistic society, where experiences of church, school, and ethnicity were not universally shared, Disney motifs constituted a common culture, a kind of civil religion of happy endings, worry-free consumption, technological optimism, and nostalgia for the good old days.

In sheer size, Disneyland's sets invited comparison with those created for the inflated "spectaculars" through which Hollywood in the 1950s hoped to recoup profits lost to television. There was only one difference, Reyner Banham argued: "Disneyland was a set for a film that was never going to be made, except in the mind of the visitor."[41] Turned loose on an ersatz set, the visitor became a temporary Hollywood insider, privy to the secrets of the giant screen. But the intimacy of the backlot also made it the perfect setting for TV and its small-screen revelations of what really went on behind the scenes. Walt Disney's first television show, a 1950 "special" broadcast on Christmas afternoon by NBC, made a vast family audience familiar with the doings in his studio during the making of *Alice in Wonderland*. "One Hour in Wonderland" also gave viewers a look at the Disney family: Diane and Sharon, then high schoolers, appeared with their father. The formula proved so successful that Disney offered another insider's peek at movie-making in 1951.

Television was the family entertainment medium of choice in the new, isolated, gadget-happy ranch houses of suburbia, and the commercial benefits of luring those families back to the movie

The castle eventually built at Disneyland gave a deceptive air of fantasy to the park. In fact, the concept was grounded in technology and history.

houses with free previews of forthcoming films were enormous. "That telecast should be worth $1 million at the box-office to *Alice in Wonderland,*" wrote one TV columnist after the first Christmas program aired. But, despite its appeal to the swelling postwar middle class, old-line Hollywood moguls and highbrows alike considered television an enterprise of dubious artistic and intellectual merit. The first major producer to join forces with the networks, Disney incurred the wrath of other studio heads bent on ignoring the competition or fighting a losing battle against "the idiot box." His espousal of TV—his intuitive grasp of the potential for profit—gave Disney's critics another reason to consign him to the ranks of the philistines. His sheepish defenders, on the other hand, put forth the curious argument that Disney "demonstrated . . . his inherent contempt for the medium" by using television to create a market for his films—and for Disneyland.[42]

In the early 1950s, Disneyland was in trouble. Within the company, Disney had found little support for what many believed to be an excursion into "honky-tonk." The planning process continued only because he paid for the work out of his own pocket. And when he approached would-be backers with his idea for a form of participatory entertainment at the furthest possible remove from television, the business community was inclined to believe rumors that Disney was not quite himself. But TV was the last hope. Walt Disney Productions would crank out the weekly series the networks had been angling for in return for heavy cash investments and loan guarantees to see the park through to completion. A written prospectus and a portfolio of patented Disney drawings were prepared in a single frantic weekend, and in the late September of 1953, Roy Disney went to New York to strike a deal. On 2 April 1954, it was formally announced that ABC—the struggling "third" network—had landed

Walt Disney and that Disney, as part of the package, was going to build some sort of "film production center" patterned after the villages in his movies. The TV show and the "center" were both to be called Disneyland.

"Disneyland" the TV show premiered in October 1954. It played on Wednesday nights at 7:30, the children's hour, and within three months it had hit the top ten. "Disneyland" became a family institution: homework was deferred, sales of frozen TV dinners soared. In Walt Disney's own mind and in its televised format, the program was not easily distinguishable from the project then under construction in Anaheim. "I saw that if I was ever going to have my park," he stated, "here . . . was a way to tell millions of people about it—with TV."[43] And so, every week, the format introduced the audience to the principal themes of the park. One Wednesday the topic would be Fantasyland, with the content made up of clips from animated films. Adventureland evenings recycled unused footage shot for the nature documentaries. But the Tomorrowland segment was perhaps the most revealing of the lot in terms of Disney's own intentions.

Under the heading of Tomorrowland, the studio prepared a behind-the-scenes preview of *20,000 Leagues under the Sea,* with an emphasis on special-effects technology. The program won an Emmy, but it was also dubbed "the first 60-minute commercial in the history of TV" and "the longest trailer ever made."[44] Nor did critics fail to notice that three additional Wednesdays were given over to progress reports from the park site urging members of the audience to plan a vacation trip to Southern California, much as other telecasts had sent viewers to the drive-in to see a new movie with which they were already familiar before the credits ever rolled. Nonetheless, while "Disneyland" served blatantly commercial

Walt Disney introduces his park and the "Disneyland" television hour to the public, 1954. From the beginning, the two propositions were inextricably linked.

ends, the show was also crucial to the creation of the mood or underlying scenario basic to its geographic counterpart in Anaheim. Through the medium of "Disneyland," the American family became part of the process of building the park and thus acquired an emotional stake in its success. It was Walt's American Versailles, but it was a part of the Wednesday night home lives of countless viewers, too. And by rehearsing the proposed features of the park, the TV show eliminated all grounds for apprehension: Disneyland—the theme park—was just as safe, wholesome, and predictable as

the living room setting in which the family gathered to watch Walt talk all about it. Going to Disneyland was just like watching that other "Disneyland" on TV.

Bob Chandler, a television reporter for *Variety*, admired the way in which the show relentlessly plugged the park and the park, in turn, gave permanent form to transient aspects of Disney's entertainment empire. But the systematic integration of the two arms of the business went further than that. Disneyland's Frontierland and Tomorrowland, Chandler noted, were "tele-creations," concepts generated for the home screen without much precedent in the existing Disney film archive.[45] Indeed, most of the brand-new material produced for the show, including a popular series on space exploration, fell into one of those two categories. Both were important television motifs of the 1950s.

The futuristic hardware explained by rocket scientists and animated by the Disney artists was not dissimilar in appearance, for instance, to the products of American industry on display during commercial breaks: a new, befinned Ford Fairlane or a push-button kitchen range heralded a future of magical ease as surely as did any lunar vehicle. Television suburbanized a future that remained, until Sputnik suggested otherwise, a strictly American phenomenon, a technological wonderland available for purchase on easy credit terms. The Autopia in Disney's park is a reminder of that consumerist vision of the world to come. Funds ran out before the Tomorrowland precinct was fully realized, but Walt insisted that this one attraction—a replica of the new freeway system that linked America's past with its suburban future—be completed in time for the opening ceremonies. The shiny new cars vrooming past the camera would make for great TV, he thought.

Frontierland represented the national past, and it was also the most popular recurring theme of the "Disneyland" program, thanks to the Davy Crockett mania of the 1954–55 season. And like Tomorrowland, Frontierland resonated to powerful themes in the suburban imagination. The ranch house, the knotty-pine den, the outdoor barbecue, the search for acres of crabgrass beyond the boundaries of urban civilization—these facts of American life in the 1950s help to explain why the western genre accounted for more than a quarter of the movies produced in Hollywood and why the cowboy film of the period was so often domestic in flavor, with the hero longing

for the stability of home and hearth. Television had a voracious appetite for old Westerns in its early years and soon demanded more, made to order for the medium. Disney's Davy Crockett episodes—the first one-hour Westerns on ABC—garnered the highest ratings of the decade (and produced a bonanza of product spin-offs) by validating suburban mobility in the person of the restless frontiersman who waxes nostalgic about home and family as he dies in the wilds of Texas. Those who wondered, in a recession year, about the wisdom of acquiring the streamlined appurtenances of Tomorrowland found imaginative comfort in Frontierland's simple, log-cabin past. Armchair frontiersmen uneasy about the nation's postwar transformation into a military-industrial power found solace in the vision of an earlier day, commemorated in their own wagon-wheel coffee tables. The eye of the camera let the living room viewer travel freely in time and space, backward to the Alamo, forward to the moon. Television was a magical picture window on the world beyond one's own front lawn, and Disneyland was conceived in its perceptual image.

The cultural historian George Lipsitz insists that the spatial sensibility of Disneyland comes from television, too, specifically from the latter's "managed gaze": just as the various segments of the televised "Disneyland" were discrete, self-contained entities, so the "viewer" touring the park could not see Frontierland from Tomorrowland or vice versa.[46] Disney's theme park planners always used an older cinematic analogy to describe the way in which the tourist was to be gently nudged from scene to scene in a narrative sequence of edited takes. But Disney planners made a major departure from this analogy: in the movies, the experience is continuous and unbroken, but in Disneyland, it is discontinuous and episodic, like watching television in the privacy of one's own home—each ride a four- or five-minute segment, slotted in among snacks, trips to the rest room, and "commercials" in the form of souvenir emporia. And it is always possible to change the channel. "Disneyland . . . is a kind of TV set," writes William Irwin Thompson, "for one flips from medieval castles to submarines and rockets as easily as one can move, in . . . Los Angeles, from the plaza of the Mexican Olvera Street . . . to the modern Civic Center."[47]

Disneyland is pure L.A., TV, high-tech, shop-'til-you-drop 1950s glitz. It is also a sober critique of that culture, couched in the visual language and the myths of the American film. It is an alternative to the city, an affirmation of the suburb, neither, and both. Mobile yet curiously inert. A glorification of technological progress, or an indictment of the shift in values accelerated by the machine. Naggingly familiar; profoundly alien. Tomorrow. Yesterday. The antithesis of art. The most complex, baffling, and beloved work of art produced in postwar America.

Notes

1 "Disneyland Dedication from Coast," *New York Times*, 18 July 1955; Bob Cummings, quoted in *Disneyland, The First Thirty-Five Years* (Anaheim, Calif.: Walt Disney Company, 1989), p. 30; Walt Disney, quoted in Valerie Childs, *The Magic of Disneyland and Walt Disney World* (New York: Mayflower Books, 1979), n.p.

2 Reporter's quote in Randy Bright, *Disneyland: Inside Story* (New York: Harry N. Abrams, 1987), p. 107.

3 Disney, quoted in ibid., pp. 108–9.

4 Julian Halevy, "Disneyland and Las Vegas," *Nation* 186 (7 June 1958): 511.

5 Ray Bradbury, "The Machine-Tooled Happyland," *Holiday* 34 (October 1965): 100.

6 Louis Kronenberger, *Company Manners: A Cultural Inquiry into America* (New York: Bobbs-Merrill, 1954), p. 28.

7 Bosley Crowther, "The Dream Merchant," *New York Times*, 16 December 1966.

8 Diane Disney Miller, with Pete Martin, "My Dad, Walt Disney," *Saturday Evening Post* 230 (5 January 1957): 82.

9 Disney, quoted in *Disneyland, The First Thirty-Five Years*, p. 11, and in Richard Schickel, *The Disney Version: The Life, Times, Art and Commerce of Walt Disney*, rev. ed. (New York: Simon and Schuster, 1985), p. 310.

10 Ford advertisement, quoted in Phil Patton, *Open Road: A Celebration of the American Highway* (New York: Simon and Schuster, 1986), p. 88.

11 Reyner Banham, *Los Angeles: The Architecture of Four Ecologies* (London: Penguin, 1971), pp. 127–28.

12 Miller, "My Dad," *Saturday Evening Post* 229 (24 November 1956): 70, 75, 80, and (8 December 1956): 85.

13 Ollie Johnston, quoted in Christopher Finch, *Walt Disney: From Mickey Mouse to the Magic Kingdom* (New York: Abrams, 1973), p. 386.

14 Ward Kimball, quoted in Leonard Mosley, *Disney's World* (New York: Stein and Day, 1985), p. 216.

15 Johnston, quoted in Finch, p. 387; Kimball, quoted in Mosley, p. 217.

16 *Railway Age*, quoted in "Glamour on Wheels," *Newsweek* 32 (2 August 1948): 56.

17 Ward Walker, "Rails Attract Myriad Fans—with Cameras . . . ," *Chicago Tribune*, 20 July 1948.

18 "Railways Freight in Old West," *Chicago Daily Sun-Times*, 20 July 1948; advertisement, *Chicago Daily Sun-Times*, 20 July 1948; "Villages Form Interesting Part of Lake Front Show," *Chicago Tribune*, 20 July 1948.

19 "The 'Deadwood Central' Runs on Time," *New York Times*, 22 August 1948.

20 For photographs and discussion, see "Scenes from 'Wheels A-Rolling,'" *Railway Age* 125 (7 August 1948): 32; "Pageant Is Main Feature," *Railway Age* 125 (24 July 1948): 78; "Speaking of Pictures," *Life* 25 (27 September 1948): 12–14.

21 Kimball, quoted in Mosley, p. 218.

22 Disney, quoted in Bob Thomas, *Walt Disney: An American Original* (New York: Simon and Schuster, 1976), p. 218.

23 Quotation in Jim Heimann and Rip Georges, *California Crazy: Roadside Vernacular Architecture* (San Francisco: Chronicle Books, 1980), p. 11; Aldous Huxley, *After Many a Summer Dies the*

Swan (1939), excerpted in *The California Dream*, ed. Dennis Hale and Jonathan Eisen (New York: Collier Books, 1968), p. 239.

24 Richard Neutra, quoted in David Gebhard and Harriette von Breton, *L.A. in the Thirties: 1931–1941* (Layton, Utah: Peregrine Smith, 1975), p. 109.

25 Michael Eisner, quoted in Charles Leerhsen, "How Disney Does It," *Newsweek* 113 (3 April 1989): 51.

26 Memorandum, quoted in Thomas, pp. 218–19.

27 Anonymous elected official, quoted in Bright, p. 41; Roy Disney, quoted in Richard Hollis and Brian Sibley, *The Disney Studio Story* (New York: Crown, 1988), p. 66, and in Thomas, p. 218.

28 Disney, quoted in Bright, p. 39, and in Thomas, p. 224.

29 David Riesman, in collaboration with Reuel Denney and Nathan Glazer, *The Lonely Crowd: A Study of the Changing American Character* (New Haven: Yale University Press, 1950), pp. v, 354.

30 John R. Stilgoe, *Metropolitan Corridor: Railroads and the American Scene* (New Haven: Yale University Press, 1983), p. 218.

31 Miller, "My Dad," *Saturday Evening Post* 229 (24 November 1956): 74; Disney, quoted in *Disneyland: The First Thirty-Five Years*, p. 16; Richard V.

Francaviglia, "Main Street USA: The Creation of a Popular Image," *Landscape* 21 (Spring–Summer 1977): 20–21; Francaviglia, "Main Street U.S.A.: A Comparison/Contrast of Streetscapes in Disneyland and Walt Disney World," *Journal of Popular Culture* 15 (September 1981): 144; John Hench, longtime vice president for park operations, quoted in Paul Goldberger, "Mickey Mouse Teaches the Architects," *New York Times Magazine*, 22 October 1972, p. 95.

32 Disney, quoted in Michael R. Real, *Mass-Mediated Culture* (Englewood Cliffs, N.J.: Prentice-Hall, 1977), p. 54.

33 Lewis Mumford, quoted in *American Society since 1945*, ed. William L. O'Neill (Chicago: Quadrangle Books, 1969), p. 41.

34 Glenway Wescott, quoted in Carole Rifkind, *Main Street: The Face of Urban America* (New York: Harper & Row, 1977), p. 187.

35 William Irwin Thompson, *At the Edge of History* (New York: Harper & Row, 1971), p. 9; Charles Moore, quoted in Goldberger, p. 95.

36 Disney, quoted in Robert Jewett and John Shelton Lawrence, *The American Monomyth* (Garden City, N.Y.: Doubleday, 1977), p. 136; Hench, quoted in Anthony Haden-Guest, *The Paradise Program* (New York: William Morrow, 1973), p. 237.

37 Hench, quoted in Finch, p. 414.

38 Mel Kaufman, quoted in ibid., p. 447.

39 Hench, quoted in Bright, p. 237.

40 Francaviglia, "Main Street U.S.A.: A Comparison/Contrast," p. 156; promotional brochure, quoted in Leo E. Litwak, "A Fantasy That Paid Off," *New York Times Magazine*, 27 June 1965, p. 27.

41 Banham, p. 127.

42 Television columnist, quoted in Hollis and Sibley, p. 60; defenders' argument, quoted in Mosley, p. 244.

43 Disney, quoted in Schickel, p. 313.

44 "Disney Does It Again," *Newsweek* 44 (27 December 1954): 60; "The Mouse That Turned to Gold," *Business Week* (9 July 1955): 72–73.

45 Bob Chandler, "Disneyland as 2-Headed Child of TV and H'wood Shoots for $18 Million B.O.," *Variety* (20 July 1955).

46 George Lipsitz, "Discursive Space and Social Space: Television, Highways and Cognitive Mapping of the 1950s City" (Paper delivered at the annual meeting of American Studies Association, Toronto, 4 November 1989). The concept of "managed gaze" comes from Lynn Spigel, "Installing the Television Set: Popular Discourse on Television and Domestic Space, 1948–1955," *Camera Obscura* 16 (1988): 14–20.

47 Thompson, pp. 13–14.

The Mickey Mouse Kachina

Rayna Green

Three hundred and more *kacinam*, masked spirits who come in the winter to Hopiland, chastise and reward The People. Those who help make the crops grow by bringing rain sometimes become Cloud People when they leave Hopiland. In their dances—which, like all dances, songs, pots, and weavings, are really prayers—they bring families, clans, and villages together. They come out of the kivas bringing food and other presents, sometimes behaving in a frightening kind of way. Oftentimes, the masked beings are almost like the Clowns who accompany them; they act in backwards, unseemly, un-Hopi ways. The masked spirits are allowed to do anything at all, rolling in the dirt, throwing dirt, and worse, making fun of people who act un-Hopi. They teach the children about being Hopi. One type of masked Clown, the Mudhead, is also a kachina. They're all sacred beings. Some of their deeds exist only in old stories.

There are many stories about Tusan Homichi, the Mouse—how once he went to war and defeated the hawk who was stealing chickens from The People. The Hopi were grateful to this tiny, plucky creature who defended them against hunger. The Mouse kachina is like that Mouse of the old stories. When Disney Studios put its version of the Mouse spirit on the silver screen, it must have been wonderful for Hopis to see him sing, dance, and perform brave and Clownlike acts, just as in their old stories and in his then-infrequent appearances in Hopiland. Worldwide, Mickey Mouse and his remarkable companions generated enormous love and admiration, so it wasn't only Hopis who seemed to understand and appreciate his magical power. In this instance, they expropriated a symbol of power from the other culture, just as theirs had been expropriated for centuries by *bahanas*, the whites who'd come to Hopiland so long ago. After Mickey Mouse began to appear in the thirties, how long or how often the Mickey Mouse kachina danced in the winter dances with the other masked spirits is not known. No one has seen him dance since the late fifties. Still, his spirit has been represented in Mickey Mouse kachina dolls, the carved cottonwood figures made to teach children the Hopi way. The true importance and power of this kachina doll and hundreds of others made for sale in a commercial market insatiable for Indian religious artifacts has little to do with their elevated status in museums and in private bahana collections.

The Mickey Mouse kachina doll pictured here embodies the spirit of the Mouse and all the kachina versions of him. Obviously, the way he is carved shows that he is a Mudhead. Cheerful and alert, he is the essence of the Hopi version of Bobby McFerrin's magic song of the eighties, "Don't Worry, Be Hopi," now worn on T-shirts throughout Hopiland. Perhaps the irrepressible optimism, bravery, and clever trickery of the screen Mickey—deeply needed by a Depression-worn America—was shaped and formed by that original Mouse spirit, sent in dreams to Disney by the kacinam, who are ever mindful of what The People need to survive. Certainly, when the Hopis pray, they pray for all beings, not just for themselves. The Mickey Mouse kachina acknowledges the power and persistence of

Unidentified artist, *Mickey Mouse Kachina*, after 1930. Carved and painted cottonwood, feathers, and string, 11 3/4 x 5 3/8 x 4 3/4 in. National Museum of American Art, Smithsonian Institution, Gift of Herbert Waide Hemphill, Jr., and museum purchase made possible by Ralph Cross Johnson

the Mouse spirit, known and needed in the world of human, animal, plant, and spirit beings. In coming to pray for and with us this winter through his dances and songs, he gives us all—bahana and Hopi—the gift of his laughter, intelligence, and holy clowning. May he teach us and all our children well.

For further information: Robert Breunig and Michael Lomatuwayma, *Kachina Dolls* (Flagstaff: Museum of Northern Arizona, 1983).

"By all Artists, it has heretofore been deemed next to impossible to make good pictures of Strange and Wonderful Scenes in nature; and that the most that could be done with such material was to give topographical or geologic characteristics. But I have always held that the Grandest, Most Beautiful, or Wonderful in Nature, would, in capable hands, make the grandest, most beautiful, or wonderful pictures, and that the business of a great painter should be the representation of great scenes in nature."

—Thomas Moran to Ferdinand Hayden, 11 March 1872,
National Archives, Records of the Geological Survey, Hayden Survey, Record Group 57

American Art

National Museum of American Art, Smithsonian Institution

To order back copies of *American Art* (formerly *Smithsonian Studies in American Art*), check off the desired issue(s) and indicate quantity. Articles and authors are indicated below. Mail to Journals Department, Oxford University Press, 2001 Evans Rd., Cary, N.C. 27513-9903. Individuals $10, institutions $15. For air-expedited delivery to foreign countries, add $5. Smithsonian Associates receive a 20% discount.

❏ Check enclosed, payable to Oxford University Press

Please charge to my   ❏ MasterCard   ❏ Visa

Acct. no. _____

Signature _____
        (Credit card order not valid without signature.)

Name _____

Address _____

City/State/Zip _____

Back Issues

___ **Vol. 1, No. 1 Spring 1987**

The Statue Near the Wall
The Vietnam Veterans Memorial and the Art of Remembering
Karal Ann Marling
Robert Silberman

Winslow Homer in His Art
Jules D. Prown

James Hampton's Throne and the Dual Nature of Time
Stephen Jay Gould

Thomas Hart Benton
A Politician in Art
Elizabeth Broun

Frederic Church's "Sacred Geography"
John Davis

___ **Vol. 1, No. 2 Fall 1987**

"The Happiest of Happy Accidents"?
A Reevaluation of Casablanca
Gary Green

Torre dei Schiavi
Monument and Metaphor
Charles C. Eldredge

Wayne Thiebaud
Beyond the Cityscapes
Andrée Maréchal-Workman

The Liberty Cap as a Revolutionary Symbol in America and France
Yvonne Korshak

Thomas Eakins and His Arcadian Works
Marc Simpson

___ **Vol. 2, No. 1 Winter 1988**

Barking Architecture
The Sculpture of Coney Island
Michele H. Bogart

Overstated Means/Understated Meaning
Social Content in the Art of the 1980s
Neal Benezra

Off the Wall and onto the Couch!
Sofa Art and the Avant-Garde Analyzed
Christopher Reed

"Endued with Rare Genius"
Frederic Edwin Church's To the Memory of Cole
J. Gray Sweeney

America's Measure of Mankind
Proportions and Harmonics
Jonathan L. Fairbanks

___ **Vol. 2, No. 2 Spring 1988**

George Bellow's *Stag at Sharkey's*
Boxing, Violence, and Male Identity
Robert Haywood

George Caleb Bingham's *Lighter Relieving a Steamboat Aground*
Nancy Rash

Mark Rothko
Heritage, Environment, and Tradition
Stephen Polcari

Henry Ossawa Tanner's *La Sainte-Marie*
Daniel Burke

William Glacken's Beach Scenes at Bellport
Richard J. Wattenmaker

American Art

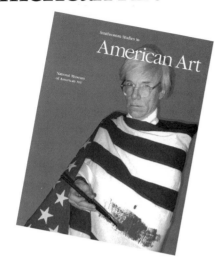

Explore the unique vision of America's artists.

Subscribe to *American Art* and explore American art in light of the cultural, historical, and sociological factors that have shaped it from colonial to contemporary times. Each richly illustrated issue contains articles of significant interest to a broad audience of professional art historians, collectors, and scholars, as well as students and art lovers. While the fine arts are the journal's primary focus, its scope encompasses all aspects of the nation's visual heritage, including decorative arts and crafts, architecture and landscape design, film and video, and commercial and graphic design.

American Art combines sound research with accessibility to the general reader. It embraces all approaches to America's rich and diverse artistic legacy, from traditional formalism to analyses of social context. Whether reflecting on specific artists or works or exploring a broad sweep of cultural trends, each essay offers the reader sound scholarship and thought-provoking interpretations.

The journal is edited by the National Museum of American Art, Smithsonian Institution, and has an editorial board of internationally known scholars.

Subscription Rates (One Year/Four Issues)

Individuals: $35/outside US: $45
Institutions: $70/outside US: $80

Prices include normal delivery. Please add $15 for air-expedited delivery (outside US only).

To begin your subscription with the current issue, send payment to the Journals Marketing Department, Oxford University Press, 2001 Evans Rd., Cary, NC 27513–9903.

A distinctive approach to Asian art and culture

from the Smithsonian Institution's Arthur M. Sackler

Gallery and Oxford University Press

Asian Art

Perhaps no other continent possesses a more richly diverse artistic legacy than the vast region of Asia. From nomads and villagers to urban citizens and courtiers, artists from dramatically divergent cultures have expressed themselves throughout time in works of profound beauty and visual power.

By exploring the arts of Asia using a thematic, cross-cultural approach, *Asian Art* provides a broad, yet detailed look at the painting, sculpture, ceramics, textiles, photography, architecture, landscape design, and folk traditions of this region. The journal's scope encompasses civilizations from the eastern Mediterranean to the Pacific islands of Japan, from antiquity to the present.

Each issue of the journal is devoted to a particular country, craft, medium, time, or cross-cultural inquiry. Through provocative opening essays by artists and scholars, in-depth yet lively articles, compelling color illustrations, detailed maps, and supplementary reading lists, new approaches to Asian art are illuminated.

Themes of Past and Future Issues	The Art of Eating and Drinking in Ancient Iran • The Art of India • A Lyric Impulse in Japan • Timur and Fifteenth-Century Iran • Buddhist Art • Raghubir Singh's Photographs of the Ganges • Japanese Craft Traditions • Games in Asian Art • Art and Performing Arts in Indonesia • East Asian Furniture
Past Contributors	Kwang-chih Chang • Jonathan Chaves • Vidya Dehejia • Kenneth DeWoskin • Lisa Golombek • Conrad Hyers • David N. Keightley • Hongnam Kim • Max Kozloff • William LaFleur • Tom Lentz • J. Thomas Rimer • Marianna Shreve Simpson • Henry D. Smith II • Wheeler Thackston • James L. Wescoat, Jr.

Subscribe now at a 20% discount

☐ Please enter my one-year subscription (4 issues) to *Asian Art* at the special discount rate:
  ☐ Individuals: $28 (reg $35)   ☐ Institutions: $56 (reg $70)
  Add $10 for subscriptions outside the US.

Name _____

Address _____

City/ State/ Zip _____

Send with check or money order to the Journals Department, Oxford University Press, 2001 Evans Road, Cary, NC 27513. For credit card orders (MasterCard, VISA, and American Express are accepted) include account number, expiration date, and signature.

Institutions may order direct from Oxford University Press or through their subscription agent. Include a copy of this form with your purchase order to receive your discount when ordering through an agent.   **AP 91**

About the Authors

Albert Boime

is a professor of art history at the University of California at Los Angeles. His most recent books include the first two volumes of his work-in-progress, a multivolume study of the social history of modern art, and *The Art of Exclusion: Representing Blacks in the Nineteenth Century* (1990). His book *The Magisterial Gaze: Manifest Destiny and American Landscape Painting (ca. 1830–1865)* is to be published in late 1991.

Elizabeth Broun

is the director of the National Museum of American Art, Smithsonian Institution. Before joining the museum in 1983, she served as curator of prints and drawings and acting director at the Spencer Museum of Art, University of Kansas, Lawrence. Her most recent book *Albert Pinkham Ryder*, published for the museum's 1990 Ryder exhibition, was co-winner of the College Art Association's 1989 Alfred H. Baar, Jr., award.

Anna C. Chave

is an associate professor of fine arts at Harvard University. She is the author of *Mark Rothko: Subjects in Abstraction* (1989), articles on Georgia O'Keeffe and on Minimalism, and a forthcoming study on Constantin Brancusi, to be published by Yale University Press in 1992.

David Corey

teaches undergraduate and graduate courses in comparative literature and film at Brooklyn College. He is currently collaborating with photographer David Levinthal on a book of short fiction and photography in the style of film noir.

Rayna Green

is currently director of the American Indian Program at the National Museum of American History, Smithsonian Institution. She has written several books and essays on American Indians and American culture and is also known for her work in museum exhibitions, film, television, and radio. A Cherokee, Green is the director of ATLATL, a Native American arts service organization.

Linda C. Hults

is an assistant professor in art history at the College of Wooster, Wooster, Ohio. Her published writing includes essays that have appeared in exhibition catalogues published by the National Gallery of Art and the Gilcrease Institute. She is currently working on the book *The Print in the Western World: An Introductory History* and a book-length study on witchcraft imagery from Dürer to Goya.

Ivan Karp

is curator of African ethnology at the Smithsonian's National Museum of Natural History. Trained as a social anthropologist, he currently conducts field research in East Africa. He is the author of *Fields of Change among the Iteso of Kenya* and the editor of *The Creativity of Power* and *Personhood and Agency*. With Steven D. Lavine he co-edited *Exhibiting Cultures: The Poetics and Politics of Museum Displays* and the forthcoming *Museums and Communities: The Art of Making a Civic Culture*.

Carole Kismaric and Marvin Heiferman

work collaboratively on publications and exhibition projects, investigating how images have come to define a shared visual language. For *Talking Pictures: Oral Histories in a Visual World*, a book they are packaging for publication in 1992, they conducted fifty interviews with people whose lives are intertwined with images.

Max Kozloff

is a photographer who has had his work shown in New York, where he lives, and throughout the United States. A writer on photography, he has published two collections of critical essays, *Photography and Fascination* (1979) and *The Privileged Eye* (1987). His most recent publication is *Now Becoming Then*, a monograph on Duane Michals.

Donald Kuspit

is the editor of *Art Criticism*, a contributing editor for *Art in America* and *Contemporanea*, and a staff member of *Artforum*. He is a professor of art history and philosophy at the State University of New York at Stony Brook. His books include *The Philosophical Life of the Senses*, *Clement Greenberg, Art Critic*, *The Critic Is Artist: The Intentionality of Art*, and, most recently, *The New Subjectivism: Art of the 1980s*. He is a recipient of the College Art Association's Frank Jewett Mather Award for distinction in art criticism.

David Levinthal

is a photographer whose works are in the collections of the Corcoran Gallery of Art, the National Museum of American Art, the Los Angeles County Museum of Art, and Atlanta's High Museum, among others. In addition to many solo exhibitions, most recently in Belgium and Zurich, his photographs have been featured in several group exhibitions, including NMAA's "The Photography of Invention" show and the "Surrogate Selves" exhibition at the Corcoran in 1989.

Lucy R. Lippard

is an author and activist. Among the fourteen books she has written are *From the Center: Feminist Essays on Women's Art*, *Overlay: Contemporary Art and the Art of Prehistory*, and *Get the Message? A Decade of Art for Social Change*. She is a contributing editor to *Art in America* and the art and politics columnist for *Z* magazine. She has curated and organized more than forty exhibitions in the United States, Europe, and Latin America.

Karal Ann Marling

is a professor of art history and American studies at the University of Minnesota. Her most recent work, co-authored with John Wetenhall, is a study of the battle of Iwo Jima, to be published by Harvard in 1991. Past books are *Blue Ribbon: A Social and Pictorial History of the Minnesota State Fair*, *Tom Benton and His Drawings*, *Wall-to-Wall America, A Cultural History of Post-Office Murals in the Great Depression*, and *The Colossus of Roads, Myth and Symbol Along the American Highway*.

Alex Nemerov

is a doctoral candidate at Yale University and a National Museum of American Art fellow in the Material Culture Program. He helped organize the museum's 1991 exhibition "The West as America: Reinterpreting Images of the Frontier, 1820–1920" and contributed an essay to the exhibition catalogue.

Stephen Polcari

is a 1991 visiting scholar of the National Museum of American Art. His articles "Mark Rothko: Heritage, Environment, and Tradition" and "Martha Graham and Abstract Expressionism" appeared in the spring 1988 and winter 1990 issues, respectively, of *Smithsonian Studies in American Art*. His book *Abstract Expressionism and the Modern Experience* will be published by Cambridge University Press in spring 1991.

Peter A. Juley and Son Collection

consists of more than 127,000 photographic negatives that document primarily American artists and works of art. Specializing in photography of fine arts, the New York–based Juley firm photographed artworks from 1896 to 1975, many of which are now lost, destroyed, or altered in appearance.

Photo Credits

Cover: Courtesy Fraenkel Gallery, Fotomann, Inc., and Jan Kesner Gallery, © Richard Misrach, 1987; 4: © The Detroit Institute of Arts; 7: AP/Wide World Photos; 11 (fig. 1): Don Wright, *Palm Beach Post*; 12: © Centre G. Pompidou, photo by Adam Rzepka and Jacques Faujour (fig. 3); 14: Photo by Kate Keller, Chief Fine Arts Photographer, The Museum of Modern Art, New York; 16: Courtesy Marvin Heiferman, New York; 22: Courtesy of the artist; 24: Photo by Peter Jacobs; 25: © Ming Fay, photo by and courtesy of the artist; 28: © and photo by Ellen Page Wilson 1989; 35: © Estate of Tseng Kwong Chi; 43: Courtesy Gerald Peters Gallery, Santa Fe, New Mexico; 47: © Addison Gallery of American Art, Phillips Academy, Andover, Massachusetts; 61–67: © David Levinthal 1991; 68: Courtesy Gene Autry Western Heritage Museum, Los Angeles; 79: © Denver Art Museum; 89: © 1990 The Art Institute of Chicago; © The Museum of Modern Art, New York; 94: Courtesy Sheldon Memorial Art Gallery; 108, 124–129, 130 (fig. 15): © Richard Misrach 1985 (figs. 12–13), 1986 (fig. 15), 1987 (frontispiece, fig. 14), courtesy Fraenkel Gallery, Fotomann, Inc., and Jan Kesner Gallery; 111–112: © David T. Hanson, 1984, 1986, courtesy of the artist; 114–115: Courtesy Castelli Graphics, New York; 116–118: Photo by Andrew Harkins, 1991; 119: Photo by Joan Broderick, 1986; 120: Courtesy Janet Borden, Inc.; 130 (fig. 16): © The Royal Photographic Society; 133: Courtesy Robert Miller Gallery, photo by Phillips/Schwab, New York; 134 (top): Courtesy Kay Haring, photo by Estate of Keith Haring; 135 (top): Courtesy Metro Pictures; 136 (top): Courtesy Sonnabend, photo by F. Scruton; 137 (top): Courtesy Marian Goodman Gallery, photo by Jon and Anne Abbott; 138 (top): Courtesy Jay Gorney Modern Art, photo © 1989 David Lubarsky; 139 (top): Courtesy of the artist and Michael Klein Gallery; 140 (bottom): Courtesy Mary Boone Gallery, photo © 1989 David Lubarsky; 142, 154–155: National Park Service; 143: © United States Postal Service 1991; 145: © 1990 New Yorker Magazine, Inc.; 146–147, 151, back cover: Courtesy South Dakota Tourism; 148 (right): Courtesy of Greta Pratt; 149: Courtesy of the Academy of Motion Picture Arts and Sciences; 153: © Joslyn Art Museum; 157 (top): Photo by Robert Killian; 157 (bottom), 158–159, 164: © Smithsonian Institute; 160: Photo by Carl Rise; 163: © 1924, Metropolitan Newspaper Service; 168, 170–171, 178, 188–189, 191, 204: © Walt Disney Productions; 172–173, 175, 188 (top, bottom), 193–197, 202: Photo by Gregory Marling; 177, 180, 182, 198–199, 200: Courtesy G. Kaye Malins; 179 (left): Courtesy Nettie Boley; 179 (right): Courtesy Ruth Disney Beecher; 183–184, 186: © Chicago Historical Society, photo by Harold S. Beach (183), photo by Frank E. Rice (186); 185: Photo by T. Harmon Parkhurst, Museum of New Mexico